TABLE OF CONTENTS

Dedication v

Foreword vi

Preface viii

Important Note From The Author ix

Introduction x

Smiley Poswolsky – How to Show Up for Others in the World 1

John Lee Dumas – Entrepreneur on Fire 7

Cathi Hargaden – Feng Shui Lifestyles 12

Dr. Carri Drzyzga – Staying Happy and Healthy 18

David Mead – The Golden Circle of Purpose 23

Chandler Bolt – Writing Your Own Book 29

Gretchen Rubin – Better than Before 34

Dotan Negrin – Piano Around the World 40

Gene Hammett – Leaders in the Trenches 45

Rick Martinez – BINK 51

Jason Zook – Jason is Up to Something 56

Joel Zaslofsky – The Value of Simple 63

Erik Hemingway – Seven Sailors 69

Hal Elrod – The Miracle Morning 74

Greg Rollett – Ambitious 80

Dave Sanderson – Miracle on the Hudson 86

Chanel & Stevo – How Far From Home? 94

Clint Arthur – As If You Were Dying   101

Erlend Bakke – Never Work Again   108

Riley Temple – The Millenial Mindest   114

Joseph Ranseth – How to Start a Movement   121

Rob Scott – Hijack Your Mindset   128

Bryan and Jen Danger – One VW Bus and The Open Road   134

Jon Nastor – Hack The Entrepreneur   144

Mitch Matthews – DREAM THINK DO   148

Stephan Spencer – Reboot Your Life   153

Nick Unsworth – Life on Fire   158

Jordan Harbinger – The Art of Charm   167

Jeffrey Shaw – Forget the Focus   174

James Lawrence – The Iron Cowboy   180

James Miller – Lifeology   186

Michael Grandinetti – Masters of Illusion   192

Gary Mancuso – How to Time Travel   198

Mindie Kniss – Heart Intelligence   203

Steve Olsher – What is Your What?   209

Sergeant Kevin Briggs – Guardian of the Golden Gate   214

Epilogue   219

ZEPHAN MOSES BLAXBERG

THIS BOOK Won't CHANGE YOUR LIFE

STORIES, TIPS & GUIDANCE FROM WORLDWIDE MENTORS

Dedication

For my late "Zeide" (Yiddish for grandfather) Bernard "Buddy" Earl Toback.
My Zeide taught me so many things about life, love and work.

Love you champ.

Foreword

Surviving is easy. Living is hard. Living life on your terms is the most difficult thing you can do, for it means ignoring all the naysayers, including yourself and being exactly who you are meant to be.

Enter, Zephan Blaxberg.

I've known Zephan for more than several years now, actually got to know him pretty well, since I interviewed him, in much the same way he has conducted interviews in this book and I've shared his story on a few different occasions on my worldwide blog, The Sunday Series.

His story is amazing, as are so many who find themselves living on the edge, maybe even tired of living, as Zephan once was, to becoming someone who is a wonder to behold, full of energy, drive and purpose and is touching and inspiring lives all over the world.

It was less than 15 years ago when Zephan was struggling with his own meaning of life, literally sitting with a knife at his kitchen table, surrounded by pill bottles, meant to control his depression, anxiety and panic attacks, but which were slowly robbing him of meaning, of any desire to live.

He was thinking about ending it all.

But unable to do the deed, it became the same moment Zephan made the decision to keep going, and to go cold turkey, no more meds, and no more self-pity for a life he didn't see going in the direction he desired. No more being lost, it was time to find his purpose.

Zephan got to work on himself, doing free-lance video work and then working for one of the largest marketing companies in the world. But it was during a short stint as an Apple store employee when a customer changed Zephan's life. After Zephan shared his unhappiness working in retail at Apple, this customer took him to dinner and on a simple bar napkin, the man showed Zephan what life could look like, the opportunity and potential of life as a full-time entrepreneur. For Zephan, it would mean giving in to what most of us suffer from - fear of risk, fear of change. In reality, the fear of going after the golden ticket – a shot at living up to our potential, of becoming the very best version of ourselves.
Zephan went all in, and went about racking up experience after experience, running a multimedia video business, traveling (or hacking travel points) around the world, working with youth groups, and asking many questions, which led to his desire to ask even more of these same questions to people who were extremely successful entrepreneurs, amazing individuals from all across the globe.

Hence, Zephan's desire to bring his will and wonder about how others did what they did and share it with the rest of the population through his podcast, The Year of Purpose Podcast.

If you are truly the product of the four or five people you spend the most time with, then suppose you amplified that number by nearly 200… especially if those people are world-and-life game changers? In the span of a three-year period, Zephan conducted interviews with 175 people, and a sampling of the best of the best are part of this book.

So maybe this book won't change your life, but maybe instead Zephan's life and his desire to give back, to share what matters in life, especially the stories of other people – will change the way you look at life, and get you to change the way you think, to alter your perspective.
In every moment is a chance to change, a chance to begin again.

No, this book won't change your life. But YOU can.

Thanks to Zephan Blaxberg, his mission, his purpose, and these stories, you've got a chance to rewrite your own.

This just might be your year of purpose.

Mark Brodinsky
Author: *The Sunday Series*
Author: *It Takes Two*
Blogger: The Sunday Series & Storytelling for Business
Creator/Moderator: Change Your Mind. Change Your Life.

Preface

This book is selfish - it's a product of my desire to make sure the information and teachings that I've discovered never dies. One of the greatest things about publishing a book is that it can live on beyond your time on this earth.

When my grandfather was on his deathbed, I watched as a frail 89-year-old man suffered from kidney failure and what we suspected to be cancer. He was coming to terms with his life and the ending that was inevitably near. I remember quite clearly one night he turned to me and said, "You have your car here, right? You can take me home tonight!" His next words cut like a knife to the gut. He asked me, "Am I going to die here?" I knew at that very moment; this man wanted his story to continue. Despite all the pain and the suffering he was going through, he wasn't ready to leave this life.

I think that it is human nature to want our story to go on, or at the very least to be remembered. This is where my inspiration for this book came from. This is where you have the opportunity and the reminder that you can change your life. I can only hope that you realize this opportunity is here and now right in front of you and not when you are laying on your deathbed.

I selfishly don't want this information to die. I want to be remembered for who I was when I was alive and in some small way. I hope the books that I publish will become a time capsule for my life and the things I accomplished on earth.

Hopefully one day my children and my grand-children and my grandchildren's children will be able to learn about who I was through my books. I know my grammar isn't perfect and I openly admit that I work with an editor to ensure that I sound semi-polished. I have nothing to hide. Sorry kids, I was never meant to be the next great novelist – I just don't have it in me.

At the same time this book isn't selfish. It is a recipe for living a great life, building amazing relationships, creating successful businesses, reducing stress, living longer and more.

As I've said, this book won't change your life, but the teachings and principles that are shared in this book can change your life should you choose to implement them.

Thank you for taking the time to read the amazing stories, and for diving deeper into the story that you are living. My wish for you is that you pull a few golden nuggets that will transform your life. To my future descendants - live a great story.

After all, the choice is yours.

Important Note from The Author

The stories contained in *This Book Won't Change Your Life* are derivatives of original stories that were shared between 2014 and 2017 on the Year of Purpose Podcast, a weekly podcast that I produced and shared on iTunes and other podcast streaming websites.

I, along with my editor, have done my best to retain the information shared by my podcast guests in as close to an un-altered and authentic form as possible.

These words stand alone in their truth at the moment they were told to me and shared with the world. It is virtually impossible to update each and every story, detail, name or website URL because of the sheer number of stories that we have compiled over the years.

I encourage you to do your research if you find that a particular story stands out or resonates with you. If you want to see where that person is now or what their business has achieved, a search engine will be your best friend.

We as humans are not designed to retain the same thoughts, opinions, or goals over the years, months, or even days. Please understand that while life may have changed over the past few years for the subjects of this book. I ask you to accept the stories, tools and advice as they were in the moment.

When I set off on this journey my goal was to find and interview entrepreneurs from all over the world who have created life on their own terms.

Please enjoy their stories.

Introduction

A 24-year-old decided to travel hack and couch surf his way around the United States to discover what type of person he would become when he stripped away the security blanket of comfort. Two months later, he emerged a different person. He learned what happens when you remove the guarantee of a warm bed to sleep in at night, the certainty of where his next meal will come from, and the convenience of knowing he would get paid every two weeks. The person forged from that crucible is the man putting pencil to paper, or should I say fingers to keyboard, at this very moment.

Life would never be the same.

When the concept for the Year of Purpose Podcast came to me I was driving home from an East Coast road trip with my cousin. He joined me for the tail end of my two-month adventure. For the last 7 days we made our way through 12 states. As we drove past the nation's capital, on our way to our home of Baltimore, Maryland, I was reflecting on the past two months of traveling and introspection.

I left nearly 60 days prior because I was burned out from being an entrepreneur. I had read books like Tim Ferriss' *The Four-Hour Work-Week* and was sold a magical story that so many other business owners fall head over heels for. It wasn't the dream of spending 4 hours a week to develop a business that attracted me, but rather the dream that I could make a six or even seven-figure income without the hardship that others had to endure.

For the record, I did build a six-figure business. I say this not to brag, but to be transparent. Rome wasn't built in a day. It took nearly six years, countless weeks of working 60 or even 80-hour weeks, hustle, and true grit to make it a reality. The struggle isn't sexy, so we don't always talk about it. I attribute a large portion of my success to the stories you are about to read. Ok, now back to the good part...

I was in the passenger seat on our return journey scrolling through Facebook when I saw a lengthy article shared by one of my connections whom I'd never even spoken to or met in real life. The article read "2015 To Be A Year of Purpose for Many" and it finally clicked. I had been struggling to "find my purpose" like so many others, but I was looking at the story backwards. The videographer, storyteller and creative in me thought, "what if we turn this concept on its head?"

One of the best pieces of advice I have ever received was to look at where everyone was guiding their focus and do the opposite. If the photographer at a wedding is photographing the bride and groom, take a look at what the parents are doing or even the grandparents. Stories are three dimensional, never black and white, so what if I could apply this same concept to life?

I was always convinced that in order to find my purpose I had to set goals at the beginning of the year. Goals like going to the gym, drinking more water, getting more sleep, meditating, etc. No wonder most people failed their New Year's resolutions - they didn't stand a chance at such a macro level.

What if we flipped the script? What if we decided that each day when we woke up, we would set a goal to live a day of purpose and intention. Then, on top of that, what if we dared to continue doing so for the entire year. As long as you wake up every day and your actions are intentional and symmetrical to your purpose here in life, you've already won. It comes down to a single choice. Will I align myself with my purpose today? If the answer is yes, you can cross another day off of the calendar that you have lived with purpose.

Many years ago, Jerry Seinfeld gave similar advice to a struggling stand-up comedian. Seinfeld told him that his method for success was each January he would hang a large Year-At-A-Glance calendar on the wall. Every day that he wrote new material, he would go to the calendar and draw a red X over the date. The idea was never to break that chain of red X's on his calendar. You see, it wasn't about making the goals at the beginning of the year and hoping you'd follow through. It's about waking up every day and making sure you cross another X off the calendar. You can't see a calendar filled with red X's looking forward – only backward.

We search tirelessly for mission statements and ways to compile our "purpose" into a simple and easy to recite mantra. The truth is we live with purpose by simply existing. We already have a purpose on this earth, whether we know it or not. The question is what will we do with it?

> "The two most important days in life are the day you are born and the day you find out why."
> - Mark Twain

Just two weeks after my life-changing trip, I launched the Year of Purpose Podcast where I set out to find people, entrepreneurs, average joes- anyone who was on a journey to create a life on their own terms.

For three years I interviewed authors, athletes, coaches, world-record holders and more to find out what it was that made them tick. The Year of Purpose Podcast consisted of half-hour long interviews that were unaltered and unedited. These stories can be found in their entirety on YouTube or any major Podcast app. With the help of my editor, I have distilled what I conclude to be the most important knowledge that if taken and implemented could change your life.

So why did I title this book, *This Book Won't Change Your Life*? It's quite simple - the book won't change your life. Only you can create change. Only you can make the choice that things will be different from here on out. I guess the million-dollar question is, will you choose to change your life?

For years I recited myself a script for how I thought my life was going to be. Find your story, flip your story, and make sure it's a good one. If you're looking for a framework to get started re-writing your story, I highly encourage you to read my first book and #1 best-seller, *Life Re-Scripted: Find Your Purpose & Design Your Dream Life Before The Curtains Close.*

Before we get going, I want to share a quote with you that has resonated with me ever since I made that choice…

> *"What do you desire? What makes you itch? What sort of a situation would you like?.. What do you want to do? When we finally got down to something, which the individual says he really wants to do, I will say to him, you do that and forget the money, because, if you say that getting the money is the most important thing, you will spend your life completely wasting your time.*
>
> *You'll be doing things you don't like doing in order to go on living, that is to go on doing things you don't like doing, which is stupid. Better to have a short life that is full of what you like doing than a long life spent in a miserable way."*
> -Alan Watts

Choose wisely.

SMILEY POSWOLSKY
How to Show Up for Others in the World

Adam Smiley Poswolsky (smileyposwolsky.com) is the best-selling author of *The Quarter-Life Breakthrough: A Guide for Millennials to Find Meaningful Work*. He is also a keynote speaker and a millennial workplace expert. His real name is Adam, but he goes by Smiley, a nickname he's had for more than 15 years. He earned his nickname in high school during the first week of running cross-country; smiling all the way while other runners puked.

Smiley was the first person I met while on my trip around the United States. When a friend joined in for the California portion of my adventure she said, "We've got to meet this guy who wrote a book that resonates with exactly how we're feeling right now." She reached out to him, and sure enough he met us for coffee. It's worth mentioning that he is a much better writer than I am, so if you're in your 20's or 30's you should really check out his book.

BACKSTORY

"Three years ago, I was 28 and the Special Assistant to the Director of Operations at the Peace Corps. I was making good money and had benefits, but I wasn't happy or fulfilled. When you have a job that on paper looks good to your friends and your parents but internally you wake up in the morning and have stomach and back pain that devolves into depression and feeling really stuck, it's a difficult place to be.
That's where my story begins and I wrote a book about the transformation and how I got unstuck and I was able to say, 'It's okay even if you have a good job to take a leap, to do something new, to experiment,' and now three years later, I'm a lot happier and I'm doing things I really care about."

From here on out you'll typically see names represented as initials so it's safe to say anything denoted as "ZB" is me talking in the interview and the other initials… well, you're a smart cookie, I'll leave that for you to determine.

ZB: Do you remember the specific day where everything just connected, and you said, this is it, this is the last day?

AP: "I was at the Peace Corps for over two years and a couple of friends told me about a program called Starting Block Institute for Organizations. They gather 20-something's who are interested in creating social change. Teachers, nonprofit folks, enterprise business, sustainable business folks, artists, and writers.

It's February and I'm at this program in LA with the palm trees and people surfing while it's snowing and freezing in DC. I was sitting on this rooftop bar with my friend and I was telling him about feeling unhappy in work but being scared of quitting my job. He goes 'Smiley, why would you be doing anything less than reaching your full potential in life?' That was the moment I knew I had to make the leap and quit my job.

That was when it all clicked and understanding that by not leaving, I was not only robbing myself of personal fulfillment and happiness, but I was robbing others of the difference I could make because I wasn't unleashing my full potential on the world. When you realize that, it's powerful."

ZB: Where did the original motivation come from to actually start writing the book?

"I started a blog around that time because going through the experience of quitting a job is intense and blogging helped get out my feelings and helped me realize other people were going through the same thing. I was working for a program in San Francisco called the Bold Academy, which is a life accelerator program where people live together for 10 days to work on themselves and meet other entrepreneurs, mentors and speakers all around this idea of clarifying your purpose and unleashing your gifts to the world. People were like 'You do these interesting blog posts; you should write a book.' And I was like, 'Ha, yeah. I'm going to write a book.'

After the program, we all write down our commitments in front of everyone on the wall. My commitment was to write a book this year, and I did, but it took a year. That's how the book was born."

"Surround yourself with people that can make you take those leaps and hold you accountable to your dreams."

"I actually scrapped the whole first draft and ended up re-writing the book because that first draft was dark, negative and uninspiring. That year was an amazing time for creation, learning and growth and I always advise people when they're launching for the first time, the first innovation isn't going to be perfect; it's a prototype. In the same way that we constantly grow, we constantly learn more about our lives; it's a journey."

"If you get too scared about what the final product is, you'll never get there."

ON PURPOSE AND BEING FULFILLED

"It's important to know that purpose is different for everyone. How I define purpose in the book is what you want to give to the world. If passion is kind of inward-looking, my passion is being healthier, writing, and meditating in the morning."

"My purpose is what I want to do for others and aligning my unique gift with who I am with the impact I want to make in the world."

ZB: Talk a little bit about different options for people who are interested in programs with like-minded people who are also seeking out a purpose-driven life.

AP: "One of the things that I talk about in the book is that you can't do this stuff alone in terms of life and living a purpose-driven life. You need to surround yourself with communities of supportive people and I've been fortunate over the last couple of years to find a lot of these aligned, intentional communities of people interested in social innovation, social entrepreneurship and social change."

"Camp Grounded is a summer camp for adults, available two weekends a year. You can't talk about work; you can't use digital technology; you can only use your nickname. It's the exact opposite of a conference. You do arts and crafts, and capture the flag, and all of those things you used to do as a kid with other adults; age 18 all the way up to 70. It's a really powerful experience. I really recommend this for college grads or people just getting into their 20's and trying to figure out where they fit."

"The StartingBloc Institute for Social Innovation allows you to meet other young people that are creating social change, other young people that are going after their dreams; that's a great program."

"I also work part-time for a program called The Hive Global Leaders Program. That's for purpose driven leaders and entrepreneurs that are a little farther along in their careers. Mostly age 25-40 who are working at large companies like Google and Facebook, or non-profits or social enterprises trying to create a better world. We do a three-day event in San Francisco to bring people together to clarify their life purpose, accelerate their impact and get the tools that they need to move forward and create a more abundant and sustainable world for everyone."

Where have you traveled in the last year?

"I got to go to London and that was my first speaking event outside the United States. I found the London audience was just as excited and passionate about this quarter-life crisis as people in the states. This is a global issue. Everyone is looking for purpose and meaning in their life and at work and it's not just millennials.

I've spoken to audiences that are my parent's age or older and they're also thinking about this. I would encourage anyone that's in this space to realize that you're not alone. A lot of people I know are on their third or fourth job where they are trying to make a change because they've developed, they want to make a difference and they want to do something else and that's okay.

I would encourage folks not to just nudge themselves but to actually empower themselves to make these changes, define purpose, and figure out what's best for them."

ON THE FLUIDITY OF MULTIPLE PURPOSES AND CHANGE

"Most people have probably done at least five or six different things because they are constantly exploring and experimenting. That doesn't mean quit your job every six months because that's not a very good strategy for making a living. We're constantly learning new things, meeting new people, having new experiences and if something ticks, there's a reason.

If I suddenly were to get excited about design innovation, that's not a reason to say 'whoa, I got to stay focused here on writing.' No. Maybe I want to do a class, maybe I want to write a book about design innovation, maybe I could combine those things and grow."

"It's all about passionate curiosity about things that ignite you and excite you and figuring out a way to incorporate that into your work."

"I find that the people that seem to be most fulfilled are constantly growing, are constantly innovating. You have to stay focused and know where you're at, but you also have to experiment and innovate. Just look at the job market now and think about what's changed in the last ten years.

We're going to constantly have to adapt and learn new technologies and learn new ways of working with people. I encourage people to be nimble, to be flexible, to experiment, and to understand the relationships between different disciplines; it's okay to try to find these synergies. Purpose is a journey."

ZB: What was your best decision and not your favorite decision?

AP: "The best decision I made was committing to finishing the book because there were a couple times where I was like, 'This is too much, I'll just blog or do a couple of websites.' But committing to something that took a year has opened up a lot of doors for speaking and opportunities to talk about these ideas and help people think about this. The book has really served as a calling card for me, so making that decision was really important."

"The decision that didn't go so well – for me the biggest challenge is focus. I sometimes say yes to different side projects and I'm still working on that balance.
You have to be willing to really focus; you have to be willing to get good at something and know what your priority is. For a lot of this last year, that's been my challenge; to say, 'What is the absolute top priority?' Right now, getting a book deal for my second book is my absolute top priority. Until now, I've been having trouble with the discipline to prioritize and focus.

There are a lot of distractions, but I find that people who are truly successful have really clear focus. Number one is the most important thing that they are working on and everything else follows that. Until this year, I don't think I've been that clear for myself and I'm really excited about that."

What advice would you impart on young Smiley?

"I would tell my younger self that money doesn't lead to happiness. I was making good money and it wasn't right. In the last couple of years, I've made far less money but I'm in the arena of things I really care about and I'm around people I care about. The potential for making income is there because I haven't put money first.

I know a lot of people that work at awesome companies like Apple and Google, and they're not happy and then I know a lot of entrepreneurs that aren't happy either."

"Until you start to not care about what others think and figure out what you want, it's really difficult to find meaning. Don't worry about what other people are doing. Focus on asking yourself the right questions. 'Who are you?' 'What are you about?' 'What do you care about?' 'What issues fire you up?' 'Who do you want to be around?' 'What impact do you want to make in the world as yourself?' 'What's your purpose?'

Those are going to lead to the answers, not what your friends are doing, not what your parents did, not what this person that's on the cover of *Fast Company* did.

What do you care about?"

KEY TAKEAWAYS

- The first innovation isn't going to be perfect
- Surround yourself with communities of supportive people
- The most fulfilled people are constantly growing, constantly innovating
- Know what your priority is
- Money doesn't lead to happiness

WHERE TO FIND SMILEY'S BOOK AND GET IN TOUCH

You can purchase *The Quarter-Life Breakthrough* on Amazon.

Visit thequarterlifebreakthrough.com and sign up for Adam's mailing list and get some free resources.

You can email him, smiley@thequarterlifebreakthrough.com.

He's also active on Twitter, @whatsupsmiley.

JOHN LEE DUMAS
Entrepreneur on Fire

John Lee Dumas (freepodcastcourse.com, thewebinarcourse.com, eofire. com/gift) is the founder and host of the *Entrepreneur on Fire* podcast, an award-winning podcast revealing the journey of today's most inspiring entrepreneurs seven days a week. Entrepreneur on Fire generates over $250,000 a month in revenue and offers a free 15-day course on podcasting at freepodcastingcourse.com. With over one-million unique listens a month, *Entrepreneur on Fire* has inspired Fire Nation to take control of their life and take that entrepreneurial leap.

WHAT IS AN ENTREPRENEUR ON FIRE?

"An Entrepreneur on Fire is somebody who is really a captain of a life they chose and they're steering their own ship. An Entrepreneur on Fire has to be open and willing to talk about their past failures. Guest's stories are the focus because I want my listeners to know that failure's part of the game. Failure's there every step of the way, and that's okay—as long as you're learning from those failures. So, we always talk about the lessons learned. And then, be open to talk about that Ah-Ha! Moment, that great idea, that lightning bolt that came through, and then walk us through the steps taken to turn that great idea into a success.

Then we're going to talk about something you're really fired up about right now. Like that's what we'll get to. Then, we get to the lightning rounds where the Entrepreneurs on Fire are going to answer specific questions about different aspects of their lives to unlock the mysterious perceptions surrounding entrepreneurship."

WHERE WAS YOUR AH-HA MOMENT WHEN YOU STARTED THIS PODCAST?

"I've experienced failure at different levels in different industries. Failure was inevitable because I wasn't inspired or passionate about anything I was doing and that was a disappointment. At first, I thought that was okay; that was just life where you weren't inspired by what you did, like, 'Hello it's work!'
Fortunately, I started listening to people like Dan Kennedy, Brian Tracy, Zig Ziglar, and Jim Rohn -- these entrepreneurs of old dispensing great information that life doesn't have to be that way."

"I listened to their audiobooks, took their audio courses, read the right books, and that led me to podcasts, which I listened to very avidly. Then I had my Ah-Ha moment. The interviews of successful entrepreneurs were so inspiring but there were only a couple of podcasts doing it and they were airing it once a week or twice a month.

I was like, 'Hello! There are people like me who are driving to work every day. At the gym three to five times a week, looking to consume this content during those times. Where's the seven-day a week podcast?' I searched for it; it didn't exist. Here I am, 900-plus episodes later, with those amazing statistics you shared, and just continuing to rock and roll and having a blast doing it."

What have you drawn from those past jobs and the military to get you through a long, hard journey?

"I like to equate it to a marathon, not a sprint. You know, having this goal and then reaching it, that's good, but it's not going to sustain happiness, there's always, 'okay, what's next?' Having this gradual realization of a worthy ideal over this marathon of life, that's what excites me."

"I definitely attribute my discipline, my focus, and my work ethic to the military, because I saw the results of all of those attributes. In 2003, we knew that we were going to deploy to war in six months. I was a tanker and in charge of four tanks and 16 men. We had 12 months of work to do in six months. I was forced to learn about discipline and really focused on hard work -- and we got it done.

I learned when you have the right mentality and do things in the right order, things can be accomplished. I applied that concept to the world of entrepreneurship, and that's really why I have had such a rocket ship to success. Sometimes people get into entrepreneurship because they think they want to be their own boss, but they're not willing to hold themselves accountable to do the work. But that's what I was able to do from day one because of my military background."

ZB: What would you say is the difference between someone running a million-dollar business versus your average person who might be listening to this podcast right now? What is preventing them from being able to achieve greatness of that magnitude?

JD: "Scale and leverage. The average person doesn't have it and the people who are running seven-figure businesses do. I'm doing what I do with "Entrepreneur on Fire" because this medium gives us the ability to reach a massive audience on a really large scale and that's exciting.

Just last month, *Entrepreneur on Fire* had a million unique listens and we've got over 15-million listens since we launched back in September 2012, in over 145 countries. That scale, that leverage is huge."

DIFFERENTIATOR: "When you have the right mentality and do things in the right order, things can be accomplished."

ZB: On Instagram, I saw you found your 2014 goals where you had planned to make $2.5 million for all of 2014. What were some of your biggest obstacles or fears, as a business owner?

JD: "Those fears are prevalent and that's one thing I focus on when I'm talking to audiences -- those fears are never going away. Don't think you're going to get to a place where you wake up and you're like 'Oh, it's an amazing day and I don't have any fear!' That's part of the game. And it was really interesting to look at that paper where I scribbled my goals for 2014. I was brought back to a place of scarcity and doubt when I was writing it. I was like, 'there's no way I'm ever going to generate this kind of money.' And it didn't happen how I thought it would.

Some things were much bigger than I expected, and other things were much smaller or non-existent. But the key thing is I wrote down those goals and I put it out there in the universe. It was really fascinating to see how close I was, where I had $2.5 million as a revenue goal, and we got $2.75 million.

I kind of wonder what would have happened if I'd written down a million dollars?"

ZB: I'll give you a quick story. I produced a feature film when I was in college, 118-page script, 96-minutes long with $1000 budget. My senior year, in 12-months, we shot, we edited, we color-corrected, we sound-designed, and we premiered it in a movie theater. Everyone told us we weren't going to do it.

If we hadn't set that lofty goal, I don't think we ever would've been able to do it. It just doesn't happen. Setting that lofty goal pushes you to be better and better and better, and it doesn't limit you anymore.

Are you worried about the future of just having a business that runs online?

"Yeah. I mean, the thing is, we live in such a virtual world that is so scalable and so leverageable as long as we just don't get really caught up. And that's the focus of 'What can I do virtually? What can I tweet? What can I post on Instagram?' and that's great in a lot of ways. Because that really allows you to reach a lot of people.

That's actually why I'm in the process of creating a physical book called *The Freedom Journal*; it's actually a journal book. The tagline is '100 days to your destiny.' It's going to take somebody 100 days to write down goals, affirmations, and accomplishments and it will get them to their goal in 100 days. It will be an amazing physical item that people can hold and that's real to them. And I love that idea.

I think a combination of both is the best way to approach the future, and never to forget that there will always be a physical side to what we do."

THINGS THAT MIGHT SURPRISE PEOPLE ABOUT ENTREPRENEURSHIP

"One of the biggest misperceptions is when people say, 'When I become an entrepreneur, I'm not going to have to answer to anyone.' You will always be answering to somebody. I answer to the millions of 'Fire Nation' listeners that are out there; they are my bosses. I listen to them, I ask them questions, I jump on phone calls with them and I respond to their emails. So that's one of the biggest misperceptions."

What do you think that everyone else should start doing to stay motivated and keep that fire burning?

"You are the average of the five people you spend the most time with, so figure out who those five people are right now. And then identify the people that are not adding value to your goal and don't kick them out of your life but kick them out of your top five. Bring in people who you do want in that top five, who are going to bring value.

Join or create and host a mastermind. I think they should be small, because you need legitimate floor time and meet for an hour every week. Invite people who have different skills in different areas, who will bring value to it.

You will really lean on that mastermind for information, for influence, and for guidance and support. There's nothing wrong with being part of bigger masterminds, but you want that one core small one with three or four people."

FAVORITE QUOTES

"Success and happiness is a gradual realization of a worthy ideal."
- Earl Nightingale

"I decided to be that change that I wanted to see in the world."
- Ghandi

"You are the average of the five people you spend the most time with."
- Jim Rohn

KEY TAKEAWAYS

- Failure is there every step of the way, learn from your failures
- Life is a marathon, not a sprint
- Surround yourself with people that add value
- Set lofty goals – write them down
- Fear will not go away

LOOKING TO START A PODCAST?

"I've been working really hard to create free and awesome courses to do just that.

We have a free course for podcasters. If you're looking to start a podcast, freepodcastcourse.com is your one-stop shop to learn how to create, grow, and monetize a podcast for free. I see the power of this medium, and I just want more people to have access to the knowledge to unlock the secrets and use them to their advantage."

Get your FREE copy of John's book, *Podcast Launch*, at eofire.com/gift.

For more free courses or to contact John, visit eofire.com

CATHI HARGADEN
Feng Shui Lifestyles

Cathi Hargaden (wealthyspaces@gmail.com) has been teaching and implementing Feng Shui for over 20 years with a diverse background in radio journalism and lecturing on health. As a health professional and entrepreneur, she has traveled extensively throughout the world, experienced various cultures and offers many real-life stories about the power environments have on people and their everyday lives. Cathi's work has helped clients increase revenue, reduce stress, resolve conflicts, build health, and more. She is the host of the Feng Shui Mastery Show podcast.

BEYOND REARRANGING THE FURNITURE

"Feng Shui for health and spiritually is complex, but it also can be simple. Feng Shui comes from an ancient book called the *Book of Change*. Our lives are changing from nanosecond to nanosecond, from the very micro particles (cells) to the macro (planets). We're changing all the time and if we can go with the flow of that change, then often life can be a lot easier.

The problems and obstacles come about when we resist those changes, and sometimes we're not even aware that there is a change or a flow. It's getting into that flow and being aware of it."

"If I said to people 'Okay, you want to make changes. You're going to have to change the way you think or feel; believe me, I'm a health professional,' it's not going to happen because people don't know what to change within themselves. But if you start saying 'Well how about changing the colors around you? How about letting go of all the memorabilia that's cluttering your house? How about putting pictures up that actually orientate you to where you want to go in your life?' then it's easier for people to change things on the outside.

And then those things on the outside start to change people on the inside, because to go from the inside outwards sometimes is too challenging."

GOVERNING ELEMENTS OF FENG SHUI

"Earth, water, wood, fire, and metal. You may think 'What's that got to do with environment?' Well, each of those elements is an energy. Some is earth energy. Fire energy is passion and action. And the water energy is represented in the north, because you're flowing. I don't prescribe to people 'You must put a picture up that's got three people in it, and two dogs and—' No. I say, 'This area is to do with this part of your life, and it is governed by these elements.'

It could be fire; it could be water. Then it's up to the person to get creative and think, there's water in that picture. I'm going to put up that picture and now when I look at it, it makes me think 'I'm on my way! I'm going somewhere in the direction I want to go!'"

ZB: This is something that is not necessarily explained by science, is that correct?

CH: "No, this IS science. This is where science meets art. Nikola Tesla said if you want to understand the universe, look at energy, vibration, and frequency. I would say if you want to understand Feng Shui, look at vibration, frequency, and energy. Because that's what it's about. It's about the energies within and without us, vibration of the place where you're living, and what you yourself are exuding and the frequency of that. The lower the frequency, the slower the energy. The faster the frequency, the more elevated."

"Think about where you're living now and who lived there before you. Think of the life they may have had. A doctor who died recently, Dr. Masaru Emoto, said that there's water in the atmosphere and that water holds memory. There are patterns in water and patterns in energy and the environment around us. Our lives are patterns as well."

"Native Indians used to cleanse the land. Increasingly in the West, we're out of touch with that; we don't heal the space.

If people buy a house and the energy hasn't been cleared, is it any wonder they sometimes start to live out the lives in the same space where there's been friction, divorce, and conflict?"

GHOST STORY

ZB: When it comes to certain energies being in certain areas, I have a ghost-hunting tour experience to share. This was on the infamous Gettysburg battlefield, where we went into this mansion that was an old hospital at the time. Hundreds of people died there, and this was not a very nice place during the time of the war.

They let us wander around and I found a way to get up into the attic, via a very odd ladder from the floor of the attic to the ceiling of the house.

I went and sat on the third or fourth rung and just kind of sat there for a moment. The group of people had electromagnetic field detectors when this extreme sadness came over me, I turned to the people who were facing me and said "Someone died in here" and just as I said that, the person who was leading the trip walked up the stairs and he asked "Who died?" I said, "I feel like someone hung themselves in here." He puts the meter right next to me and it's going off and lighting up.

People in the group said that at one point, my face went pure white and they took a photo of me. You can see this gray sort of cloud next to me and you can't really tell what it is. I said, "I think someone hung themselves here." The guide asked, "Boy or girl?" and I said, "Girl." And he said, "A girl hung herself about three inches to the left of your head." It's amazing to me, because I had gone in completely skeptical, and the fact I was able to not only detect gender, emotion, but also occurrences in that room, I fully believe that you can tell what has gone on in a place if you are sensitive enough to it.

CH: The people themselves aren't really in the room, it's the patterns that are left behind. I called it "energetic debris."

ON FEELING ILL AND BEING STUCK

"I've been in over a thousand homes, and I look around at the environment and I'm thinking 'Yeah, that's why you're ill. Have you looked at the dead plants? Have you looked at all the paperwork and the chaos here?' But people don't see it because they're in a habitual way of thinking, and they're living out a pattern."

"I CAN'T TEACH YOU ANYTHING BECAUSE YOU ARE SO FULL."

"Before you even start doing any Feng Shui, clear the clutter of things of the past that are not sentimental, but no longer are needed. That mentality of 'I've got to hold onto things because I may never get them back again.' It all comes from a mindset of frugality and this creates a rigidity that causes the rut they are in."

You are storing yourself in a box, which means you're frozen because your life's on hold. You've got to create space around you for new things to come in.

"Get yourself a compass and find out where north is and where north is, I want you to put a picture of where you see yourself going. Let's just keep it simple, in the next year, where would you like to be going? Is it a picture of a nice big boat going off to the Caribbean? Is it a picture of a family? A picture of fame? Are you a person whose health is compromised at the moment?

Then you'll want a lot of nice plants and flowers and things that create a sense of nature. Your environment is setup to give back these messages all the time."

ON HAVING A TV IN EVERY ROOM

"What exactly is the TV broadcasting? 'Buy me. Buy this. Do this. You're not healthy, so you need our product. You are not intelligent enough, so you need this.' These are the messages compounding people's subliminal brain channels through the ears, through the eyes, through these other senses, and hence, people become self-fulfilling prophecies of what the TV is telling them.

People think they're not that gullible, but we've all been programmed, so my invitation is for people to start programming where they want to go in their life.

Get themselves focused on a purpose and set it up in their homes to take the control back from the corporations, from the government, and bring the power back into their own living room."

GOOD VIBRATIONS WITH COLORS

"I've just been in central London over the weekend. I walk in, and it's very, very noticeable that many people are dressed in black. And I thought why is that when we have just a host of fantastic colors in our palette that we choose black? And black absorbs everything. If there's any depression or any kind of wanting thoughts, it absorbs all of that.

You've got a blue t-shirt on. That's very good. Blue is very good for communication. You actually eat certain colored foods in the season in which you live. So, for example, over in England, we would be having red and orange foods in the summer, because that's to do with fire energy.

Then we'd have maybe orange foods like the pumpkin and the sweet potato in the autumn. In the spring, we'd be having loads of greens, because that's the spring energy. In the winter, a lot of black & purple like root vegetables. You can actually work with the seasons as well and nutritionally organize your body."

INTERNAL FENG SHUI

"I do meditations with people where they can psychologically take themselves in and around the organs of their body. Each element is represented by an element and a color. This has been really effective for people because they've been able to bring in the power of color, the power of aroma through their own imagination and calmed down all the different organs in the body.

People often self-sabotage; a lot of autoimmune diseases are caused by creating not-good thoughts in our head. What's happening is people are disconnected from the rest of their body. This connects people with the organs in their bodies. What I'm trying to do is bring the Feng Shui not only to the environment, but internally so that the two come together. In the end, we have to look at the whole picture."

Tell me about services you offer and how you can go in and help somebody make a change.

"I had one client who wasn't my regular client – I was standing in for a colleague. This client was a solicitor who tried to commit suicide many, many years ago. My session with him was his final session. He didn't want to return to his business, and I said 'Describe where you work. What is it you're looking at every day? What's on the wall in front of you?' He said, 'It's just blank.'

I said, 'Well, why don't you put up a picture there that communicates why you're turning up to work every day? What's the vision? Where is it you want to go?' And right away, I could see this man's face change instantly. He was thinking about his family and where he wants to go with them.

That man skipped out of that office. You could see he was going off to implement these things."

KEY TAKEAWAYS

- Go with the flow of change
- Change from the outside in
- Vibration, frequency, and energy govern our lives
- Our lives are patterns
- Clear the clutter of the past

FREE WEBINARS

- Five Steps to Creating Wealth Thanks to Feng Shui
- Five Feng Shui Keys to Attract that Special Relationship
- Being in the Right Place at the Right Time

Sign up at Feng Shui Mastery Show (fengshuimasteryshow.com)

CONTACT CATHI

- wealthyspaces@gmail.com
- wealthyspaces.com
- Facebook.com/wealthyspaces
- Twitter.com/cathi888

DR. CARRI DRZYZGA
Staying Happy and Healthy

Dr. Carri Drzyzga (drcarri.com) is known as the Functional Medicine Doc, the go-to expert on finding the root causes for health problems so you can feel normal again. She's a chiropractor, a Naturopathic doctor, host of the popular podcast, the *Functional Medicine Radio Show,* and author of the hit book *Reclaim Your Energy and Feel Normal Again: Fixing the Root Cause of your Fatigue with Natural Treatments.* Dr. Carri's newest program is Entrepreneurial Fatigue: How to Fuel Your Brain and Body for Entrepreneurial Success. Her private practice is Functional Medicine Ontario, located in Ottawa, Ontario.

What is functional medicine and why is it important for us?

"People don't really know what functional medicine is because they haven't heard of it. It's about finding the cause, then fixing the cause, so that you can feel normal again. Finding the cause enables us to understand that everything in your body's connected. And from a purely biochemistry standpoint, to understand how hormones interact with the brain which interacts with the digestive tract, which interacts with everything else. So, to really find the underlying cause of where symptoms come from and then to fix that, which would include things like diet changes, getting the right amount of exercise and sleep, taking the right vitamins, herbs, supplements, stress management—all of those kinds of things to get the body back into balance to reclaim your health. Not only to feel normal again, but to reach a whole new state of health.

It's not band-aid medicine, which is what typical medicine is these days. It's medicine to find the cause and fix the cause so you can feel normal again."

ZB: So, this could really impact a whole variety of medical issues, right?

CD: "Absolutely. Any symptoms that you're having are a warning sign that something is out of balance in your body. And a lot of times, people will ignore symptoms, like 'I have some heartburn, I'll just take some Tums,' or they're starting to feel tired, so they blame it on stress. They're medicating themselves with caffeine and sugar. Symptoms come from somewhere, and when you ignore them, symptoms get stronger and stronger and it's like if you don't feel the pebble being thrown at you, one day you're going to have a brick thrown at you.

And that's usually when patients come in to see me, when they've had the brick thrown at them."

ZB: Low energy seems to be a big issue. I'm reading here there's four common nutrients that some people are deficient in and that can cause that? What are those?

CD: "Fatigue is very common, and I suffered with fatigue myself, so I have my own story about how fatigue affected me and how I had to treat myself to figure out where my fatigue was coming from.

A common story I hear when patients come into my office is that they've gone to their family doctor, had some testing done to find out where their fatigue is coming from, and their bloodwork comes back and everything's normal and the doctor suggests maybe to take a vacation, take three months off of work, or they recommend anti-depressants."

"That's a very common story when patients come to see me, but they know deep down inside that there is something out of balance. One of the things that I look for are nutrient deficiencies and a very common one is Vitamin D.

I live in Canada and anyone living in Canada pretty much has a Vitamin D deficiency. But you could be living in Miami and still have a Vitamin D deficiency, and the only way to know is to have your blood levels checked. Vitamin D is known as the sunshine vitamin, so if your levels are low, it'll be like your body has gone into hibernation mode and that's where the fatigue comes in. That's one of the very common nutrients that I find as being deficient."

ZB: I actually have a good friend who's just tired all the time. And he just kind of accepted it as being the truth in how he's going to live his life. And it could be something as simple as taking Vitamin D?

CD: "Yeah. The other ones I find are B12, magnesium, and zinc. Those are the four ones that I often find with my fatigue patients. Now that's just part of the puzzle; functional medicine is a puzzle we have to put together.

Nutrient deficiencies are one piece of the puzzle of fatigue and usually there's other things going on too."

How do you hold your patients accountable?

"For some people, you have to dangle a carrot in front of them to motivate them. For other patients, they need to be whipped in the behind, and that's what motivates them. So, it's a very individual thing. For some patients it's a manageable step-by-step process to reach a goal. Sometimes, it's also just figuring out how much the patient can manage, too, and still be moving forward and still motivated. It's quite tricky because everybody's so different."

"For some people, the real root cause is in their brain."

"It could be an imbalance between the neurotransmitters. It could be their brain is just not getting enough oxygen. People tend to breathe from their chest instead of belly breathing and they tend to hold their breath too.

It could be that the brain isn't getting enough blood. A lot of people have cold hands and feet and that's a sign of poor circulation, but that also means your brain is not getting enough circulation also and enough glucose to fuel it."

ON SLEEP

"The Centers for Disease Control, the CDC in the US, has found that sleep deprivation, which is six hours of sleep or less a night, is a public epidemic. Sleep deprivation weakens your immune system, it makes you hungrier, so you tend to gain weight, it puts you more at risk for having cancers, heart disease, and diabetes."

"Some of the causes for sleep deprivation that I see are pure lifestyle factors, like staying up too late watching TV, or being on the computer, tablet, or your cell phone. Because the light from those computer and cellphone screens are much brighter than your typical television screen, you're creating an imbalance of melatonin, which is your sleep hormone.
If you're not getting enough of sleep hormone, you're not going to sleep very well. There can be imbalances within the body, too, that is driving poor sleep. When a person has that attitude of, 'I'll sleep when I'm dead,' it IS a ticking time bomb because one day your health is going to just tank."

ZB: What sort of allergy problems do you see in people?

CD: "Food allergies and food sensitivities very commonly undermine people's health. I have one patient who had severe stomach pains for four years and she had had every test done. She was seeing a gastroenterologist and a gynecologist just to make sure everything was okay, and they ran every test they could, but could not find the cause.

So, she ended up in my office and we were at a point of checking for food sensitivities. I put her on an elimination diet, and she found out that she was sensitive to coconut. As soon as she took coconut out of her diet, the pains were completely gone. Like just gone. Absolutely, completely.

We could take ten people and line them up, and let's say they might have a sensitivity to eggs. Well one might have fatigue from eggs, the second might have aches and pains in their joints and think that they have arthritis when actually it's just a food sensitivity. Another one might get migraines and headaches from eating eggs, while another one might get depression. The next one might have anxiety and the next might have skin rashes."

"The thing with food sensitivities is they are the great mimicker because they can create any symptom in your body."

"If you're struggling with your health, what I want you to get out of this is to have hope because your symptoms are coming from somewhere and it's just a matter of finding the right doctor, running the right tests and figuring out what the real cause is."

TOP TIPS FOR IMPROVED FUNCTIONAL HEALTH

"The first and the most important is the mindset that your health is your most precious asset and to make it a priority and to take responsibility for it. Number two is diet and food. Food really is your medicine and the most important thing that can impact your body. Take small steps.

Have an extra serving of vegetables on your plate. If that's the small step you take, that's perfect because you're going in a better direction with your health. And then the third is getting back to sleep. The research on sleep says that the ideal amount of sleep is between seven-and-a-half to nine hours of sleep. One thing that has helped the majority of my patients is very simply wearing an eye mask when you sleep at night because it blocks out bits of light creeping in around your window blinds, light from your alarm clock, from your electronic devices.

All of those light bits of light blind your melatonin production. So simply wearing an eye mask gives more people a deeper sleep and they'll wake up feeling more rested."

How do people learn more about you?

Website: drcarri.com
Podcast: *Functional Medicine Radio Show*
Facebook.com/DrCarri/

KEY TAKEAWAYS

- Health is your most precious asset
- Focus on better sleep
- Eat more vegetables
- Eliminate food sensitivities
- Look for vitamin deficiencies

DAVID MEAD
The Golden Circle of Purpose

David Mead (propel-inc.com) works with leaders to help them create an environment where people feel safe and that they belong and show up to work because they want to, not because they have to. In 2009, David partnered with Simon Sinek, a world-renowned thought leader, and now travels internationally, helping organizations shift their perception around why they exist, what leadership really looks like, and how our human biology plays into it all.

Where does the foundation for figuring out who we are and why we're doing things start?

"I've been working with Simon Sinek for the last few years and he came up with a very simple concept called the Golden Circle where every organization, and even your own career, operate on three levels—what we do, how we do it, and why we do it. People are usually really good at talking about what we do and how we do it, and we're obviously clear on what we do, it's the products we sell, the service we offer, the title that we hold, but very few individuals and very few organizations can clearly articulate why they do what they do."

"Why really comes from our past experience. It's not aspirational, it's not 'What do I want to do with my life?' It's looking at past experiences where you have felt at your best, where you felt the most fulfilled, where you felt like you were doing something on purpose and getting the specifics of those stories and figuring out the common thread.

What is it that ties all those things together? What are the commonalities? Who are the types of people always around me? What was the contribution I was making in every single one of those situations that made me feel like I was really at my best, like I was really doing something that was more of a calling than anything else?"

"When we can find that pattern among those specific stories, that's really where the seed of the Why comes from. It's figuring out in what sort of situations do we need to place ourselves in order to feel at our best. What sorts of things do we need to be doing so we feel like we're the most fulfilled? And when we figure that out and we can clearly articulate that, then we can project that into the future and say, 'Okay, so now that I know what it takes for me to be fulfilled, now I know which situations to put myself in. I know what types of people to surround myself with and I know what to avoid.'
That's where it all starts."

ZB: It's interesting that you bring this up, because for a good majority of my life, video was my thing, but I had this moment where I was trying to figure it out if video is what I love because everybody's like "Oh, my gosh, you're so amazing! You do really good work!"

I came to the answer that I really liked it because a lot of people thought I was good at it. But I couldn't quite piece together what I enjoyed about it. I was telling a story in my business mastermind group and all of a sudden, the person leading the group had a lightbulb moment. She said, "You like telling stories. It's not that you like video. You like storytelling." And everything just clicked into place from there.

Why is it so difficult to articulate why we do what we do?

"The Why comes from the part of our brain that does not control language; it controls feelings and beliefs, which is what the Why is. So, it's hard to talk about why we do what we do, which is why we so often resort back to the What and the How. When you say, 'Why do you do what you do?' 'Well, to make money.' Yes, you need money to live, but it's just a result. It's not why we do what we do."

BACKSTORY

"I went through some stuff in my life where things kind of blew up and I ended up finding myself at the Apple Store where I worked with a lot of great people. I usually don't tell this part of the story, but I was walking to the back room after my shift was over one day, and I was just sort of talking to myself and as much as I loved the people and the environment, I just couldn't afford it.

I had a wife and a brand-new baby, and they couldn't take me on full-time and it just wasn't working out. I said under my breath, 'Ugh, I really need to find another job.' And a buddy of mine heard me, and he said, 'Hey, my best friend just started this new company, and basically what they do is door-to-door summer sales. You can make a ton of money for three months to hold yourself over until you find something else.' I hate sales, but I was kind of desperate."

Zephan cutting in here for a second – most of you know that I too worked for the Apple Store and had some very transformational moments come out of my time working there. I thought it was interesting to bring up the fact that David worked there too, and this is not part of my story. Back to the good stuff…

"I went to this company and when they discovered my background in corporate training, they hired me to run their training program. So, about a week after I started, they told me they were going to have an event and they were going to have a speaker come in, and the speaker happened to be Simon Sinek.

This was back in 2009, before anybody knew who he was, but when I heard Simon speak about WHY and the Golden Circle, I was like, 'Holy cow!' It's not like it was anything new, but it was something that I understood, and the way he put it into words so simply is what really hit me."

"I took the idea of purpose and showing up to work because you want to and not because you have to and contributing to something bigger than yourself and put it into a training manual that I was writing.

Simon came back into town a couple months later and I gave him a copy of it just to show him what he had inspired. He called me, and he was like, 'Dude, you heard me speak for forty-five minutes and you turned it into that?' He asked me to come and help him on the side while I was still working for this other company to put together the online Why Discovery Course, which is now on his website.

In the meantime, the company that I was working for, they didn't get it. They weren't interested in the culture I was trying to help them build, and they let me go. This gave me the opportunity to go work with Simon full-time and that's where all this started."

DAVID'S "WHY"

"My Why is to propel positive change so that people can progress toward the things that really matter, which is why my company is called Propel."

"There's a difference between causing something to happen and allowing something to happen."

"What I picked up on was that every person on Simon's team was NOT somebody who said, 'I'm really inspired, what can I do to help?' It was somebody who, on their own, said, 'I love that. I'm just going to do it on my own.' And we found out about it and it said, 'Hey, come do it with us.'

Rather than trying to cause something to happen, just do it. Simon has started a movement and a movement doesn't mean you have to be on the team of the leader of the movement; just do it! If something inspires you, just do it independent of the leader. And if the leader happens to notice that you're doing something great and they say, 'Hey, we would love to work together,' awesome. But when things are meant to happen, allow them to happen.

Don't try to cause them to happen; it just doesn't work."

HOW TO GET STARTED ON MANIFESTING YOUR "WHY"

1. **"Talk about it.** Communicate it. The reason most people don't talk about it is they don't clearly understand it enough to be able to talk about it. It's not an easy thing to do, but the more you do it, just like riding a bike, the more practice you get, the easier it becomes. As you start to tell people about the thing that you're working toward, you'll inspire other people who believe in the same thing, who want to help you get there and you will naturally attract other people who share your common values and beliefs.

    Alone, you're not going to be able to do anything great; none of us can. But when we talk about it, when we can begin to attract other people who believe what we believe and want to help us build the world that we imagine, together, we can accomplish anything."

2. **"Start using your *Why* as a filter for every decision you make.** Every decision will either get you closer to or farther away from your Why. So, when you're going to make a career decision, or decide to partner with somebody or hire somebody, always go back to your Why and use it as a filter and ask yourself the question, 'Is this decision going to get me one step closer to the world I imagine or one step farther away from it?'"

How do we go about not getting discouraged by the inevitable naysayers?

"There were plenty of people that said we would never land on the moon. There were plenty of people that said there would never be horseless carriages; pick your innovation and there have always been naysayers. The point is not to try to convince everybody that your idea's great, the point is to surround yourself with people that do believe it's going to happen.

Who cares what everybody else thinks? If it's something that you believe in, go for it. Apple is a great example. Apple doesn't really care if you buy their computer or not; they are more interested in surrounding themselves with people who believe what they believe, who are interested in creativity. Don't worry about the people that don't want what you want. Go after the people that do."

ON BEING AUTHENTIC AND BUILDING TRUST

"Tell the truth. You know, most of us don't flat-out lie to people, but we bend the truth. We tell little white lies and sugar-coat things a little. Don't do it. There's no better way to present your authenticity than to just tell the truth. And it takes practice and it's tough. When your girlfriend says, 'Do these jeans make me look fat?' What are you going to say? There are ways around it. You can say, 'I like the other one's better.' Just tell the truth."

"Don't pretend like you're good at everything. Nobody's good at everything. Admit what you suck at! Don't admit that everything is fine when it's not. We don't trust people who have all the answers. The interesting thing is, most of the things we're not good at, we don't really like to do.

So, if we tell people that we're good at everything, they'll ask us to do everything and we'll hate half the stuff we do. Tell people what we're not so great at, they'll have us do more of the stuff we're good at and they'll get somebody else to do the stuff we suck at."

The Biology Behind the Golden Circle

"If you look at a brain from the side angle, the outer section of the brain that corresponds with that What level of the Golden Circle is the neocortex. This is the part of the brain that controls rational thinking and language. The center two seconds of the brain that correspond with the Why and the How level of the Golden Circle is the limbic system. This is the part of the brain that controls our feelings like trust, loyalty, love, all the other ones, and it's responsible for all of our decision-making, all of our behavior, but it doesn't control language.

This is the reason the Why is difficult to talk about, because it comes from a part of the brain that controls those feelings or those beliefs, but it doesn't control language. What we usually do is default to what we do and how we do it because that's where the language lives—in the What. Emotional questions are tough to answer, like, 'Why do you love your girlfriend?' What we're attempting to do is to try to put these feelings that we have for another human being into words from a part of the brain that controls feelings but does not control language. That's the disconnect that we struggle with.

KEY TAKEAWAYS

- Know your Why
- 'Why' is a core belief
- Tell the truth
- Communicate your why

FOR MORE INFORMATION

- David's Website: propel-inc.com
- Simon's Website: startwithwhy.com
- Simon's books: *Start with Why* and *Leaders Eat Last*
- Podcast: *Start with Why*

CHANDLER BOLT
Writing Your Own Book

Chandler Bolt (self-publishingschool.com) is the host of the *Self-Publishing School* podcast & the author of 6 bestselling books including his most recent book Published. He's also the founder & CEO of *Self-Publishing School*, the #1 online resource for writing your first book. Through his books, podcast, training videos, and *Self-Publishing School*, he's helped thousands of people on their journey to writing their first book.

BACKSTORY

"You know, it's funny. I actually hated writing. I never really imagined that I'd ever write a book and, to be honest, I was a horrible writer. I always made Cs or Ds on my papers in college and high school, and my friends would churn out a two/three-page paper in like a couple hours and it would take me sometimes all night, and I'd just be staring at a blank Word doc having no clue what to say. It's like staring into the screen of death."

"My friend and I put our first book out there and it took off. It topped David Allen's *Getting Things Done*, the number-one time-management book on Amazon. Our book made close to $7000 in the first month, and it started bringing in $2000-$5000 a month of passive income, and when I dropped out of school, the book was paying the bills and keeping my head above water.

It really opened my eyes to what a book can do in terms of revenue, passive income, and being an authority. It's gotten me on podcasts and has brought in thousands of leads for my businesses."

ZB: Was your decision to drop out of school partially because you realized there's some good business opportunities here?

CB: "Yeah, absolutely. And it wasn't all because of the book. I actually planned to drop out of school before the book happened, but that definitely affirmed things. I'd already done a couple businesses before that, but I kind of saw, 'Okay, this is the future and I can really help people and make a lot of money from this.' So, that took me on that path."

ON COLLEGE DEGREES

"I think a lot of people are realizing that the whole college degree thing is kind of a fallacy. A lot of people were going out of state and getting $100,000 in debt for a degree that didn't get them a job.

It's great if you want to be a doctor, if you want to be a lawyer, if you want to be certain things where those degrees are necessary, but for a lot of other things, you can achieve it by either going in-state, going to a technical school, or maybe not going at all."

"Part of me wishes I would have dropped out a little bit earlier because I was running a business and got tired of learning how to run a business from professors who'd never run a business. I wanted to learn by doing, and I wanted to learn from people who were actually doing it, so that's why I dropped out."

ZB: Talk about other things that happened as a result of publishing that first book.

CB: "There's the authority, there's getting on blogs and podcasts, and the book drew in thousands of leads for courses and other online products. That's huge. It's a glorified business card. Would you rather do business with someone who hands you a business card or someone who hands you a book and autographs it? It's an inroad to relationships or people who you really respect and want to learn from."

"People don't like to admit it, but publishing a book is an accomplishment your parents are proud of, your friends admire—it's these intangibles where you think, 'Wow! I've done something that's had success and that's actually making money.'

For a lot of people, it's that foundation they can build on. It's not so much about the book, it's the opportunities the book opens up for you."

How hard is writing a book?

"Your first one is, by far, going to be the hardest, but it's still not that hard. The average book size right now is about 15,000 to 20,000 words, so that's a good target. That's a good size that sells well online right now. It's shorter, easier to digest, and easy to read."

"If you just chip away a little bit at a time, it's not that difficult. The good news is that you can speak your book into a mind-mapper. A mind-map is basically a brain-dump of what you're thinking about. Spend 10 minutes on a mind-map, and then 10 minutes on an outline, 10 minutes per chapter, and then speak it.

You'll have like an 80% written book, and then all you have to do it polish it up or bring in an editor. That's going to be a quality book. A lot of people miss that upfront step and just start speaking and then it's just is all over the place. If you have a little bit of guidance and direction, you can actually speak the book pretty easily."

How long does it take to speak 15,000 to 25,000 words?

"The average person talks about 150 words a minute, and so if you average that out, that's anywhere from about an hour and forty minutes to two hours and forty-seven minutes."

What sort of realistic time frame are we looking at to write the book?

"My brother and I wrote our very first book in one week, and that was 225-plus pages. My second book, we went from book idea to bestseller in two and a half months. It took us 16 days total to write, spread out over a month, writing every other day. That's a realistic timeframe.

Our program called *Self-Publishing School* takes people from book idea to bestseller in three months. We allot a little over a month for writing. It's pretty fast-paced, but once you get into this process, people discover it's a lot easier than they think as long as they have the discipline to keep going."

"It's easy to start, but several days in where you're not close enough that you're motivated to finish is the danger zone; that's when people give up. But once you pass the half-way point and you start seeing the finish line, then it gets so much easier."

ZB: Do you ever get people who really want to write a book, but they have no clue what to write about?

CB: "It actually happens all the time and our program's not cheap, but I think people trust our process. What I've found is most people go into the program with an idea or two that they could write a few pages on and that's all they've got. Then they do the mind-mapping for 30 to 45 minutes and then they're like, 'Wow, I've got so much more about this topic than I thought and now I can see it and it looks way less intimidating,' as opposed to people look at a book and they think, 'Oh, wow, that's just some huge, mammoth task that I can never accomplish.'"

ON DETERMINING WHAT WILL SELL

"A lot of people look at a popular niche and think, 'There's too much competition. I can't put a book in there' and it's actually the exact opposite. That's a greenlight that it's a good niche, and you just have to carve out your spot.

Our first book was about time management -- massive niche, there's a lot of books on that. We just carved out our niche, which was productivity and time management for entrepreneurs or for people who create their own schedule. So that's a niche within a niche, and we specifically targeted those people."

"If all else fails, there are four main categories that always sell books:
1. How to make more money.
2. How to lose weight or how to get fit.
3. How to be more productive.
4. What to do when you just got dumped or how to have better relationships.
Those are the pillars of books that will always sell."

ZB: Have you ever worked with people who have a hard time sharing their story with the public?

CB: "Yeah, definitely. There's a lot of fear and anxiety attached to that and even if they're not sharing a personal story, sharing your work is personal. There's this big fear of, 'I'm gonna put this out and people are going to slam me with bad reviews.' The reality of that is that it's just not the case.

We have weekly hangouts with our members, and we were doing a hangout last night and one of the members was talking about his book, about how he put out to his network that he was writing a book and about his deadline. He said, 'If I don't finish it and put it out by this date, you can kick my you-know-what' and the cool thing is people started reaching out.

He found an editor and people who wanted to help him."

"Everybody faces the same fears when they're about to finish and publish a book. But people are not going to judge you; some of them will actually be jealous. What you'll find is everybody has those fears and by embracing that, stepping up to the plate, getting the courage to put it out there, and letting people know, people will jump on board and they'll be much more supportive than you ever imagined."

How does Self-Publishing School work?

"The program itself is interactive and hands-on. We have videos, tutorials, checklists – you name it. There's a membership portal where you go at your own pace. But what I think is the most valuable part, and it's the part that's missing from a lot of online training programs out there, is the community. It's a really live community of people and we help pair people up with accountability buddies.

We give you a doc that you can use to set your goals for the week, and then you have a weekly call with your accountability buddy. We have a higher level in the program where we have coaches that you can get on the phone with every week."

"And then we have the weekly hangout where we share stories and answer questions. We'll bring on students – like last night – we brought on a student and he shared his story and how he overcame his fears and how the community was able to pull him through that. We have an easy calendar that's set up where you can be successful by spending 30 minutes to an hour tops a day.

And then we have a calendar that takes you step-by-step through the process. It's A to Z – how to write, market, and publish your book, all the nuts and bolts of what you need to do."

How can people check out this program, learn a little bit more about what you do and find your books?

Website: self-publishingschool.com

KEY TAKEAWAYS

- Learn from teachers who are doing what you want to do
- Books can be your calling card
- The first book is the hardest
- Carve out your spot in a popular niche
- Find a supportive community

GRETCHEN RUBIN
Better Than Before

Gretchen Rubin (gretchenrubin.com) is one of the most thought-provoking and influential writers on habits and happiness. Her next book, *Better Than Before*, is about how we change our habits. Her books, *The Happiness Project* and *Happier at Home*, were both instant New York Times bestsellers, and the Happiness Project spent more than two years on the bestseller list, including at number one. Her books have sold more than two-million copies in thirty different languages.

On her blog she writes about her adventures as she test-drives ideas from contemporary science and ancient wisdom about building good habits and a happier life.

BACKSTORY

"One day I was stuck on a city bus in the pouring rain, and I had one of those rare opportunities for reflection that you don't often get in the tunnel of everyday life. And I thought, 'What do I want from life anyway?' and I thought, 'I want to be happy,' but realized I didn't spend any time thinking about whether I was happy or whether I could be happier.

As often happens with me, I become obsessed with the idea and want to do a huge amount of research, so I ran to the library the next day and got this giant stack of books and started researching happiness. Before too long, I realized that it was a deep, rich subject and I really wanted it to be my next book. I decided I would spend a year to think about everything I wanted and tried to learn about happiness, whether we can make ourselves happy or how we can make ourselves happier, and then try it out and see if I would be happier."

"Something that all happiness researchers tell you is you need to have novelty and a challenge to be happy. I thought, 'No, I like familiarity and mastery, so I don't think novelty and challenge are going to be important for me.' But to test that, I decided to start a blog and I've had it for eight or nine years all about happiness, habits and human nature, as well as the books that I've been writing on those subjects."

ZB: Do you think we're losing sight of happiness because we're not being present in the moment?

GR: "That's a very interesting question and speaks to this idea of mindfulness and asking yourself if you're as happy as you can be. Many highly esteemed people have said happiness is not something you should aim for. But you don't hit a target by not aiming at it.

When you ask yourself what you can do to be happier, you make it much more likely that you are going to bring about those changes. I think, for most people, there's some low hanging fruit that doesn't take that much time, energy, and money, and really can make a big difference."

ZB: Is happiness something that is actually fairly simple and we're just forcing it?

GR: "There's this study that asked people what's important to you about work. And it turned out that money was not in the top three or four. And then people were asked, 'What do you think other people value most about work?' and they said other people value money. We tend to think other people value money more than they do. My sense is people understand that just having more money is not going to make them happy; they get the idea that it's how you spend it and it's the decisions that you make. That doesn't mean that people are necessarily following that understanding and spending their money wisely in the way that is going to have the biggest happiness bang for their buck. But I don't think there are many people that think that simply making more money, past a certain level, is going to make them happier."
"One of the greatest luxuries that money can buy is the freedom not to have to worry about money."

"If you don't have enough money, it's a big, big worry and it's a big negative. Then once you have enough, then other things begin to matter and decisions you make around money matter more. Like are you spending your money on a new bicycle or on cocaine? That's going to make a difference in your long-term happiness."

What are the biggest obstacles preventing us from being happy?

"I think one of the biggest obstacles is loneliness which should be studied and/

or addressed more. One of the things that comes up most often when I'm talking to people is what do you do if you're in your thirties and you move for your job to a place where you don't have family and you don't know anybody? For a lot of people, it's harder to make friends because people are really busy with a bunch of different things so it's hard to maintain relationships because friendship takes time and energy. And then sometimes people have a very active social circle, but they're missing a romantic partner. For many people, they want both of those elements of relationships."

"Ancient philosophers and contemporary scientists agree that we need to have strong, enduring, intimate relationships. We have to feel like we belong, and we need to be able to confide. We need to be able to give and get support. And when you look at the people who are happier, they tend to be people who have more strong relationships."

ZB: I read recently that the reason people have an urge to text while driving is because they're alone.

GR: "You know, I wonder if this is related because one of the things that struck me when talking to listeners of my podcast, *Happier with Gretchen Rubin*, is they say listening to my podcast in the car is like hanging out with a friend. People say they feel connected to you in some way."

How did *The Happiness Project* go from being a book to becoming a movement?

"It's interesting because when I was talking to people around me about this subject, there were two reactions. One was, 'Well the story of your happiness project is not going to be interesting because you're so ordinary.' They would say that in a loving way. And other people would say, 'You're so idiosyncratic; no one is ever going to identify with you.' So, there was this feeling that it's not going to strike a chord with anyone. But what I found out is people seem to be more responsive to someone else's story than big scientific studies or philosophical treatises. When I was writing *Better Than Before*, I found it so instructive just to talk to people about their experiences or other people's memoirs. So, someone like Benjamin Franklin or Saint Thérèse of Lisieux's memoir called *Story of a Soul* is extraordinarily influential to me."

"One person's story taught me more about myself that just about anything else."

"I think the reason *The Happiness Project* took off is because of this idea that if I really thought about the things that are most important to me and the very specific, concrete, manageable things I could do as part of my everyday life, these are the things that I could do. And some of them are really small. Like in our household, every time someone comes or goes, they get a real hello, meaning everybody comes to them and really speaks to them and hugs or kisses them. I started this because we were in a really bad habit of people just sort of grunting out 'hey!' from across the room and not really paying attention when people came and went, and I really did not like that.

I wanted to have a more tender, attentive atmosphere in our household. It's made a tremendous difference in the atmosphere of our household just in terms of the feeling of lovingness and connection. And that doesn't take a lot of time, energy, or money, so I think that's why it caught on."

ZB: Tell us about your book, *Better Than Before* and how we can change our habits.

GR: "The idea for this book came on gradually because I noticed that whenever I talked to people about happiness, whenever they were talking about a big happiness boost, or even a big happiness challenge that they were facing, they very often pointed to something that at its core was a habit issue. Like, 'My problem is that I'm exhausted all the time.' Well that's really about the habit of getting enough sleep.

So, I got more and more drawn into the subject of habits and the related issues of willpower, self-control and procrastination. And then I had lunch with a friend and she said something that got me obsessed with habits. I was asking her about her habits, and she said, 'This is the thing. I know I would be happier if I had the habit of exercising. And what's weird is when I was in high school, I was on the track team and I never missed track practice, but I can't go running now.' I thought, 'Why?' because it's the same person, it's the same behavior. At one time it was effortless; now she can't do it. What is going on with her habits? With that, I really wanted to come up with a framework that would explain everything I saw on habits."

ZB: So why do we find it so tough to create a habit for something that we love to do?

GR: "A habit is a kind of expectation and in the course of writing the book, I came up with a framework that categorizes how people react to expectations.

The four categories include: Upholders, Questioners, Obligers, and Rebels. The biggest tendency, and the one my friend falls into, is for Obligers to readily meet outer expectations, but struggle to meet inner expectations. When my friend had a coach and a team, she had no trouble showing up. But when it was only her own inner expectation for herself, it was very hard for her to follow through. If there's something you really love, yet you find that you never are following through with it, give yourself external accountability. For example, a friend of mine loves to read, but she never makes time to read. So, she joined a book club that held her accountable to do that reading."

"Just the fact that you love something doesn't mean it's going to happen."

"The ideas in this book, for many people, have been huge because you don't have to worry about priorities, motivation, or sacrifice. If you have trouble following through on something that's important to you, give yourself external accountability.

On my site I have a starter kit for people who want to start a group for people holding each other accountable. Think about AA or Weight Watchers. When a group comes together, they don't even have to be working on the same habits, but it's just the idea that you know that someone's going to be like, 'Hey, you said you were going to spend more time learning how to play guitar. Have you been practicing guitar?' Knowing that you have that external accountability, for many people, is really the crucial thing that's going to allow them to stick to it. So, you need to figure out why something's not happening, so you can bring about circumstances that will allow it to actually happen."

Are there any particular habits that we need to have as a foundation to make ourselves better?

"In the book, I talk about 21 strategies that people use to make or break habits, and it's the same strategies whether you're making them or breaking them. All of them are really powerful, and the one you're pointing to is what I call the *strategy of foundation.*

Certain areas of behavior go directly to self-mastery and when you're trying to give yourself a good habit, you need to use self-mastery. Eventually, you'll have it as a behavior to go on autopilot, which is excellent, but until you get that cemented in, you have to use your self-mastery."

"Self-mastery allows you to do the things you want to do and not do the things you don't want to do."

"Four areas of behavior go directly to self-mastery; they have special priority because they're going to make it easier to do anything else you want to do. One area to think about is eating.

1. Eating. Weirdly, one reason that people overeat is that they don't eat enough. They skip breakfast, they skip lunch, and then they're so hungry that the just grab anything, any junk food you can because you have to eat. You have to be satisfied in order to have that self-mastery.
2. Sleeping. If you're exhausted, it's very hard to use your self-mastery. And this is when you get into people who are getting by on four hours of sleep every night and then they're standing there at midnight in front of the freezer, eating an entire pint of ice cream to recharge their battery. Most adults need seven hours; it's really important to get your sleep.
3. Moving around. People often think they're too tired to exercise, but exercise actually boosts energy and self-mastery; it doesn't deplete it. You want to be up and moving around as much as you can.

4. Outer Order. This one surprised me. For most people, outer order contributes to inner calm and a sense of inner self-command. Many people feel like if they throw away their junk, if they put things in their proper places, if they get rid of things that they don't use or love, if they clear off surfaces, they feel more in control of themselves."

"Habits are 40% of our daily life."

KEY TAKEAWAYS

- Aim for happiness
- Money buys the power not to worry about money
- Focus on strong, enduring, intimate relationships
- Give yourself external accountability
- Develop your habits

CONTACT INFO:

- Website: gretchenrubin.com
- Podcast: Happier with Gretchen Rubin
- New Book: *Better Than Before*

DOTAN NEGRIN
Piano Around the World

Dotan Negrin (pianoaroundtheworld.com) has lived a life that is completely outside the box. Frustrated with the routine nine-to-five lifestyle in 2010, he took all of his savings to travel around the world and pursue a career in music. Since then, he has traveled to more than twenty-four countries lugging a 500-pound upright piano and meeting more than 10,000 people. He now lives in New York City and performs regularly around town.

ZB: Where were you in life when you first were just like "I'm going to take all my stuff and hit the road and get a piano and a truck?"

DN: "This was 2010 and I had been out of college for two years, graduated when the stock market crashed and there was a lot of fear in the air in New York City. I jumped around from job to job without feeling any sort of fulfillment. And after two years, I felt like I had wasted time and wasn't on track for a specific thing I wanted.

At the start of 2010, my dad's friend, an artist, offered me a job to drive his truck from New York to Miami to drop off his paintings to Art Basel. I completed that job, got paid really well and that week I got a phone call from a friend living in the Dominican Republic and he wanted me to come down. So, I took the entire $400 and flew to the Dominican Republic and had the most incredible adventure of my life! It was this trip when I fell in love with traveling, adventure, and the spontaneous spirit of adventure. I rode motorcycles in the rainforest and met local people in small towns.

Then I flew back to Miami because I had to drive back to New York with all the paintings. I came back to New York with a couple of hundred-bucks profit in my pocket. I started to think, 'Oh, this is amazing! What if I can make money and travel the world? That would be the ideal life for me!'"

"I kept working for the artist and did deliveries for him while figuring out how I can do this. After about six months, I felt miserable again. I didn't feel like I was doing anything that was gratifying. Throughout that six months, I came up with this idea to travel around the world and play piano. I could make money and travel and it would be this amazing adventure."

"It was August 2010 when I started playing piano on the streets and I was actually a pretty bad piano player. I would go on the streets and I'd push this piano like five to ten blocks just to play in City Hall Park and I'd make like fifty bucks and maybe like ten dollars an hour, but I started meeting people.

What made it so much fun is I was meeting people from all over the world. I just kept doing it. In September of 2010, because I was fairly new to moving the piano, the piano fell back and landed on my hand and broke two fingers.

I was out of commission for three months. I saw this as a big turning point – 'If I don't do this now, I'm never going to do it.'"

"It was the most glorious experience of my life."

"I had saved up around twelve-grand, bought a box truck on eBay, set it up with carpeting, a cooler, a little closet, my piano and a ramp. Then I just hit the road. I was living out of this box truck and still wasn't that good of a piano player, but I played every day for four or five hours.

In five months, I traveled 15,000 miles through 36 states and 200 cities. It really changed my life."

ON BEING FEARFUL

"I was so fearful. Even when I first started playing piano in New York, I was embarrassed to be looked at. Like, 'What am I doing?' I felt like such a fool. But I saw it as something extraordinary and something that no one else was doing at that time. 2010. I wanted to do something extraordinary with my life. Yet every day, I was fighting this fear. There were days I wouldn't want to go out and did not go out and play because I was so scared, and I didn't want to move the piano.

Eventually, I learned to love it because it brought me so much joy and the benefits far exceeded the fear, and that's why I kept going at it."

"When I first started traveling, the fear was deep because people would tell me 'Don't go to New Orleans! They're going to kill you there!' I heard stories like that even with Mexico too. I told people the reason I did it is because it's challenging. I can live in New York and go to work doing the nine-to-five, but I'm just going to be stuck in a box of routine."

ZB: From my own experience, at the end of the day, traveling is not really as scary as people think.

DN: "If you don't travel, the only way to know about the world is to hear about it secondhand. I once met a woman. This was on that first art delivery in 2010. I was in South Carolina and stopped to get a burrito. It was just me and this old woman at this restaurant. I was talking to her about traveling and she was like, 'I don't understand how you can travel like that.' I asked if she had ever traveled and she said, 'No. I've never been outside of this little town in South Carolina.' I was shocked. But then, she was like, 'Have you watched the news and seen what goes on in the world? I have no interest in going out there.' All of these images on TV and secondhand information created this negative impression of the rest of the world."

The first month that you're traveling, was there any one thing you learned that really surprised you, whether it was about yourself or about traveling?

"Realizing that the world isn't this dangerous place, but in fact there are more good people in the world than there are bad people. There are more nice, generous, friendly, open people in the world than there are people who want to hurt you. 95% of the people in the world just want to live and enjoy life and it's just 5% that are giving it this impression that the rest of the world is a bad place."

"But in terms of learning something about myself, one of the biggest things I've learned is how to interact with the world and starting to realize I've always been a very outgoing guy. I'll talk to everybody. I talked to drug addicts and people that have been living on the streets because I'm curious about their stories, I'm curious about who they are and what they've learned."

"I actually became friends with this one guy in Albuquerque and it turned out he played drums. I had a couple of drumsticks, and I gave him a bucket and I said, 'Hey, man, let's play.' He was so inspired by playing bucket drums, we ended up playing together, and he ended up robbing me. But then I found out he was a drug addict and that's why he stole the money.

I knew where he was sleeping that night, and I showed up there. Not to hurt him or anything, but I wanted to ask why? He told me he was an addict and thought I was going to hurt him. I was like, 'No, whatever, it's $40. I don't need to punch you or anything.' It turned out I had met him during the week he had just gotten out of jail."

ON GETTING UNSTUCK AND FINDING PURPOSE

"We all have this fear and a voice inside our heads that get in our way. The only way for us to really know is to just go out and try things because that's the only way we're going to know if we like these things."

"At the same time, finding a passion is great, but if you want to make it your living, it becomes a whole different animal, because not all passions can be monetizable. **When you're dependent upon your passion to make a living, it changes that passion.** It becomes difficult, and you start to not like it as much anymore. That's what I've discovered over the years.

I started to not enjoy playing piano, because I was so dependent upon piano to make a living. Because I had this box truck, I've done moving jobs to supplement my income. My original goal was to find a way to travel the world. make money and be able to work remotely. I've been on this journey since 2010 and I still haven't figured it out. Playing piano is not a great source of income."

"Failure isn't a failure unless it's the last thing that you've ever done."

How did you get on "The Situation Room" with Wolf Blitzer?

"I still play piano on the weekend in New York because of the amazing people. Just about every person there has an amazing story or good contacts. So, I was playing piano on the streets, and I met this woman who worked for CNN and she loved my story and put me on Wolf Blitzer. I have about twenty-five other stories like that. Because of my appearance on Wolf Blitzer, I did a commercial for Goodyear Latin America. They flew me to Peru, and it was an amazing experience."

"Playing piano around the world has opened up so many different opportunities. Just last month, for example, I facilitated a $150,000 marketing deal with two people I met. One of the guys has a startup company, and I'm friends with the creative director of the marketing company. All of this because I play piano on the streets and meet people."

ZB: For every drug-addicted thief, there's twenty stories of meeting amazing people.

DN: "My favorite story of all time is when I was playing piano in the streets of Portland, Maine, and this guy who was a drummer approached me. Dan loved what I was doing and invited me to his family's home, located on this beautiful pristine island. I drove two hours north, took a ferry, met him and we drove to his house. And there I was, eating dinner with three generations of this family; it was like a family reunion.

We had zucchini from their garden and fish they just caught off the coast. It turned out the entire family was musical. That night, Dan and his older brother were scheduled to play with their band at a small local bar where a hundred people come and dance. They invited me to play with them and set up a keyboard for me. I ended up playing the whole four-hour gig and it was the first time I ever played with an entire band. It was an incredible experience with people dancing; it was such a fun time."

"At the end of the gig, the older brother comes up to me and he hands me $200 and goes, 'Here, thanks for playing.' It was the most spontaneous experience I've ever had in my entire life, where I just said yes to everything that came my way and it brought me such an incredible experience of discovery."

What do you think the world needs more of now more than ever?

"I think people need to realize that they can do things on their own, that they need to take the leap, and get over the fear and that voice inside your head and try to do something that they really want to do and not give up on that.

There'll always be that fear, but it's only a bump in the road. Now more so than ever in the history of the world, because of the internet, we all have this accessibility to do something great with our lives and also be individuals, rather than just be part of a company."

Where's the best place to follow you and to see a couple of those videos of your trip?

YouTube: Piano Around the World
Website: pianoaroundtheworld.com

KEY TAKEAWAYS

- Travel is easier than you might think
- Most people are not out to hurt you
- Be spontaneous
- Meet people and grow your network

GENE HAMMET
Leaders in the Trenches

Gene Hammett (leadersinthetrenches.com) previously ran a multimillion-dollar business that struggled in the beginning, so Gene started focusing on the right parts of the business for extreme growth. Gene is the host of the *Leaders in the Trenches* podcast, where he has conversations with leaders for leaders.

ON FAILURE

"Failure is something that we all go through, and it depends on how you meet that failure, how well you come out the other side and how quick you come out. The things I went through would cripple most people."

What does it take to get to a multimillion-dollar business?

"I ran a sports travel tour company that I started in 2001, so the first full year was 2002. but the first—it was toward the end of that—the first full year was 2002. I had about two million in sales that first year. I had five employees, some contractor employees, and when I did the taxes in 2003, I realized two-million in sales is not a lot of money, because I was paying money to employees, I was paying for advertising, and I was taking home about $30,000, which was a huge jump for me, because I came from a corporate job in sales where I was making about a $150,000..."

"I share this with you because I want you to understand it wasn't easy. It was something I had to go through to get a multimillion-dollar business that was not only multimillion in sales, but also very profitable."

"I hired a coach and that coach asked me questions that no one was asking me, and I focused my business on the right customers and the right events, and I got rid of a lot of things that were costing me money and headaches. That's when I actually felt like I had made it my business. It took me about four-and-a-half years to get to that point."

"You know, every time I've hired a coach, I didn't have the money. Now, maybe I had the money in an account somewhere and I could do this, but when I was making $30,000 and I was paying bills, it was all gone. I had nothing extra. And the leap of faith to actually hire a coach is the kind of move that you have to take to be successful.

That's the kind of move that scares the crap out of you, but it really is meant to challenge your courage; are you meant for this? Because if not, go get a job. Go hide away in some cubicle somewhere and just go do that. But don't try to be an entrepreneur, because if you don't have the courage, you won't be able to do it."

"I actually hired a coach about this time last year, and I spent $25,000 total. Within six weeks, I had made that one back based on what I had learned in working with that coach, and the moves I made. And I was truly committed to making a change and showing up differently every time I got a coach. And I was there to learn, I was there to put it on the table, be honest, and say 'This is what I'm afraid of, and this is what the problem is,' because when you hold back, you're not going to get what you want."

What are some of the qualities that you look for in a coach?

"I'm real big on industry-related coaches for most people, but sometimes people need a new perspective and you can't do what everyone else is. I had a client that came to me, he had a coach in the mortgage industry. And he was doing what the mortgage industry coach did, and that's what they did for everybody, but it wasn't working. When he came to me, he was like, 'I come to you because I want new things, new ideas, and a new challenge.' And that's what we created for him. He's got the most successful business he's ever had in all of his life, because of the work we did nine months ago."

"But as far as my journey to finding coaches and what I tell people to do is you've got to have your questions straight. You've got to know what you're going to do and compare because you're about to spend a lot of money. Coaching at the higher levels, you're going to want to take in their content, you're going to see what they believe, you're going to see if you fit into that. I'm also looking at the clients they have, if the clients are getting the results that I want.

Are the clients the type of people that I am coming into this? And there's a lot to it, but that's a pretty good start when you're actually looking at this. I would also say someone that's actually run a business before. Because there's a lot of coaches that come from corporate, and they have never run a business. They've had money thrown at them; they don't really know what they're doing. Having that experience that I had 10 years ago and ran it for nine years was monumental in me running my business and me coaching my clients now."

ON FEAR AND LIMITING BELIEFS

"I had a lot of fears and limiting beliefs that were holding me back. My core speech that I give when I go to corporations is called The Trap of Success. I was trapped in my own success of making a decent living, and when I say decent, I was making $400,000 a year. That's really decent for most people. But I was trapped in that.

I did not want to venture out, even though I was unhappy. My wife came to me and said, 'How long are you going to do this? Because we both hate what you're doing.' And we did both hate what I was doing, but it was paying the bills, it was putting money into the retirement accounts, it was putting money into the savings, and it was allowing us that lifestyle, and I was trapped.

My fear wouldn't allow me to let go of that until something happened one day where I didn't have a choice, and I had to let go of everything to really create a life of purpose."

Is there one small change that we can make in our businesses or in our lives that would have the biggest impact on getting us unstuck?

"It's really about your own thinking. You've got to be willing to think differently, and I just noticed that over and over, when I wanted success, it was because of what I was thinking. It wasn't because of what I was doing, it's about how I saw the world, how I saw myself. Your inner critic is a jackass.

I said something different on my website, leadersinthetrenches.com, and you'll have to go to it to find out what I said. Every time you decide you want to raise your prices, it's not because of anything other than your inner confidence. And if you want to go out there and pick up the phone to sell something, the only thing stopping you is you. It's not someone on the other line, it's your thoughts. If you want to speak on some stage—I speak a lot for my business and I teach my clients how to speak—and the only thing holding them back, is just the inner critic that keeps them from taking action."

This not only applies for business, but in making big life decisions as well.

"I remember when I was 24-years-old buying my first house. I was pretty successful coming out of college, and I was able to save money for a down payment because I didn't spend any money, like most kids that age, and I was buying a house. And I was buying a house in a very nice neighborhood and it was very stressful. But I remember my boss turned to me and said, 'This is not a big deal, just go buy this house. It'll be the best decision you ever made.' But I second-guessed myself, 'Is it the right house? Am I prepared for this?' And it turned out to be a very good decision, because I bought a house for like $130,000 in a great neighborhood. I made about $70,000 over about three years—but if I had it today, it'd probably be worth three times what I paid for it."

What was the biggest decision to date you've had to make where you might have had those voices come up and tell you "I don't know if you should do this?"

"When I became a coach. Just to give you some context here, this was in 2010, I had been running a business from 2001 to 2010. On January 15th, 2010, I lost $3 million in one day. That's the failure that really set me back. I lost my house, I lost my savings, I lost my confidence—I lost everything. And I probably really needed therapy because it was so hard.

I was questioned by the Secret Service, I was questioned by other attorneys, I was spending money left and right; it was just insane. A couple of months after that, I was looking for what I was going to do next. I had no money, essentially, and nothing else to do, and I said, 'I want to make a difference.' The decision before me was, 'Do I go back into the same career?' – I really didn't want to go down that path – or, 'Do I go get a job, do I start another business?' What I ended up doing was kind of a hybrid. I ended up training as a coach — most coaches don't have any training whatsoever – but I'm proud that I went through this process because it really helped me understand myself so that I can serve my clients better. It was either that, or therapy. I joke around and say investing in coaching was a much better ROI than therapy because it actually launched a business for me. It launched a way for me to be the person I am and live my purpose. That decision was hard to make, though, I'll be honest with you."

"I was worried if they would accept me because of what I'd just gone through. Who wants their coach to say, 'You know what, I just lost $3-million? Let me help you run your company. Let me guide you, let me support you.' I was so worried about that, but then, I actually called my coach that I had a long time ago and had a real conversation with her. I said, 'What do you think?' and she goes 'Well, I'm going to tell you, you're used to making a lot of money – coaches don't make a lot of money until they cross a certain barrier.' Which is true, most coaches make less than a $100,000 total, ever. But she said, 'If you're willing to do this, people will accept you and your story, your experience will bring so much to those conversations that you will be a successful coach if you're willing to put in the work and build your business.'"

And it hasn't been that long. Just under five years, right?

"Five years, yeah. I got a job too. I got in sales, sold a bunch of stuff for other people and made some money. I helped a guy sell his company, and it's not like I cashed out big on that at all, it was just the confidence I needed to help him get some key accounts, help him get some cash flow, and helped really clarify that business. I went out on my own about three years ago. And since then, I've been tracking really well with my own business, because the most important thing is not my income, but it's the impact I'm making for my clients; that's what I focus on."

ZB: I had someone email me from as far away as Sweden and to know there's someone on the other side of the planet whose life I might be impacting, is extremely rewarding motivates you throughout the whole process.

GH: "Absolutely. It's fantastic. It boosts my day when I get those emails from clients thanking me for the work we did."

"The thing about it is I do a lot of work in the areas of sales and marketing to help people get speaking gigs, but what they thank me for is the person that they've become because of working with me."

"They thank me because they now have a level of confidence, they thank me that they can now figure out some of these things on their own, and that's what real coaching's about.

A lot of coaches will tell you what to do and that's because they're not trained on true coaching, they're just accepting some title and really what they're doing is consulting. They're looking at your business and they're telling you how to run it. And the problem with that is most people are not transforming, and so, they become very dependent on the decisions from that coach, and that's really doing people a disservice."

ABOUT LEADERS IN THE TRENCHES PODCAST

"I was talking to my wife about what it's like to grow and run a business. Not the starting part; there's a lot of hype and excitement about a new idea. But what happens when all of that excitement dies down and you actually get in there and start working it? You get in there and start making the phone calls and sending out emails and creating videos and creating podcasts—whatever it may be—and it doesn't go your way? And we talked about this for a while, and she's told me that I need to support that segment of the market that is completely covered up with all the things they need to do and can't get it all done.

They can't get traction, but they're working really hard, and they're not making it. I was having a conversation with a client about his, and I said, 'I want to work with business owners, the leaders of their companies who are in the trenches,' and he goes 'Oh, leaders in the trenches!' and I'm like, 'Oh, that's pretty good.'"

RECOMMENDED RESOURCES

"I've got free stuff on my website, leadersinthetrenches.com/freestuff. I've got a list of resources for speaking to serve your business, to get clients, you can go to a training course right there. I've got the seven steps to get speaking gigs. And I've got the Inner Critic audio program, and a couple other things that would help you increase your sales in your business."

What should we be doing with our lives?

"We should have the courage to truly live our purpose.

Go and figure out exactly who you are because most people are unaware of how they see the world.

They're closed in some box; they limit themselves. I help a lot of people get speaking gigs who will come to me and say, 'Well, I can't speak for free!' or some people will go 'I can't speak at all!' 'I can't speak here!' 'I can't speak there!' and it's all just some story that's in their head.

My wife is a professional speaker, because one day she decided, 'I'm going to be a professional speaker, and I'm going to make my way in this world.' And now she is; now she's living her purpose. Even when I give her ideas, 'Hey, you could go into this market,' she goes 'Nope! I'm right where I'm supposed to be. This is what I'm here to do, and I'm going to do it.'

People should have the courage to go after what they really want, and they should have also the courage to let go of the things that are holding them back and not allowing them to live the life they want to live."

KEY TAKEAWAYS

- Being an entrepreneur takes courage
- Consider hiring a coach in your field
- Being successful doesn't mean a big salary
- Know the difference between coaching and consulting
- Live your purpose

CONTACT INFO:

- Website: leadersinthetrenches.com

RICK MARTINEZ
BINK

Rick Martinez (projectbink.com) is an award-winning entrepreneur, nurse, veteran speaker, and the founder of Project BINK. He brings a wealth of experience and tremendous passion for impacting lives. His early business success prompted San Antonio Business Journal to name him one of the city's 40 Under 40. His first company, a medical services contracting company, would go on to become one of the US Small Business Administration's Top 100 companies. Rick was awarded the prestigious Jefferson Award for public service, further embodying his spirit of giving back and serving others.

BACKSTORY

"I've been a registered nurse since the early '90s and a few years into my practice, the entrepreneurial bug really started biting. I started a staffing company, nothing sexy about it. I think what really started to morph me was when our clients—when we moved away from private staffing, meaning your regular city hospitals, and moved into government staffing—what that means is we actually put doctors and nurses in military hospitals all over the country and what that meant is our client changed.

Our client was no longer just somebody who needed assistance; these were soldiers and our mission changed. It became—it always was very heartfelt, but now it was a heartfelt, compassionate, even patriotic sense of what we did, and the company grew."

"I was activated by the United States Army in 2006 and 2007 as an army nurse and sent to Washington DC to work at Walter Reed for 18 months. That's where the nursing and veteran thing really start to come together. I was an ER trauma trained nurse and I didn't go to an ER setting; I went to a floor at Walter Reed where we took care of amputees and talk about an 'Aha!' moment. Talk about where you suddenly look at things differently. That's where I think I started to understand that there may be a bigger calling somewhere."

ZB: Why do you think so many people work for a few years and then are hit by the entrepreneurial bug, the travel bug, or the purpose bug and really start to question everything?

RM: "That's a really thought-provoking question. I think it's just the human condition. I think, for the most part, we all ask those questions. Whether we're in a job that we like or don't like, we always ask 'Why am I doing this? What does this all mean?'

My last kid is about to leave the nest and we start to ask different questions; it's part of our growth. When we're children, the questions are always 'Why?' 'Why is the sky blue?' But as we grow, the questions morph into the What's. 'What does this mean?' 'What should that mean?' Sometimes it takes those moments where we step into a hospital and see a kid who was just blown up to make us ask those questions; sometimes we ask them intuitively; and sometimes it's moments that cause us to ask those questions."

ABOUT PROJECT BINK

"I go to Walter Reed and I'm now an active duty army nurse for 18 months, and my company's still in San Antonio. We're still growing. We have about 30 people on our staff in our office in San Antonio and we staff about 500 to 600 employees, doctors and nurses, at military bases all over the country. I'm doing my thing, the company's growing, I come back, and I have this realization that it's time to do something different. I ended up selling my company.

The thing is, after I sold it, as an entrepreneur, there was this real emptiness. It's like, 'What did I do?' and 'Where do I go now?' I started to ask, 'What does this all mean?' This is where my real journey into seeking deeper meaning started because I didn't have a job anymore; I was no longer at Walter Reed. All of a sudden, I didn't know where I fit. I was searching, searching and I've always been a fitness buff; I like to stay in decent shape. I entered a weightlifting competition up in Austin, Texas back in 2012 and, again, I was searching for meaning, to coin Victor Frankl. And I had an accident.

It was a weird accident, but the essence of it was, in the middle of a lift, 225 pounds crushed my right leg. It was that accident that opened my eyes. It was an awakening for me that there's a bigger picture out there. There's something more and I was focused on the wrong things; I was focused very internally with this arrogance. The accident really was an awakening that 'Hey, hey, hey! There are others out there. There's a bigger picture.' I made the conscious choice of not feeling sorry for myself, of really exploring it."

"After a reconstructive surgery and some rehab, I went to an event in Cincinnati and it was about 30 people, and afterwards, I'm standing around talking to Sam Horn. And she asked me, 'What happened to your leg, Rick?' and I said 'Oh, I had this accident' and I'm making—I'm trying to divert away from it, and her eyes pierced right through me, and she said 'Rick, what happened?' and it gave me chills then and it gives me chills now because it's like she knew something was different, something had changed. And I told her the story of my accident, and my awakening, and I was sharing it for the very first time right there.

As I'm saying the story to her, reenacting the weight falling on my leg, and I flicked my wine glass with my finger and it made this sound, this 'bink' sound and it resonated up in the air. And we stop for a second and froze and she said 'That's your sound. That's your word!' And I said, 'What? What do you mean?' And she said 'Bink, you had a bink moment.' And it just felt right. Because to call it an 'Aha!' or an epiphany, it's just — cliché and it meant so much more to me."

"Project BINK was birthed during that conversation, because here's what she said to me next—and then I'm going to be quiet—she said 'Rick, that story. If you were to tell that story again, if you were to share that story, your piece of your journey, how you changed and morphed and how others can, do you think it could impact somebody?' And I said, 'I think it could.' And she said 'Rick, it's your moral obligation to now tell that story,' and that's what happened. I went home, and the entrepreneurial fire kicked in and Project BINK was born, and that was the genesis of the project and this business now."

ZB: How could other people create this moment for themselves? Is there a way people can at least open themselves up to the possibility that they can find some better answers?

RM: "I think the operative part of what you just said is 'open up;' that's where it begins. We are so busy in the grindstones of our lives – we're hustling, we're building, we're creating, we're raising families. What I'm afraid of is one day we look up and our noses are gone. Where it starts is being able to open up, being able to revel and receive everything else that's going on; it's important that we do that. The moments are always out there happening, it's just a matter of us tuning in, becoming more aware, picking our heads up, smelling the roses. Sometimes it just means stop, slow down, take a second, take a minute, take a vacation, and look around, see what's happening. That's where those moments often happen. I think where it begins is just awareness. Looking up, opening up, and taking in everything around us."

"It's in all those small moments that the richness of life really comes out and we get to find a deeper meaning and maybe a sense of purpose in that."

THE BINK PROCESS

"We actually formed a company and our first product was a book that talks about the theory of life purpose. Not my theory, but just what we've been taught, that purpose script, if you will, that we're supposed to find and live. Then it talks a little bit about the story of how sometimes purpose is thumped on us. And then at the end, it talks about a process, a simple four-step process by which we can decode those moments and help us individually make sense of it.

The first step is to be aware that something has happened. Good or bad, some moment has happened. The second part of that is the I of the B-I-N-K, it's that "it means something." Imagine my accident, it could have meant a lot of things, but for me, it meant that there's a bigger message out there. Give it a positive meaning; we get to choose."

"The B and I are internal, while the N and the K are external. The N part of this, it's 'new action.' In other words, don't do what you've always done, or you'll get what you've always got. Take some new action as a result of the awareness of the meaning you've applied and do something new. For me, it was I started to write, just in a journal. I didn't say, 'I'm going to go write a book,' I just started to write in a journal. And I actually have it right next to me, it's a little journal I got. It was a new action and that new action cascaded into a book, which leads us to the final step of the process of K, and that's 'knowledge sharing.'

For me, what that meant was I had this moment, I became aware, I gave it a positive meaning, I began to take a new action of writing every day in my book, and the knowledge share was, 'Okay, now I've got to do something with what I've learned,' publishing the book.

The knowledge share for anybody else could be joining a group and sharing your story, mentoring, teaching, guiding, starting a podcast—but it's a shame for us to learn something from that process of the moment and then keep it to ourselves because what I learned is that it's not meant just for us. If we can impact others, isn't it then our moral obligation to share it? That's the essence of the B-I-N-K process."

"Human beings are meaning-making machines. We make everything mean something. Make it mean something positive."

KEY TAKEAWAYS

- Open yourself up to possibility
- Be aware of your life, slow down and take in where you are
- Accidents happen, you get to choose how they shape you
- Share your newfound knowledge

CONTACT INFO:

- Website: projectbink.com

JASON ZOOK
Jason is Up to Something

Jason Zook (buymyfuture.com) formerly known as Jason SurfrApp, Jason HeadsetDotCom and Jason Sadler, is an unconventional marketer and entrepreneur. He created I Wear Your Shirt, a company that used sponsored t-shirts to promote businesses on social media. And in 2012 and '13, he auctioned off his last name to the highest bidders. Jason recently wrote a book about his entrepreneurial journey, but in a very unique way. Frustrated by the confusing landscape of book publishers and book agents, Jason self-published and raised over $75,000 through sponsorship for his book, *Creativity for Sale*—before a single word of the book was written or a single copy was sold. Tired of living a life that felt prescribed to him by society, Jason used his out-of-the-box thinking and ingenuity to create multiple profitable internet-based businesses. He is a public speaker and entrepreneur at heart and lives a life of intention and continues to strive to make a living doing what he loves.

BACKSTORY

"I always had this feeling growing up that I was different. I had this feeling something about me was unique or that I had more to offer the world than going to a job and sitting in a chair at a desk and working eight hours a day and then going home and that was it, that was my existence. And as I left the 9-to-5 world and I gave my brain the permission to be like, 'Okay, let's get weird. Let's do some stuff that's different, let's be okay with not fitting into the status quo of society.' And when I Wear Your Shirt came into my brain; it was a culmination of all these different things that I thought would be interesting.

At the forefront of that, it was really telling stories. I've been a storyteller ever since I was a little kid, always trying to entertain my family, having fun and being the jokester. And with I Wear Your Shirt, every single day, I got to tell a different company's story in my own way, being unique, and trying to bring some humanistic nature to advertising, which didn't really exist and still—in my mind—social media has now become, 'Hey, here's our discount codes. Here's our story'—they're putting all their stuff out there in a normal way. Very rarely do you find these awesome wins.

I think there was something that was missing there and for five years, I tried to capture that and made over a million bucks wearing t-shirts, which is ridiculous, and have had a lot of different other projects come along the way."

"For me, the way these crazy projects happen is, when somebody says 'yes' for something absolutely ridiculous, it's empowering. The more that people give me permission to do that by giving me money for these things or saying yes or agreeing to contracts or whatever, every step along that path is 'Oh, okay, let's get crazier! Let's do more things that are interesting.'"

"I was a nobody from Jacksonville that wanted to get companies around the world to pay me to wear a t-shirt. That's a little bit audacious, but I was like, 'Why not? Why does it have to be some celebrity? Why can't it be just a normal person who is willing to put themselves out there?' I think a lot of people get stuck. They think 'I have to have a big following. I have to do all these things.' No, you don't; you have to have the courage and you have to have the work ethic and you have to be willing to hear a bunch of people tell you 'no' when you're getting started.

I was just able to push through all that stuff and say, 'Alright, let's keep going.' And that's what continues to drive me through all my ideas; I want those things more than I'm afraid to do them, and that's the lens that I apply to everything that I'm doing."

Is there any secret-sauce to figuring out how to create a business out of the thing that you have so much fun doing? I think that some people out there would look at what they love doing and they wouldn't be able to figure out how you can make money off of it.

"In the beginning, I was really excited to try and film videos every day, because that's what I did. I filmed a video every day, I took photos, I tweeted, I was on Facebook, and I was on a live video show. But as that progressed, I wasn't passionate about those things; I wanted to tell the story.

I wanted to find the interesting nuggets about these companies and share those, and then all of those things that I did were the vehicle to express those. That became what I call building a 'career dungeon' around myself. As an entrepreneur, you start your own business and you're like, 'I'm going to have all this freedom!' and now, all of a sudden, I was working 14 to 16-hour days, I was editing video for six hours, and it was miserable. Every day was like, 'What did I do to myself?' I could do this from anywhere, but I'm locked into all these hours."

"Reflecting back upon that and looking at the type of businesses that I have now and the things that I do now is more along the lines of I really want to follow just a hint of passion. It doesn't have to be the thing like, 'Oh my gosh I love this thing.' I use the Mark Cuban quote, 'follow your effort, not your passion.'

Where will you put your effort every single day? What do you want to put work into? For me right now, the world I'm in is writing. I love writing. And over the past two years, I've written almost a million words—in the past two years. And I was never a writer before that. I never read before that; I didn't have any experience. I don't even have a journalism background of any kind whatsoever. But I found that that's a really fun way for me to express my thoughts and to tell stories nowadays."

"If anybody is thinking about 'I want to try X, Y, Z thing,' make sure you want to put your effort toward it. Make sure it's not *just* something that you're passionate about, that just lights a fire under you. That is important, but a lot of times, it won't lead to a good business and then you're going to hate that passion because you're going to have to be a slave to it, which is not what you want. You want to find something that you're willing to put effort into."

ON HAVING MONEY

"I realized over the years, my values were not necessarily about money in that having a certain amount of money, to me, doesn't really matter. *What does matter* is having enough money that I can have the control and flexibility to travel or that I can help support a cause that pops up that a friend of mine's doing on Indiegogo or whatever and not have to worry about that stuff and not have to think about it. And, of course, having my pills paid. The freedom to not have to worry about my bills."

SUCCESS AND VALUES

"I've only realized my core values as of the past year or so. I think, as guys, it's something that a lot of us don't think about a lot. We're more like, 'We're going to take care of you, we're not going to think about ourselves. We've got to kill the wooly mammoth and we've got to make sure that there's a fire and then that's it.'

But how do we feel about the wooly mammoth? How do we feel about the fire? I'm really starting to look into some of that stuff and defining that for me and saying 'What are my metrics of success? Okay, now how does my business relate to those?' and then, really, those metrics become a filter. And then everything that you do gets passed through that filter. If it doesn't make it through, if you see something like wearing hats for a living. 'Hey, does this give me the freedom of flexibility? Is this fun for me? Is this something where I'm giving value and it's something that I care about?' 'Hmm, probably not; it's chasing the money,' that idea goes away."

"I think it's really good to be able to establish those things and then be able to look at them on a continued basis because they change. It's okay if you define them once and you're like, 'Oh, here's what I thought they were a year ago, but now I've evolved as a person, so here's what they are,' and that's a constant evolution and change that's perfectly okay."

ZB: What came after wearing a bunch of shirts for a couple years?

JZ: Towards the end of I Wear Your Shirt, which ended in 2013, I had an unfortunate family situation. My mom called me on Skype, which never happens and she's like, 'Your step-father and I are going to get a divorce,' and this was unfortunately my third father at the time and I was like, 'Oh, man, that really sucks.' I didn't have a lot of attachment to him and my mom explained a little bit of the situation and it wasn't good. And at that moment, the storyteller entertainer in me came out and I was like, 'Oh, screw that guy, I'm going to sell my last name and mush it in his face in the public eye.'

I got my mom to crack a smile in a moment of sadness, and that was really it. This was April of 2012 when that happened. And then four or five months later, I'm sitting in a Panera Bread and I was like, 'I don't really want this last name, Sadler anymore; it had never defined me – I've had three last names, but I don't want to go back to any of them. I don't know how to pick a last name, but I want to find my identity.' Just looking at the White Pages wasn't going to do. So, I launched a website called Buy My Last Name—the domain was shockingly available. I started an auction at zero dollars. I built up a small email list, building some buzz about it and it launched and was up to $33,000 in the first 24 hours."

"It was timed well enough that I had been on social media for four years, I had been building my brand for four years, I had been in a bunch of press and media outlets for four years. I couldn't have done that idea five years ago; no one would have had any interest. The last name thing went off really well the first year. I was on the first page of USA Today, I announced it live on Fox & Friends, just a ton of press. I did the last name thing a second time and that led me to my book."

A UNIQUE BOOK PUBLISHING MODEL

"I was like, 'I want to write this book, but I don't want to get a publisher. I don't want someone to tell me what book I want to write. It's my story. I don't want someone to edit out something of my life just because they think it won't sell on a bookshelf or something.' I said, 'Let me try and do some type of crowdfunding with sponsorships.'

And basically, offered up a spot at the bottom of every page that's a hundred and forty characters in length, like a Tweet, and I sold the pages starting at $600 and then counted them down $3.00 less each page.

By the end of the 200- page book, the last page would be $3.00, and then I thought, 'Hey, most people don't read an entire book, I don't.' And I launched it and five months and 5000 emails later—and by 5000 emails, I mean people emailed me and asked questions – I pitched it to people who were sponsors of I Wear Your Shirt. There was so much going back and forth and explaining; I was selling something intangible."

"Not a great business model. I'm like, 'Give me $600 and you don't get anything for eight months, and you still don't even know what you're going to get because you can't actually see it until it's done.' That was a hard sales pitch. But it worked. I was able to raise $75,000 in five months. I basically wrote myself a book advance authors would never get and with full control and I wrote the book Creativity for Sale."

"It has *not* gone on to be a bestseller, it has not hit any lists, but I've moved over 10,000 copies on my own. I get emails probably once or twice a week from people who said that this book has an incredible impact on them. It was a labor of love, but I didn't want to ask somebody permission, I wanted to do this in the way I wanted to do it."

What is the author name that this book was published under?

"I did another auction for Buy My Last Name. The big call out was 'I'm writing this book, it's going to be on the front cover of the book.' A surfing company called SurfrApp, basically a Yelp for surfing and they're trying to build this surfing ecosystem. It was Jason SurfrApp on the front cover of that book. That's my Amazon bio."

What is buymyfuture.com?

"What I've realized over the years is I love creating new products. I love making things. It's fun, I solve problems for people. They give me money for those problems that I solve, and that feels awesome. But I don't love the constant cycle of, 'Okay, now I've got to market. Now I've got to do all these things, promoting and sales funnels and all this stuff.' I don't love it and it feels icky to me. It got me thinking, 'Okay, what could I do, based on some of the projects I've done before that would be crazy but would also be akin to me but would give people value?' And so, I am launching a website called buymyfuture.com, where for $1000, people can buy one-time access to everything I will ever create for the rest of my life, plus you get the eight things I've already created.

The way I'm spinning this to people is the past eight products are worth about $2500.

The next six products that I'm guaranteeing that you can see on buymyfuture.com—two courses, two books, and two other web apps—are worth about $2500 each. It's about $5000 in value for $1000."

"The beautiful part to me is that if you invest $1000 in me, I'm not going anywhere. This is the stuff that I love. I create things for three subsets of people who want to be more creative, who want to take action in their business and lives, and those are people who want to make money with the stuff they do and maybe in interesting ways. I think there's really interesting ways that you can make money and that's what I'm building around. For me, this is my opportunity to say 'Okay, for two weeks, September 22nd to October 6th, you can invest in my future.

You can invest in me, spend a thousand bucks. You get a ton of stuff.' And then there's also going to be some really cool stuff with a community that's involved. I'm going to do quarterly calls with this community, so I can dig in and see what they need. I want to get out of this cycle of having to sell every new product that I make and just do this once a year Buy My Future for a thousand bucks—which I think is super affordable for all this stuff; I'm selling my future."

ON BEING STUCK

"For people listening to this, if you're sitting on the edge of, 'I don't really like what I do, I want to do something else.' It doesn't have to be a huge leap. You don't have to think about it like in the classic action movie, jumping from one rooftop to the other and, 'I may not make it!'

Why not jump one step up a flight of stairs to the next one? Take that leap, which is a side project, which is something you can do in your spare time – a really small best version of whatever your idea is.

I think side projects are incredibly important. I think it's also important to quit side projects. I think it's important to make space for other things in life so that you can do more things. And I think that quitting allows for space—and a lot of people don't think about it that way. They think quitting is failure, and to me it's not. I'll start working on a project and be, 'Mm, nope' and then, I shelve it. It's not worth the time."

"If anybody's listening to us and they're thinking 'What can I do with this? How can I start my own thing?' Start small. The smallest version that you can do of that. Taking that risk? You will see the benefits of it. It'll be hard, for sure, to make those decisions, but there's so much that comes out of that that's positive that you'll never even be able to see if you don't take that chance."

WORDS OF WISDOM TO YOUR YOUNGER SELF

"I would say 'Dare to go bigger,' because there were a lot of times when I had opportunities to work with bigger companies and I was afraid because I still felt that 'I'm a nobody from here.' And that's a self-limiting thing. No one said that about me. No one did. I was the one who was thinking that. So, take those limits off, dare a bit bigger. Take a second and define your values. What really helped me do that was a book by Pam Slim called *Body of Work*. It really helped me start to chip away at that stuff."

"The other thing I would tell myself is 'start writing.' Every day just start a daily writing practice, because it has led to a lot of opportunities, and it sparks a lot of ideas. I'll start writing about absolutely nothing – I'll be writing about outside, the things that I see and then it'll lead to 'Oh man! Idea!' my brain connects some dots and then, boom, a creative idea happens. And it's only because you're stimulating it. You're not reading the Facebook feed, you're not reading Twitter, you're not watching cat videos on YouTube, you're actually doing something where your brain is kind of like crunching numbers."

KEY TAKEAWAYS

- Be unconventional
- Find something that you're willing to put effort into
- Reassess your success metrics
- If you don't want to take a huge leap, take a small step
- It's okay to drop a project, learn and grow from it
- Avoid self-limiting thinking

BOOK RECOMMENDATIONS:

- *The Obstacle is the Way* by Ryan Holliday
- *Body of Work* by Pam Slim

CONTACT INFO:

- Websites: jasondoesstuff.com, buymyfuture.com
- Book: *Creativity for Sale*

JOEL ZASLOFSKY
The Value of Simple

Joel Zaslofsky (valueofsimple.com) is the curator and simplifier behind Value of Simple, The SimpleREV Movement, and the *Smart and Simple Matters* podcast. In March of 2012, two years after his personal renaissance shook him awake, he quit his cushy job to help people simplify, organize, and be moneywise. When he's not enjoying nature, making his wife smile, or playing with his two young sons, he's living intentionally being paleo and experiences curating.

BACKSTORY

"I'm almost 36-years-old and for the first 36 years of my life, I was totally sleepwalking through it. I had a great middle-class upbringing in St. Paul, Minnesota. My parents provided everything for me. I went to a great college, met a wonderful woman, got a cushy corporate job, and everything was just clicking along. When I was 30, my wife told me she was pregnant with our first son. After the euphoria of, 'Sweet, I'm going to be a papa!' wore off, I realized, 'Wait a second, I'm going to be a father, and there's a lot of things in my life that are not conducive to being a good father.'"

"That was the first moment in my whole life where I completely stopped and thought, 'Where do I need to go in order to be a good father?' and I realized my current trajectory was not going to take me where I wanted to be. I was addicted to video games, routinely staying up until three in the morning, then went to work at that cushy corporate job for 11 hours. I wasn't really physically or emotionally available when I got home, and I thought, 'You're going to be a horrible, horrible father!' That was the day I decided to give up video games completely; I don't do well with moderation.

I'm very much into find a paradigm, find a mindset, do it, rock it, and don't worry about the alternatives that are out there."

"My wife coined this time in my life my personal renaissance. I started experimenting with paleo and minimalism and a whole bunch of other things. I had become version 2.0. Before my wife told me she was pregnant, I never aspired to be anything other than what I was, but once that safe bubble was popped and I looked outside and thought 'Hey, there's pretty cool people that are doing some pretty cool and unconventional things, maybe I should start exploring a little bit,' and life got really nifty."

ON GOING PALEO

"The weird thing about going paleo was it wasn't just the food aspect of it; I did it from a holistic perspective, from a lifestyle perspective in terms of how much time I spent outside, how much sunlight I got, what activity I got. Not just walking with my dogs but doing bodyweight exercises. What I was doing before with my food, in general, was working for me, and I didn't necessarily feel better when I started the paleo lifestyle. I just knew from a scientific perspective that it made a lot more sense. From a longevity perspective, it made a lot more sense for me to start being outside more and eating crappy food less.

I'm six-foot-six; I've got a lot of frame to spread food over, but from inside, I can't really tell what's going on and since I don't know, I want to do long-term what's best for my body because I want to be on this Earth for a long time. The perspective of what's going to be best for me long-term and what's going to allow me to be the most generous, most grateful, most contribution-oriented dude that I can be, that started with paleo and has since extended way beyond that; it's just a general life mindset."

"I'm not paleo orthodox; I can't quite cut out dairy and I'm not convinced, based on what I've read and heard, that milk, cheese, and yogurt are detrimental to me personally. Generally, they might not be conducive to a healthy lifestyle—I'm not ready to declare that either. It's all about nuance. You figure out, 'In general, this paradigm works for me.' There's a set of boundaries that constricts me in a good way. I can push against those boundaries to some extent, but I've locked myself into a certain way of thinking, being and doing in interacting with people, and I love that. **There's a sense of liberation in that restriction.**"

"The problem with life these days is it seems limitless."

"You and I can connect with any of the 7.2 billion people living on this planet. It's awesome! But at the same time, it can be overwhelming. How do you place a certain filter through which you view life or the intentional way in which you go about life? That's what I've been challenging myself and others to do for the past five years. How do you have that filter in your head?

Whether it's the type of person you associate with, the kind of food that you eat, the type of meaningful work that you do that gives you purpose and is of value to other folks. It is an enormous challenge and I need something to constrict me to the point where I'm not just allowing my diverse interests, passions and skills to constantly wander off and be like, 'Maybe I should learn how to do graphic design because I'm not very good at it,' but maybe other people can help me out with that. That's why I have friends, that's why there are other people in the world who are amazing at it."

How do we set that line for restricting our lifestyle? And if that line's been set, how do we break out of that to realize that there's much more out there?

"It's contextual to each person. It depends on your personality, it depends on your resources, it depends on who you have in your life, whether you have kids, whether you have a family, whether you love to travel, whether you're a homebody—there's so many different variables that go into it.

Where's the comfortableness of restriction without fearing that you're missing out? And that fear of missing out is powerful. And I can see it on social media, I can see it in a lot of the relationships that I deal with on a day-to-day basis. I feel it sometimes too! Especially when it comes to people. I just love hanging out with people. I'm heavily extroverted, so from a relationship perspective, I need to restrict myself. From an energy perspective and from a relationship perspective, I have to very intentionally restrict how much time I spend interacting with people, otherwise zero will happen, because I'll just be chatting it up with everybody all day long.

Whether you're an entrepreneur or whether you work in some company environment or whether it's not even related to work, maybe it's just the neighbor down the street who just wants to chat your head off all the time. You just have to choose, 'How do I want to show up in the world? Do I want to consume conversation? Media? Do I want to create? Do I want to create podcast episodes? Do I want to create courses and products, build communities?'"

"It's really figuring the lens through which you view the world and what kind of contribution you're trying to make, and then structuring your lifestyle around that."

DEFINING SIMPLICITY

"I love asking people this question: What does simple living mean to you? And for some people, it's living in a tiny house in a rural environment with really nothing around. For other folks, it's just having the lightness of not being tied down by possessions and being able to freely travel the world. For other folks, it's out in their back-yard gardening with their little kids and cultivating the land together and growing something.

Simple living physically takes on a lot of different forms. And then we're not even talking about mentally, emotionally, spiritually, intellectually and what that landscape looks like. A lot of people's conception of simple is also sparse but doesn't necessarily have to be. When I think of simple, I think of vibrant. I think of nature, I think of things that are constantly growing and evolving. That's my version of simplicity. What about you, Zephan? What does simple living mean to you?"

ZB: For me, simplicity is, what are the bare minimums that you need? We haven't even put curtains up in our house. We have blinds on the windows in our bedrooms, but if you went into our kitchen, it's not something out of *Home & Garden* or anything like that. You're not going to see curtains and valances and flowery things everywhere.

I've got three or four photos that I took and printed them out on photo paper at Kinko's and glued them to a $2.00 canvas thing and stuck them up on the wall for decoration. From my standpoint, it's been a lot of, "How can we use stuff that's already out there without being very materialistic and buying all this stuff we don't need?"

JZ: "That's the premise of the shared economy or collaborative consumption. We have plenty in this world. We have plenty of electronics, we have plenty of food, we have plenty of gold; it's a distribution issue. How do we get it to the people who need it? We have the technology available to show people 'I have this resource. I don't need it anymore; but I know somebody in my community does.
How do I get it into the hands of the person who needs it, whether I'm selling it or whether I'm just happily gifting it?'"

"That's one of the reasons why I'm so encouraged about the direction of our culture is that people are more collaborative. Not only are we distributing resources in a better way, but also, you're meeting cool people and you're building a sense of community with every transaction. It's not just financial and personal, there's a social aspect to it too. Cultivating the roots of people to come together and build something together while you're distributing back and forth."

IT'S ABOUT NEEDS VERSUS WANTS

"That's a big thing with me: What is it that I need? I'm constantly questioning, do I really need that relationship? Do I really need that sugar that I'll binge on every once in a while? And a lot of times, the answer is no. And then the questions become, 'How do I remove the excess from my life so that I focus on the things that are most important?' I don't have a lot of the answers, but just continuing to ask myself that question 'How do I remove the excess, so I can focus on what's important?'"

Is your family fully 100% behind you?

"My needs are minimal, but my family's needs aren't. I'm not the guy who dictates how our family lives because Joel thinks a certain way. My wife is not a minimalist, she doesn't do paleo, there's a lot of things in which we've agreed that we're going to have different kinds of lifestyles. She works at Best Buy's headquarters just a mile away from where I am right here. I'm a solo entrepreneur working out of my house. The way that she eats is pretty typical for Americans; I eat paleo. There's a lot of lines—from a capability perspective—we're amazingly compatible from, but it's having the self-awareness to think just because you live a certain way doesn't mean everyone else needs to."

"The way I live is very different from how my family lives. Sometimes that's difficult for me, when I see there are a lot of toys around the house and I think, 'Maybe we shouldn't have so many.' Or I see how many books we get at a library and I think 'Let's just focus on one or two for the next week and intensely appreciate the one book and get to know it and cut the rest of them.' I'm just trying to help change some of the underlying structures and systems that promote complexity in life because I want the default of sustainable choice to be the easy one."

ZB: I've got to bring it up because these were cool in getting back to my roots was barefoot running when I discovered Vibrams.

JZ: "I'm tempted to just go bolt and be like, 'Hey, Zephan, I'll be right back! Give me 15 seconds, I'm going to go get my Vibrams and hold them up to you!' I got my first pair five years ago and although I normally only run if someone's chasing me, I do love to be outside in them. Just feeling the earth on your feet. When I'm outside or when I'm in the backyard or when I'm just walking around the neighborhood, I'll go barefoot in the summertime when it's not cold here. You're literally touching the ground and feeling that tactile feel—how many times do you get that? That's something that's very primal, that has a very grounding and connecting feeling to our environment."

KEY TAKEAWAYS

- There is a sense of liberation in restriction
- Find what simple living means to you
- Remove the excess, focus on what's important
- Just because you live a certain way doesn't mean everyone else needs to

---

CONTACT INFO:

- Website: valueofsimple.com
- Podcast: *Smart and Simple Matters*
- Community of simple living: simplerev.com/local

ERIK HEMINGWAY
Seven Sailors

Erik Hemingway (familyadventurespodcast.com) has a family of eight, and they wanted to try something radically different while homeschooling their children. They sold their home, 99% of all of their possessions, and set out on a three-and-a-half-year adventure, travelling, sailing, and living abroad. After 17,000 miles, 25 countries and one baby later, they run the Family Travel podcast and even worked on a book.

BACKSTORY

"My wife, Rachel, and I have always been passionate about travel. We traveled before we got married and then, after we were married, we made a couple short trips abroad. And travel was just always a part of our life that we were fascinated with, and once you get bit by the travel bug, it's definitely hard to shake."

"We had been married for fifteen years and I was working as a construction project manager, a very stressful job, working long hours, being involved with our church, kids playing sports – it felt like everything was just a whirlpool of activities. I stumbled across this book in 2000, it was called One Year Off, written by David Cohen. He and his family had sold their possessions and had taken a one-year trip around the world. That was a huge lightbulb moment for me."

"We had limited ourselves to, 'Well, maybe next year, we can go here for a week or here for two weeks,' because you're trying to fit it into the rest of your life. But when I saw this example of somebody who actually put their life on pause and carved out this year to take this adventure, I thought, 'That is exactly what we need to do.' So that's how the idea started. Mixed in there were lots of road trips with our kids as they were growing up, so our kids were pretty familiar with travel."

How did you prepare to take a whole family and to be able to support them throughout this whole trip?

"I quit the job that I was at, started my own business in order to streamline our finances and strategize on how we were going to build up to this trip. We didn't even know what this trip was going to look like at that point. Fast forward to 2007. I had an offer to take a job in Costa Rica with a friend and we decided this is our way to travel. We picked up the family and moved to Costa Rica and ended up down there for a year and a half, and as the real estate market was collapsing in the US, it wasn't far behind that it started to slow down a lot in Costa Rica as well. We were very fortunate to have sold a couple of commercial buildings in Arizona right before the downturn.

We had some savings, and we thought, 'Well, there's no point in going back to the U.S. right now, because there's nothing going on for me as a contractor, so let's dust off this sailboat idea.' So that all came together very quickly. We found a boat in Greece. We had done a little bit of lake sailing on a small boat in Costa Rica, but never sailed on an ocean, no idea what we were in for as far as maintenance or anything like that. I flew to Greece, looked at this boat, just to see if we would fit, and we had it professionally surveyed where they do an appraisal and look for any problems. Everything came back clear, so it was like, 'Well, I guess we're out of excuses. Let's just do it.'"

How did you keep up communication with friends and family?

"The number one drawback to nomadic travel is the long periods of time where you don't see family and friends, I mean, there's Skype but it's not quite the same as being in person. And it was always easier for people to come visit us than for us to pack eight people on an airplane and $10,000 in plane tickets. My parents came and visited us when we were in Turkey and Israel after our baby was born. Two different groups of friends visited us in Israel. But it just wasn't possible for some family to come visit. So, it was probably a three-year period where we didn't see our immediate family and missed weddings and the birth of babies. That's definitely one of the challenges of traveling."

Tell us about home-schooling your kids.

"Through our podcast, we've talked to a lot of families that are traveling in all kinds of different ways, and a trend seems to be emerging from longtime travelers. It's called 'unschooling,' or some people call it 'road schooling,' and it's where you don't place a lot of focus on, book-work or busy work or academics, as far as, 'We've got to get through this biology book' or 'We've got to get through this history book,' because you're living in such fascinating places and you're seeing so much culture and history. So many facets of your life are subversive education that you focus on what it is right in front of you."

"So, we didn't hit the books really hard for those few years. When we came back to the United States, we wanted to give our kids some academic tests to assess the damage that may have been caused by not hitting the books. We were blown away by the fact they tested at or above their current grade level. They had been learning the whole time, just a totally different style of learning."

"Everybody learns differently, but the travel lifestyle really lends itself to subversive, fascinating education opportunities."

"I'm not going to bash on the school system, they do the best they can with the hand they've been dealt, trying to educate a massive population. They teach to a test, because they have to have numbers and percentiles that qualify. They're not necessarily designed to give kids a lot of life skills."

"Life is about learning."

ZB: What are the top two or three things that you learned through that whole adventure? And what are some of the things that your kids took away from that?

EH: "For me, it would be patience. We were all in a lot of uncomfortable situations in new surroundings, and it just took a lot of patience for us to learn to work together. Being with the family with five or six kids in 350-square feet will try your patience, and you have to learn how to give a lot of grace to each other, a lot of benefit of the doubt. So, we really learned how to work together as a team. But it took a lot of fights and apologies – there's no room to pout or throw a tantrum on a boat, you have to deal with attitudes right then, and then you move past it. I think we all learned that."

"For our kids, it was a fantastic foundation to build a huge amount of confidence in who they are and what they can accomplish. When we were sailing across the Atlantic, that's a big undertaking, and we talked about it as a family. We were like, 'Can we do this? Is this something we're comfortable with?' It was a big deal. My son, my daughter and I did the sailing. Somebody has to be awake watching for other boats 24/7. And the Atlantic crossing is an eighteen-day passage, so you don't see land for almost three weeks. They 17 and 16 at the time and they actually sailed us across the Atlantic. You walk tall when you sailed your family across the ocean. That's a huge confidence-builder. There's not much you can't accomplish after that."

ZB: So how do you start over fresh when you get back home?

EH: "When we left, we were so committed to this adventure, we weren't really concerned. I was willing to spend all of our savings for this adventure, because I knew it was going to impact our family. We had sold our house, cars, everything already, but we did keep one business in Arizona, which we still have.

In the back of our minds, we knew when we came back that we were going to be starting over, so we chose North Carolina. We sailed up the Cape Fear River, lived on our boat for a couple months until we could find a house, and we still had some savings left. We had enough money to start over. We moved into a house with two air mattresses and I got back into construction. It's incredible how fast you can accumulate when you get back into the US."

ON FINANCING THE ADVENTURE

"When we were living on our boat, you have no hotel, no utilities, no auto insurance, no gas for your car, sports for the kids, and we ate out very little. Our family was living on about $1400 a month.

There are so many little things that eat away at your finances that are out of the picture when you're traveling. All of our guests were blown away by how little you can spend."

"It is very freeing and super-rewarding."

ZB: What advice do you have for people to live life on your own terms and to take advantage of all it has to offer?

EH: "I really have been trying to solve the issue of fear because that's what it all comes down to. You're not really afraid of running out of money, you're afraid of starving because you have no money. Your mind makes these huge what-if problems that, realistically, will never materialize. We don't push that travel is for everyone, but whatever lifestyle you want; you just need to take steps to make it happen. You need to tackle the fears head on.

What we did is we wrote down on paper our biggest fears with the whole situation. When you see the fears, you can address them, and you can plan for them the best you can, and then it's done. You don't have to fret about it, you don't have to let them spiral out of control at two in the morning when you're lying in bed."

"And if travel is your thing, don't make it a someday or a 'Gee, it would be nice.' You have to make it a goal. There is a huge shift when 'we could do' becomes 'we will do this,' and that was finally what pushed us over the edge. We picked a date on the calendar, we started selling stuff, and you'll be surprised how the momentum will pick up behind you and you are just encouraged by the fact things are in motion. The pieces will fall into place."

"Another huge shift for us is when we realized that we were going to have major regrets if we did not do this adventure. We thought, 'Are we out of our minds to take this much money and live this way, to take our kids out of their surroundings?' And then we thought, 'Are we going to regret, when we're 60-years-old, and we'll be like, 'We should have really done that.' Both of us agreed, we would have major regrets. That was the shift for us, 'Okay, let's do it.'"

KEY TAKEAWAYS

- Travel isn't always expensive
- Whatever lifestyle you want; you just need to take steps to make it happen
- Tackle your fears head on
- Ask yourself what you will regret not doing later in life

CONTACT INFO:

- Podcast: familyadventurespodcast.com

HAL ELROD
The Miracle Morning

Hal Elrod (facebook.com/groups/MyTMMCommunity) is the number-one bestselling author of what is now being widely regarded as one of the most life-changing books ever written, titled *The Miracle Morning: The Not So Obvious Secret Guaranteed to Transform Your Life Before 8AM*. It is also one of the highest-rated books on Amazon with over 900 five-star reviews.

BACKSTORY

"When I was 20-years-old I was in sales. I had gone from being a radio DJ, which was like my dream, and then a buddy of mine was selling Cutco Kitchen Knives, and he was always bugging me and saying, 'Hal, you'd be great at selling Cutco!' and I was like, 'Dude, I'm a radio DJ, I'm not a salesman at all.' I took the gig and 10 days later, I broke this all-time company record where I had sold $15,000 of kitchen knives in 10 days, which was more than anyone else in the company had ever done. A year-and-a-half later, I was one of the top salespeople for the company and I was always asked to give speeches."

"And after a speech one night, I was driving home, and I was in my brand-new Ford Mustang, which, at 20-years-old, that was like the dream car I could afford. Driving home that night, I was hit head-on by a drunk driver at 70-miles an hour, and the worst was yet to come as my car spun off the drunk driver and the car behind me crashed into my door at 70-miles an hour.

I died for six minutes. I bled to death on the side of the freeway as it took them an hour to get me out of the car. I was in a coma for six days, broke 11 bones, and when I came out of the coma, I was facing a pretty unimaginable reality. I was told I'd never walk again, and I'd have permanent brain damage. I had to choose how I was going to respond to what happened to me."

"There's that old saying, 'Everything happens for a reason,' but I think what I figured out was that the reason isn't predetermined, like we're often conditioned to think, 'Why did this happen to me?' and we're asking our friends, our family, God and actually looking for an answer that is predetermined when the reality is, everything happens for a reason, but it is our responsibility to choose the reason. We can choose reasons that are victim reasons, like, 'Oh, bad things happen to me all the time. I'm unlucky.' Or we can go, 'This sucks. This is the worst thing that's ever happened to me, but I'm going to make this my greatest comeback. I'm going to use this adversity, turn it into an advantage, I'm going to help other people' – however you want to do that."

"For me, I just realized that I can't change what happened to me, which is true for all of us. Everything that's ever happened in our lives, you can't go back and change it, right? You can either feel bad, sad, depressed or get angry. The only intelligent choice is to accept all things that you can't control, and you only focus all of your energy, all of your emotions on the things that you have control over. I decided, 'If I never walk again, I'll be the happiest person you've ever seen in a wheelchair. Because, if I'm in a wheelchair, I might as well be happy.'

But I'm not going to put my energy into my fear. Never walking again is the worst-case scenario, but I'm going to accept that, because it doesn't have control over my emotions. I'm going to focus all my energy into walking again, because that's what I want. I thought about walking, I visualized it, I dreamt about it, I prayed about it, I talked about it. I accepted the worst-case scenario but put no energy into it once I accepted it.

I don't think it's a coincidence that three weeks after the crash – my femur broke in half, my pelvis broke in three places – but two weeks after I came out of the coma and was being told I would never walk again, the doctors came in with a routine x-ray and they said, 'We don't know how to explain this, but your body is healing at an incredible rate, and we're going to let you take your first step in therapy tomorrow.'"

"I went from never walking again to taking my first step three weeks later. I left the hospital after two months and got back to work in my sales job. I finished that year as the number six rep in our company. And, to me, it wasn't about me, it was going, 'hey, this is universally true for any human being on the planet that we accept what we can't change, be grateful for everything that we have, and then focus every day on making progress towards our goals, our dreams, our highest vision for our life. And when you do that, you can't fail.'"

ZB: I think it's a lot of positive attracts positive, and also not accepting the script of what most people would settle for.

HE: "Yeah. I always say positive thinking doesn't solve your problems, but it puts you in a peak physical and emotional state to solve your own problems, and that's really what it is. Not to mention, all the metaphysical benefits of the law of attraction. There's definitely truth to that. I believe the mind/body connection; I don't think my positive thinking and my profoundly quick recovery is a coincidence."

"We can cause disease with our negative thinking and stress, or we can cause healing with positive thinking."

What's up with the 52-mile ultra-marathon?

"Let me set the scene. In 2008, when the US economy crashed, I was what most people would consider successful in terms of my income. I left my $100,000 a year position to be an entrepreneur. There was risk involved, but after a couple of years, I was back up to almost where I was income-wise.

I wanted to be an author; I wrote my first book, *Taking Life Head On*. My big dream was to be a professional speaker. I gave my first speech for $2500. And then I launched a coaching business. I was doing sales coaching and business coaching in my mid-twenties. Bought as brand-new house, bought a sports car, and met the woman of my dreams. I was in the best shape of my life physically; I was 5.7% body fat, which I used to joke 'I'm going to get 5.7% tattooed on my bicep or something.' I was working very hard in every area and I was happy."

"Then the economy crashed, and I lost over half my clients. I had to short sell my house. I went from being a debt-free Dave Ramsay student to having a $53,000 credit card balance in six months. And it was getting worse every day. For the first time in my life, I got deeply depressed, to the point of thoughts of suicide. I hated my life, because I felt hopeless. I kept trying to fix it. I would accept it, 'I'm at this low point. It's only going to get better.' Then it got worse. And then I'm like, 'Okay. *This* is my rock-bottom, I'm going to fix it. I'm going to change it!' and then I lost another client – and on and on and on."

"A friend of mine said, 'Hal, if you want to fix your life, dude, you need to exercise. Go for a run every day and listen to an audiobook on business. You can figure out how to get more clients and turn it around.' I just wanted some advice on making money and keeping my business going; I didn't want to go for a run every day. And on my first run, I heard a quote from Jim Rohn that turned everything around. And it was the catalyst for turning things around faster than I ever thought possible."

"Jim Rohn said, 'Your level of success will seldom exceed your level of personal development.' And in that moment, I realized, 'Hmm, I'm not dedicating time every day to my personal development to become the person that I need to be to create the success I want in my life. I'm just waking up, going into my office, working all day long, and going to bed. And maybe watching some TV in the evening, that's it.'

I had this epiphany. I'm going to go home and I'm going to figure out what the world's more successful people do every day for personal development. Like, 'what are the most effective personal development practices known to man?' And I'm going to pick the top one or two, and I'm going to start doing those. After an hour of online research, I came up with a list of six. You've heard of all of them: silence, meditation, affirmations, visualization, exercise, reading, and journaling. None of those were new to me, so I was kind of disappointed."

"And then it hits me. Number one, I don't do these every day. Number two, what if I did all of these? Like none of the research I did showed me any human being on the planet that was doing more than two or three of those. I thought, 'What if I did all six? That would be the ultimate routine!' I woke up the next morning, even though I wasn't a morning person, I did all six and I felt unstoppable. And what's interesting, and this is what everybody reports with the *Miracle Morning*, it's like Day 1 is a game changer, and you're like, 'Holy cow, if I feel like this every day, it's only a matter of time before my outer world reflects the way that I feel!'"

"In less than two months, I more than doubled my income. I went from being in the worst shape of my life to thinking, 'How can I get my fitness at the highest level?' and I thought, 'I'm going to do an ultra-marathon.' Fifty-two miles in one day. I started it right away, I started training, and five months later, I completed it in one day. I went from being scared, depressed, and hopeless in a scarcity mindset to feeling unstoppable and that happened day one."

"I started calling this quick financial, physical, emotional, and mental turnaround my 'Miracle Morning' because it happened so fast, but it was never going to be a book! The rest is history, as they say. What I realized is that this is so effective and equally universal – meaning, if you're at rock-bottom like I was, or you have an $80-million net worth and you're a bestselling author or you're anywhere in between – it is applicable to everybody."

What's your advice or tips with sticking to this and holding yourself accountable?

"One of the most important chapters in the book is called 'From Unbearable to Unstoppable.' It's about how to integrate any habit into your life in 30 days. I've been a coach for a long time; I have a group coaching program with 200 members, so I'm always creating content for them. I realized that one of the most important things for us to be able to master as human beings is the ability to change a habit; either get rid of a bad habit or implement a new positive habit. But most people suck at it. Think about New Year's Resolutions. A great example of how bad we are at that is if you go to the gym the first week of January, it's packed with all these people with their

New Year's Resolutions. But go to the gym two weeks later and half the parking lot is empty, because people don't know how to stick to a habit."

"In the book, I teach the psychology of this, and the most effective way to implement a new habit. There are three 10-day phases. The first 10 days is the unbearable phase. The second 10 days is the uncomfortable phase. And the third 10 days is the unstoppable phase. Usually, the first few days, people are fired up if they're excited about the new habit. But you will hit a wall, whether it's on day four or six, but you'll go, 'Alright, the initial excitement wore off and now I'm realizing this is something that's out of my comfort zone. It can feel unbearable and you're like, 'I'm not a morning person! I can't get out of bed!' But because you're going into this new habit with the awareness that it's going to be uncomfortable for a period of time and then get better, it's a game-changer.

The second 10 days are uncomfortable because it's still not a picnic, it's still easier to not do it than to do it, and that's where you have to stay committed. The beauty of it is, it's no longer unbearable. You're not hating it, you're not defying it with every fiber of you're being, you're just kind of like 'Eh, I don't really want to do it.'

And then finally, the unstoppable days, days 21 through 30. This is where you wake up one day, and there's no resistance. There's no hating it; it's not even uncomfortable. In fact, it's the opposite. You're fired up!"

"I think we're over 100,000 people now that do the Miracle Morning every day around the world and over 70% of those people have said 'Before the Miracle Morning, I was not a morning person in my entire life.' Most of them said 'I've tried to become a morning person multiple times. I've failed every time until the Miracle Morning.'

If people understand that it's 30 days, stay committed, understand the emotions you're going to go through, stick with it, be optimistic, think positively, and know that somewhere between day 21 and 30, you will hit a stride, you will be fired-up and unstoppable."

KEY TAKEAWAYS

- Everything happens for a reason, but it is our responsibility to choose the reason
- Accept all the things that you can't control, focus your energy on what you can control
- Focus every day on making progress towards your goals
- Master the ability to change your habits
- Unbearable - Uncomfortable - Unstoppable
- Positive thinking doesn't solve your problems, it puts you in a peak state to solve your own problems

CONTACT INFO:

- Facebook.com/groups/MyTMMCommunity
- Book: *The Miracle Morning: The Not So Obvious Secret Guaranteed to Transform Your Life Before 8AM*

GREG ROLLETT
Ambitious

Greg Rollett (www.gregrollett.com) is the founder and president of Ambitious Media Group, an Orlando-based media marketing company. As a kid from Tamarac who was expected to work construction or bartend for the rest of his life, and instead, tried to be a rapper, then an internet mogul. Now, Greg's the head of an agency competing with billion-dollar media companies from his home in Winter Park, Florida by empowering millennials in every crack and crevice of the planet to live out their dreams.

BACKSTORY

"I wasn't the poorest kid, but I was far from the richest kid. I knew that I wanted what some of the richer kids had: the car, the Tommy Hilfiger polo with the popped collar, the gold chains. Those dudes were getting the chicks, going to the cool parties, and I want some of that! I knew I wasn't going to get the support from my family. My dad wasn't going to lay down $50 to go buy a t-shirt. That sounds insane when you're trying to put food on the table."

"I knew from a very young age that I had to do it myself. So, I started working a series of jobs; I was a stock-boy at Target, I worked construction, and I waited tables. This was during the heyday of dirty south hip-hop, and as a little white senior in high school, I decided I wanted to be the next Master P. I studied his model of success and that became a theme throughout my whole career. I look at people, I look at their success, and I look at how I can model what they've done.

I started a record label in high school so that I could make a CD, go to the party on Friday night and sell it for five bucks. I'd sell a hundred of them. You make $500 in a night, and you're like, 'Holy crap! I got $500 in one night! That's a car payment! That's new shoes, that's the gold chain, that's the Tommy Hilfiger polo! That's all of that!' *That* was pretty awesome."

That parlayed into a cool career. We got to tour the country and these companies started reaching out to us. We were doing cool stuff and we got 'big' on Myspace. Coca-Cola reached out to me and said, 'Do you want to jump on the phone with us and do some consulting?' I was 21."

"What it came down to is I just had this passion and ambition and knew nobody was going to do it for me, so, I just went out and did it."

ZB: I think that's half the battle; you just have to dive right into it. I think everybody's just waiting for the perfect time and the perfect time is never going to happen.

GR: "Yeah, and it doesn't matter if it's business or it's just life, and it's a lot of what we talked about at Ambitious with our clients. 'I want to lose weight, but I'm going to wait until after the holidays.' 'Why? What are you doing today?' I think it's an easy excuse in our mind to say 'Well, I'll do that when...' but that fictitious date just keeps getting pushed back further and further. 'I've got so much work to do. I'm backed up. I'll wait until there's time.' *It always happens.* You really have to think about 'What am I doing today?'"

DO ONE THING

"I don't get to go to sleep at night until I've done one thing that improved myself today from yesterday."

"That could be one email to somebody to create a relationship. That could be one sales copy. That could be one phone call I make – one thing. Do one thing today that makes you a better person today than you were yesterday.

The cool thing that happens is it starts to snowball because that's 365 ways that you're getting better than you were the day before. But you're 100% right that you've got to get rid of that roadblock that is right in front of you that you keep saying, 'Well, I'll do it tomorrow.' 'I'll do it when I feel better.' 'I'll do it when I...' and you really have to break out of that pattern.

The day-to-day really gets in our way and we get comfortable with it. It's much easier to go to happy-hour and have drinks Friday at 5:00 than it is to go home and study or to listen to your podcast or to take action on the stuff that you heard in the podcast. Much easier, because it's part of our routine to just wake up, go to work, go to lunch, go back to work, go to the bar, than it is to do anything else."

"The action has to start today, not a fictitious date in the future; that date never comes."

ZB: One of the things that prevented me upfront from figuring out my direction is I didn't have a clear message of what I was doing at the start. I'm a grown man now, and my parents still have no clue how I manage to do it. When people find out I own a video production company, they're like, 'So, do you do weddings?' I'm like, 'No, I don't do any of that!' Did you ever have trouble with your message and figuring out what exactly it was you were doing? Because when Coca-Cola calls, you have to be able to tell them what you can provide.

GR: "I was at a mastermind meeting last week out in Scottsdale with all multimillion-dollar businesses up to billion-dollar businesses. I have no idea why I'm in this room. I'm listening to them talk, they don't know what they're doing. They have the confidence to know that if they put one foot in front of the other, they're going in a forward direction.

A lot of my current employees are former musicians, artists, and entertainers, and here's why: When we were trying to book gigs, no one wanted my band to play at their bar. No bar is like, 'I can't wait for this white rapper to play at my bar!' No one wanted us to play."

"There's no roadmap. There's no blueprint. We had to just figure it out. I had to sell them on me as, 'I'm going to sell drinks, I'm going to sell tickets, I'm going to get people in your bar because you have me here.' So, 99 out of 100 said 'no,' but the one that said 'yes' had a hell of a good show and we had a really good time. I think it's that forward progress, that one foot in front of the other, which sounds easy, but it's really difficult to do in real life. Don't let people stop you. You're going to fall flat on your face.

With Ambitious right now, it's the first time I'm going after venture capital, I've always been self-funded. I have no clue what I'm doing, but I'm pitching guy after guy after guy. My pitch today is better than my pitch yesterday, my pitch tomorrow is going to be better than my pitch today and at some point, somebody's going to open their wallet and I'm going to pop champagne. You said you just finished your book and you're going to party today. I'm going to have that same party!"

"This interview is better than the interview I had yesterday. But I did one. I've done a lot of them now, but I keep doing them. Every time I do one, my message gets more refined and I keep talking about it. If you don't have clarity on your message, how you get clarity in your message is just by continuing to talk about it. Talk about it to anyone and everyone. Go to the bar, buy some stranger a drink, and talk his ear off about your thing. Then go to the bar tomorrow night and tell another guy about it.

You have to continuously talk about it. When you talk about it publicly, it starts to create accountability. Because now they're going to see you at the bar and they're like, 'So, how's that project going?' Once you start to create public accountability, you have to do it. You have to talk about what you want to do, and it starts to set things in motion."

"The crazy thing that happens is if I start talking to somebody at the bar tonight, he might not be the right guy, but he knows someone. His cousin's brother's sister's friend's uncle has something similar. You start to set things in motion and the world starts working for you, but you have to be confident enough to break out of your comfort zone to talk about what you really want to do. That's what we did. I talked about my music everywhere we went. I also made it relatable.

This is something really key. Every musician in the world says, 'My music is different. I sound like no one you've ever heard of.' Then I don't want to buy your music because I don't want to buy a CD no one has ever heard of. You have to relate it to the audience and what they want. Instead of saying, 'We're a hip-hop rock band and we do some funk;' people are like, 'I have no clue what you're talking about.' I'd just be like, 'Are you a fan of Linkin Park?' 'Yeah.' 'We sound like them.' Instantly relatable and they go, 'I'm a huge fan of Linkin Park!' or they go 'I'm not, but my brother is. I should introduce him to your music.'

Find a way to make it relatable to the person and it's really going to find a way to create an inroad with them, create rapport with them, and then they can help you. If they don't know what you're talking about, they can't really help you."

What are some of the struggles or obstacles that you've seen that relate to this whole idea of figuring it all out?

"You have to tell your story and use media to perpetuate that story and get momentum because me just telling one person at a bar is just one person at a time. Media allows you to get in front of thousands of people, tens of thousands of people, hundreds of thousands of people at once. We talk about two different types of media out in the world. There's mass media, which is your radio, TV, newspapers and even things like podcasts and stuff. But then you also have direct media, which is just as important. Direct media is an email you send to all your customers; a Tweet you send to all of your followers or a piece of mail."

"Find those moments in your life that are relatable moments that everyone goes through. Find the points of vulnerability. When I tell my rapper in a rock band story, I talk about going on a 15-city tour a month after I got married, and taking all of the wedding money to buy a new trailer, t-shirts, hats, CDs, stickers – everything to go on this 15-city tour, and two days before we were supposed to leave, the band breaks up. That's a point of vulnerability.

I slept on the couch for three months. My wife hated me. My wife's parents hated me.

It was a very, very bad situation. I talk about these points of vulnerability because it shows that my life isn't all peaches and cream. Look for those points of vulnerability in your life. What are those moments? What are the faults? What are the other things? Where did you go to school? Were you from a small town or were you from a big town? Were you in the military? People love talking about their dogs; it creates an instant connection. Did you go to a university? The point is to have something to instantly bond on and connect with."

"Now use all of these different elements, and put them into your story, and you're going to instantly create rapport with people. People buy from an emotional standpoint. Tell your startup story. That's why I love Kickstarter. Kickstarter's got all the videos up there with people saying 'Here's a problem that I had, here's why my life sucked, here's the product we created, here's the path to do it, and here's how you can come with me.' Now you're bringing people on your journey. Find those connecting points in your life, all those different pieces of the story and find ways to insert them into media."

How do we leave a legacy behind or leave the world a better place than how we found it?

"I'll answer that by sharing one of my most favorite stories. Prince Harvey is a hip-hop artist out of New York City. He lives in a small house with eight other guys. There's not a lot of money to go around, and he wanted to record his debut album. He had a Mac laptop, and his hard drive crashed. This is the point where most people would do the, 'I'll just wait until Christmas and get a new computer.' 'I'll wait for my tax refund check and get a new computer.' 'I'll wait until I can borrow my buddy's friend's sister's computer' – every excuse in the book, and they would give up on making that album."

"Prince believed in that if people heard his words, his beats, his music, he knew that it could change them, it could affect them positively. And that it could get him out of his living situation. He believed wholeheartedly in this message that what he did is he traveled an hour to the Apple Store every single day and used their computers for three months to record his album. He brought a thumb drive, plugged it into a computer, and worked on his album.

He got kicked out of two stores and finished the album at the third store. He made all his beats using his mouth and recorded them in Garage Band. After three months, he's got an album and a story worth telling. He started telling people he was secretly recording an album in the iTunes store. Now, you've got guys like Russel Simmons, a hip-hop god, who's tweeting about him. He got Talib Kweli tweeting about him. He created a great album and a great story about it, and now people won't stop talking about this guy."

"That is how you overcome obstacles that are in your way. Don't give yourself excuses. If you're a painter and you want to paint and you can't afford canvas to paint on, go find a brick wall. Where there's a will, there's a way. If you have something passionately burning inside you that you need to share with the world, change the world, then it is your responsibility to find a way to make it happen. Most people don't have something worth fighting for enough to make it happen."

"During your Apple days, you might not have believed enough in the cause to go make it happen, but then, one day, you're like, 'I believe in the cause so much that I'm going to make it happen.' And that's what this guy did. Well, now, he's also building a legacy around it. Now he's building a story, he's building his brand, he's starting to book shows and he's starting to gain publicity. It's steamrolling, steamrolling, and all he's doing is telling a story."

"Find the thing that's worth fighting for, and then freaking fight for it! Kick down some doors!

Don't be scared of what other people think. I think there's an insecurity of, 'If I go to record something in the Apple store, grandma's going to look at me funny. If grandma's looking at me funny, I shouldn't do what I know I need to do to change the world.'"

KEY TAKEAWAYS

- Do one thing today that makes you a better person than you were yesterday
- Talk about your product, create accountability
- Make your product relatable
- Find connecting points in your life, different pieces of your story and find ways to insert them into media

---

CONTACT INFO:

- Email: greg@ambitious.com
- Websites:
    ambitious.com
    gregrollett.com

DAVE SANDERSON
Miracle on the Hudson

Dave Sanderson (davesandersonspeaks.com) is the managing partner of his firm Dave Sanderson Speaks Enterprises based out of Charlotte, North Carolina. On January 15th of 2009, he was the last person off the plane that crashed into the Hudson river, best known as the Miracle on the Hudson, and was largely responsible for making sure many others made it out safely. In addition to speaking and training, he conducts workshops and currently working on his next book, *Moments Matter*, in which he discusses how applying 12 key resources was a main factor that turned a potential tragedy into the Miracle on the Hudson; taking a tragic experience and turning it into an opportunity to grow and contribute.

BEFORE THE CRASH

"It was 11-degrees and snowing in New York City where I was for work. I was working at a distribution center that day, doing distribution system checks and the distribution center opened at 2:00am in the morning. Our day started early, and we got done around 10:00 that morning, and I was scheduled to be on a 5:00am flight, not the US Airways Flight 1549 that day."

"About 60-seconds into takeoff, I heard an explosion, and that's when it all started happening. But I wasn't that startled because I fly so often; I know planes lose engines. I know a plane can fly on one engine, and we're in New York City, so they're just going to turn around, go back to the airport to get another plane.

But when he crossed over the George Washington bridge, I looked out the window, and I could actually see people's faces. That's how close he was to hitting the bridge. I knew at that point it was a little bit more serious than I anticipated. And then he said his famous words, 'Brace for impact,' and I knew that this probably wasn't going to turn out very well for us."

ZB: Was there any other major announcement other than 'Brace for impact' as to what was about to happen?

DS: "No, that was one of the greatest things that happened on that plane. He only said what he had to say. He said, 'This is your captain, brace for impact.'

I truly believe if he started telling people what was going on and explaining 'This is what we're going to do,' people would have freaked out. But no one did anything. People were very quiet. They were really introverted at that point, because I think everybody knew at that point that if you're going to crash into the water, it's probably not going to be a very positive outcome.

Everybody was checking in with themselves and saying, 'Okay, I'm going to get things squared away pretty quick, whether it's with my creator or with my wife or husband.' And so, I think him saying the least words possible was one of the saving graces of that day."

WHAT WENT THROUGH YOUR MIND?

"Once I realized this could be a real tragic situation, I may not be coming back was: Number one, I prayed. I prayed for three different things. And the last thing I prayed for was for God to forgive my sins, because I want to at least have a shot to get into heaven. I didn't want anything out there that might muck it up at that point. But the second was the whole movie of my life was going through my mind. When you talk to people who are on their deathbed and they may come back, they'll tell you the same thing.

It's amazing that when you think you're going to die, in that last moment, you can see so many things, you have total clarity on what your life was about and what you did in your life. And the last thought I had before we hit the river and crashed into it was, 'I hope my wife pays the mortgage off,' because I told her from day one, 'If I die, pay the house off.' That's the one thing we haven't done yet that we need to accomplish. And then we crashed into the river. It was about 70 seconds after he crossed over the George Washington bridge until we crashed into the river, and that was one of the most surreal 70 seconds of my life."

What happened from the moment the captain makes the announcement to the first time you get to contact your family?

"When we hit, at first, you don't think you're coming back. I went back in my seat and I came up and saw light through the window, so I knew I wasn't dead, and I knew I had a shot. But when the plane hit, the bottom of the plane was stripped off and somebody tried to open that back door, so we got water coming in immediately.

Now you've got water anywhere from ankle to waist-deep, depending on where you were on that plane. I was towards the back of the plane."

"The first thing people usually say is, 'I thought you all got on the wing and went home.' Nothing in life is that easy. People were going up the seats, walking down the seats, going down the aisle and all that. But it was my time, my aisle. But when I hit the aisle, something happened that changed everything, and I heard my mother speaking to me in my head. And my mother passed away in 1997, but something she would tell me as a child popped in my head: 'If you do the right thing, God will take care of you.' And that's the last thing I heard from my mother on that plane: Do the right thing.

That's why I waited in the back of the plane before I made my way out, because I was all right and I knew, physically, I could get out. Other people weren't that fortunate. Other people were having some challenges getting out because of where they were and just the logistics of it all."

"But once we got everybody out, I went up to 10F to get out, myself, and all of a sudden, I looked up and there was no room on the wing or the boat for me. I couldn't get out of the plane. That's why I was waist deep in thirty-six-degree water for about seven minutes on that plane. I was actually holding on.

There's a picture that was shown on Good Morning America that was the first picture shown from the plane crash of me holding on to the lifeboat. And the reason why is because the Hudson River's got a very fast current. The plane is actually floating down the river. As the plane was floating down the river, the little lifeboat was also floating out into the river. And no one, including myself, reads the instructions.

Who reads the instructions? It's actually tethered to the plane. But no one knew that. They kept yelling 'Hold on, hold on,' that's why I held on to the lifeboat as close as I could to the wing for about six/seven minutes people could start getting off from the wing and moving down and that's how my story started. Because I was on the plane for seven additional minutes waist deep in 36-degree water, holding on to the lifeboat, until it was my time to go."

"The left side of the plane was facing Manhattan, so I was facing Hoboken. I'm going to Jersey and that's how I ended up being in New Jersey, and those folks did a tremendous job because they had to pick me up and carry me to the triage center, because I couldn't walk. You can go all day on adrenaline, but once you're out, I couldn't feel a thing. I'd been in the water now seven/eight minutes and I couldn't move. That's how I got there and that's how I got to the triage center and also to the hospital."

"I didn't talk to my wife until 11:00 that night, because it took about five hours for me to warm my body up. At that point, I heard her story about what was going on at home which was probably as exciting if not more exciting than what I had going on. She had to deal with all the media at home.

I did an interview that night from the hospital bed with Katie Couric. She interviewed me and I was on CBS, but my wife doesn't watch CBS. What somebody did was they called my wife and said, 'Your husband's alive, he's on CBS,' and all of a sudden, once your name is out, they can google you anyplace.

And all of a sudden, ABC, CBS, and FOX show up at the house with cameras wanting to interview my wife, who knew nothing. She had just gotten home and she's clueless to what's going on. That's how I got to my wife initially, and then I got back to Charlotte the next day and first saw my family. When I got back that next day."

ZB: Have you found that your sense of grit has really driven you to do more things outside of that situation that have contributed to your success?

DS: "Most definitely. I had the honor and privilege of being head of security for a gentleman named Tony Robbins for five years. I was an assistant for another five years. Ten years, I was with Tony, traveling with him all over the world, and you get that mindset that you can basically do anything if you control the way you manage your mind. He calls it state management. That's one of the things I talk about now, how to manage your state in the appropriate way at the appropriate time, which is a skillset that everybody could have, but few people really employ.

One thing this gave me was a strong reference to be able to handle anything, and life is not easy. There are things being thrown at you all the time, whether it's financial, relationships, whatever it may be. And you've got to deal with it. I've dealt with it beforehand okay, but now I deal with it with a whole different level of certainty.

One of the things I talked about that day, your level of certainty when something's going on really can help you turn it into a positive outcome. One thing I've learned in my life that the person with the most certainty in the room is the one that's going to be seen as the leader. He or she will be the one making the decisions, because everyone will gravitate to certainty because everyone's got so much uncertainty. I think certainty was one of the biggest points of reference I came out with on that day."

ON BEING IN THE MOMENT

"I call it the power of focus in that moment. People like me who were in the corporate world always live in the future. That was before where I'm at now. And I was always living for the future. Corporate people are all about the next step, but what you realize after you face your personal plane crash, whether it's a heart attack, stroke, whatever it may be, all of a sudden, you get back to the present.

You focus in on the power of the present. If you can focus in on that present moment and don't look at it as if it's any worse than it is, look at it as it is. And deal with it as it is. That day, we all dealt with it as it was. It could have been a lot more tragic than it was. This thing could have gone a whole different direction, but Sullenberger showed the power of focus.

When you have six minutes to make a decision that involves 150-plus people's lives and you can focus in on that moment, and then, execute and not lose it, that's a tremendous skill set that I gained from him that day. The power of focusing in on that present second, that present moment. That's why my next book's called *Moments Matter*."

ZB: You mentioned you had been in the corporate world. Was leaving the corporate world related to these events?

DS: "Indirectly. It happened about four years after. I wanted to leave them immediately after, but I still had a wife and kids in college, expenses and health insurance to pay for. But about a week afterwards, it hit me in the face on two different occasions.

The first occasion was the one-year anniversary of the plane crash, when we released our first book, in which I wrote a chapter. We were doing a book launch at the Barnes & Noble in Times Square. We were talking, sharing stories and I discovered my company never even called me that night.

There were other companies flying people in to help them and make sure they had clothes and give them time off. My company basically said, 'Are you going to go back to work next week? Do you want to fly to Michigan next week?' So, that's when I went, 'Alright, I'm just a number,' but I decided to have a job."

"Fast-forward to three and a half years later, the Wednesday before Thanksgiving, and I was trying to finalize a transaction. I was working with somebody from Costa Rica and somebody from India; I was working with a lot of good people. But when I needed help here locally, everybody else had already gone on Thanksgiving vacation.

Here I'm the one that's doing it, and everybody else will get paid. I'm like, 'This isn't right,' and I threw my phone and broke it. I said, 'I got to get out of here or I'm going to die of stress.' And that's when I made the decision to leave, and I left about two months later."

ZB: What lessons have you pulled away from all this that could be helpful to others in designing their own future on their own terms?

DS: "One thing that really was a stark change in my life was the way I managed my time. And, as you may have gleaned with some of the things I've shared, I was driven. I was a top producer in every company I was with. My dad always said, 'Make sure you take care of your family. That's the number one thing you do. Make sure they have what they need.' So, I worked and worked and worked and worked and there were times when I wasn't around, especially for my eldest daughter's activities in school. She and I were butting heads at that point. We were not really doing well, and people tell me, 'Hey, 17, girls can get that way,' but I think a lot of it was that and I wasn't there for her. But after the plane crash, I realized, 'I've got to be there for my family. I can't keep working at this pace and working for somebody else's glory. I've got to take care of my family, and the only way I can to that is work for myself and control my time.'

So now, the biggest change is I manage my time around family events, and then everything else goes around it and that has changed the relationships I have with my kids and my wife. That's probably the major thing."

"Second is not only knowing that I have a story, but my, 'How can I impact one more person?' And the other part of it is to enjoy the process.

A lot of people forget that second part of it and part of the book's going to be about how you can make these goals all day long, which I did, but I never enjoyed the process. If you put it together and enjoy the process, it's a whole different framework on how you approach something and get so much more creative on how to do it. And I talk about the skill of resourcefulness. As I look back and tell my story about that day, I realize all these little resources that I used that day. Like when I yelled at the lady on the wing because I needed to change the way she was looking at things to get her unstifled. Or making multiple pathways when the seats broke. Resourcefulness was probably the major skill set that got everybody through that day.

So now, I talk about that and teach people how to be resourceful when you think you have limited resources. In Moments Matter, we offer 12 resources that I and others used that day and you can use in your own life or in business when times get tough. Anticipation was a key skill set that day. We all had to anticipate what the next move may have been if someone had been injured or Captain Sully anticipated, 'If I don't do it just right, I'm going to topple into New Jersey.'"

How can you transform tragedy and change that into a winning mindset?

"I've thought about the different strategies I've used to take the pathway to growth instead of depression. The way I did it was go out in the street and focus on giving back to the Red Cross, making sure that they can have the money they needed for someone else who was going through a tragedy, whether it was Haiti or a tornado or Superstorm Sandy, whatever it may have been.

That's what I did and that's one of the key strategies. Focusing, not on yourself, but focusing on how you can give to somebody else, and all of a sudden you change your perspective.

I talked to a lot of military guys and gals when they come back who are going through that questionable stage. Now they're back, what are they going to do? And they're depressed because they've had structure all their life. Now, all of a sudden, they have no structure. They've gone through something. I tell them to go get it out. I tell them to go out and speak about it, whether it's a church, whether it's a United Way function, whatever it may be. Talk to people like you on podcasts. Get it out. Because the more you get it out, the more you can start processing it in your mind – 'Yeah, it was bad. Yeah, I was lucky I made it. But I did make it. And now how can I add value to somebody else who may be in that same situation?'

All of a sudden, you're thinking about somebody else. That's one of the key strategies I talk about and teach about, taking it from PTSD to PTGS – Post Traumatic Growth Syndrome."

WORDS OF WISDOM

"When you're given the opportunity to lead. When you're given the opportunity to speak, speak. When you're given opportunities in life, take advantage of the opportunities. And that's probably the number one thing I tell people now. You have opportunities all around you, but most people don't take advantage of them. They're either scared or they're too worried about the way they're going to be perceived. But I tell you what, when you take that chance, take that step, take that path because you don't know where it's going to lead.

I remember what my first mentor told me. I said, 'I want to be a leader,' and he said, 'The fast way to get anything in life is to put yourself around the peer group of the people you want to be because they will elevate you.' And that's how I started my mission and my travels to become a business leader.

Put yourself around peer groups, the kind of people you want to be, and they will elevate you to that level. That was one of the greatest pieces of advice I ever got."

KEY TAKEAWAYS

- Do the right thing
- Control the way you manage your mind
- The person with the most certainty in the room is going to be seen as the leader
- There is power in focusing on the present moment
- Focus on how you can give to somebody else
- There are opportunities all around you, most people don't take advantage of them.

CONTACT INFO:

- Website: davesandersonspeaks.com
- Facebook: Dave Sanderson Speaks
- Book: *Moments Matter*

CHANEL & STEVO
How Far From Home?

Chanel and Stevo (www.howfarfromhome.com) are two creatives with one wanderlust and zero reasons to stay at home. They're currently traveling around the world on a quest to see how far from home they can get, literally to see how far they can travel from Johannesburg, South Africa and figuratively to see how far they can push themselves outside of their comfort zones.

BACKSTORY

S: "We were all talk no action for some time. We'd been together for about four years before we left on our journey. Chanel was always keen on traveling the world and she'd always drop hints and I was like, 'I guess we should do this, but I don't know.'"

C: "I would try to brainwash you when you were sleeping."

S: "In 2014, we attended the Design in Durban, Cape Town and we witnessed a talk by Mr. Stefan Sagmeister about the power of time-off and how it's so good for creativity. We both come from the creative industry, having worked in advertising. Chanel was a creative director and I was an art director, so this really caught our attention. His speech hit home made us realize that this is something that we can do, that it would be beneficial for us. We saved money for an entire year. That meant we didn't go out; we became hermit crabs at home. Then a year later we quit our jobs, which was very tough."

C: "Quitting was the hardest because we both loved our work and had reached a

94

level of comfort where it was almost too comfortable. Despite the excitement and the stress of advertising, we had routines and it was the same thing every day. When you're at that point, your creativity isn't being stimulated, it's not being challenged. After hearing Stefan's talk and seeing the benefits of it, we thought, 'We're relatively young and don't have much to lose. Why the hell not?'"

S: "It's not a decision that you make overnight, so we gave it some thought and spoke to family members. They were encouraging, but it was bittersweet at the same time. So, we followed our gut and felt that if we took a sabbatical, there could be potentially so much more we could do. So many doors could open, or at the very least just getting to see the world."

ZB: What was it about that talk that compelled you to say, "We have to do this?"

C: "The one thing that spoke to us, was the freedom to experiment and do whatever you want. We saw how Stefan did incredible projects in Bali and he got to do anything he wanted. No client brief, no deadline, besides the one year. You just have complete freedom and for us, that is the unicorn that we're after. We can get up when we want to and we sleep when we're tired, we eat when we're hungry and we create when we're inspired. This trip gave us opportunities and inspiration because you're taking in so many different cultures; our work has never been better, and our thinking has evolved."

S: "Stefan also spoke about how good it is to get away from your routine, your daily life and as a creative person, this is essential because we're doing the same things every day. If you take time to step back, take a deep breath and reflect, your thinking clarifies, and you're open to new ideas, which is important for a creative person."

ZB: How did you guys prepare for this?

C: "The first step was figuring out what we *specifically* wanted to do, because the idea of travelling the world is too big. We put together a wander list, which was our version of a travelling bucket list. We wrote down the things we've always wanted to do, which informed us on what we needed to research. Then, we could see how much money you need to take a road-trip around Norway.

Through our research, we found a company called Workaway who pair up hosts with volunteers; the host offers accommodation and food, and the volunteers stay there in exchange for three to four hours of work a day.

This worked like a dream for us. We worked at a Husky lodge in Norway with 70 huskies. We went mushing with them, took a road trip up to the North Cape, which is the northernmost point of Europe. All it cost us was two flights to Norway.

When you look at it like that, it is doable, and you just have to choose what you want to do. You can't do everything, but you choose the specifics and you go from there. We created an itinerary and we said, 'We'll be in Norway in May, and then let's go spend my birthday in Copenhagen in June and so forth.' You just start mapping it out."

S: "Once we decided on most of this, we had to get rid of pretty much everything."

C: "At the end, we were left with four bags, one bag full of camera gear and three bags of clothes and miscellaneous items. I recommend rolling your clothes because you can fit more in. Create a bunch of piles of things you have to take, you want to take and things you don't really need and go from there. We were amazed by how little we truly needed. We're leaving stuff behind now as we go. I've left shoes in Athens because I didn't need them anymore and I thought, 'This is just weighing me down.' Our rule is, if it enhances your experiences then it's worth it, everything else you don't need."

ZB: Talk a little bit about financials and how your perspective of money has changed since you started this trip.

C: "We use an app called Trail Wallet that was created by other travel bloggers that helps us budget monthly. At the beginning of the trip, we took all the cash we had from savings and from selling our possessions and then we decided to divide this between 12 months and stick to those monthly budgets because you can easily go broke after six months. We balanced it out where some months, we lie low and do things for free, like taking out our cameras and going for a walk. Other months, we planned more trips into Italian cities or Copenhagen or Stockholm or whatever it may be."

S: "When you have a good idea of what you want to do and where you want to go, you can figure out how much that's going to cost and you've just got to stick to the budget."

C: "You don't have to do all the touristy things. You don't have to eat at the most expensive restaurants. We were dining like locals in all these places because we're checking out all the street food. It's three Euros for a hot dog versus 20 Euros for a massive meal at a restaurant two shops away."

S: "Another thing we did, is we've arranged some of our transport ahead of time, which is beneficial because the earlier you book, the less you pay. The downside is that if you start to like a specific place and your ticket out of there is booked already, you can't extend your stay. These are things that we are discovering, but it's saved us money in the long-run."

C: "For accommodation, in addition to using Workaway, we use hotels.com, Airbnb, and Hostel World, always going with the cheapest route. The purpose of the trip is not to stay in luxurious accommodations in all the cities we visit. We just want to have a bed and somewhere to stay, so that we can go out and explore. We always take the cheapest route."

S: "Our second destination was Norway and Norway has to be one of the most expensive places in Europe and possibly the world. We're heading off to Thailand and we're looking forward to the exchange rate. We're coming from South Africa and the South African rand isn't as strong as we wanted it to be; it's 15 to 1 to the Euro. If we could do this again, we would go for cheaper countries with better exchange rates to our own."

ZB: How long have you guys been on the road?

C: "Almost eight months."

ZB: "And the original plan was a year?"

C: "The plan was a yearlong sabbatical, but at the moment, we have no idea what the plan is. A year will be marked in February when we are going back to South Africa. We have a wedding and a couple of prior arrangements that we have to attend but other than that, we're not entirely sure what is next. We like it that way. We're trying to stay in the moment and enjoy the ride but, if we had it our way, we probably wouldn't give up this life."

S: "We'll do it for as long as we can."

ZB: It sounds like you're having experiences that most people only dream of. What were some of your favorite experiences? Did you ever run into any scary experiences or anything like that?

C: "We've done most of Europe and that's been a huge part for us because we both have European roots; it was all about getting to the roots and seeing the beautiful cultures. Europe is convenient because you hop on a train and 10 minutes later, you're in a different country. We've done Austria, Germany, most of Scandinavia, Norway, Sweden and Denmark, Greece and Italy and most recently Turkey."

"We sailed for five days through the Greek Isles and met up with some friends there. We got to hang out with friends from Johannesburg who were holidaying in Istanbul, so we dropped everything to go see them and it was rewarding. We worked at a dog training facility in Italy, close to Florence, which was incredible.

The zest from living with such selfless people was eye-opening for us.

We did a month in Sweden. We also decided to unplug completely from the internet that month. Our month in Sweden was hard because the weather wasn't great; it was five-degrees in the middle of summer. One of our Workaway experiences was cleaning toilets and doing laundry. We've got that, rain outside, and we were completely disconnected from the world. That month was an eye-opening experience."

S: "It was hard, but it was good."

C: "Then, working at the Husky Lodge in Norway and driving up to the North Cape and spending my birthday in Copenhagen and eating at Noma. We've had some incredible experiences."

S: "Lots, we saw the midnight sun in Norway, which is something we had been wanting to see for a while, and it blew our minds away. It seems that every place we go we say, 'This is our new favorite city.'"

ZB: Have you guys been safe the whole trip? How's it been?

S: "We've been perfectly safe. Everything has been good."

C: "We both love South Africa, but the crime rate is incredibly high, especially in Johannesburg which was our hometown. We are used to knowing boundaries and knowing what you should and shouldn't be doing. Going into city centers at 11:00 at night, not the best idea. We're very prepared for that already.

The only miserable situation that we've had was coming from Munich to Salzburg, we got stuck at the border because of the refugee crisis; that hit us so hard. All trains were cut off and we'd booked a train previously, so we knew nothing about it. We had to somehow get a bus and then find a German lady who would help us, and it was a bit of a mission, but we did it. Besides that, we've always got each other's back."

ZB: How are you documenting this trip? What are you going to do with this story when you go back home at the end of the year?

S: "We like to stay present. We haven't really thought about how or what we're going to do with our story and if we're going to take it anywhere. We started off with Instagram because it seemed like the perfect fit to document our travels. The nice thing is that we're growing a community on our Instagram account and they're giving us things to do. If we say we're going to Istanbul in two days' time, we get so many..."

C: "Suggestions from locals."

S: "We've met up with a few people, and it's almost becoming a new way of traveling for us which is interesting and eye-opening because you can connect with so many people. We're also blogging at the same time which we love and it's like a diary for us. Chanel does most of the writing because she is a great writer."

C: "A diary and a portfolio for our work. As we take photos and create art and meet up with people, that's where we document everything. It's also where we house our wander list. As we do things, we cross them off. Steve spoke about this community that we built up. As people suggest things to do and places to go, we're adding that to the wander list. It started out with 69 items and it's grown to 350 things to do. We need to get to it and do all these things!"

ZB: What advice do you have for anyone who sees you two and says, "Man, I dream of doing this."

S: "Why haven't you done it yet? We've learned that this doesn't close any doors, it opens doors. Whether you're making friends with people all around the world, or you're getting to see different places and different cultures, you're learning that every culture has a different way of doing things. It shows you that you don't have to do something a certain way, there are other ways to do things and they can all be as successful as the rest."

C: "Don't fear the financial side of it. There are ways around it by using services like Workaway. You can stay with family and they'll cover all the costs that you need. There are ways around it, so you don't have to be worried about that."

S: "With a little bit of financial planning, and having no ties back at home, like you don't want a cell phone contract that you have to pay, or a gym contract that you have to pay – these are some of the minor things that you need to think about. Plan for a year or a year-and-a-half. Find someone to do it with; it's so much easier than traveling alone. Have fun and be curious because you just need to learn, learn, learn, that's the whole point."

C: "Also, be prepared for the hardest part of this trip, and that is saying goodbye to the people you meet. We've been in tears saying goodbye to huskies and their owners and it's tough because when you get such a great relationship going with people like this, you become part of their family, and you're there for four weeks and then you leave and then it's like, 'I might never see you again.'

S: "On that note, people will help you out. We found that you're really not alone when you're traveling because of the connections you make with people and the human spirit, it's very good. We've been offered places to stay, we've been offered food, we've been offered all sorts of things."

C: "People stop us on the road when they see we're looking at a map. They say, 'Can I help you?' It's like, 'Yes, please. I have no idea how to pronounce these things.' It's so cool."

ZB: If you could pick one place as a starting point to recommend to people, which city or country do you think people should go to?

S: "That's tough. One of our favorite cities other than Salzburg, Austria that we love is Copenhagen. Copenhagen is so cool. The people are very friendly, it's a beautiful city and I would suggest renting a bike to go around it. If you can afford it, do a bit of Scandinavia, and then work your way down into Europe."

KEY TAKEAWAYS

- Take time to step back and reflect
- There are ways around the financial cost
- Find someone to travel with
- Have fun and be curious
- You're not alone when you're traveling

CONTACT INFO:

- Website: howfarfromhome.com
- Twitter
  - @howfarfromhome
  - @stevodirnberger
  - @chanelcartell
- Instagram: @howfarfromhome

CLINT ARTHUR
As If You Were Dying

Clint Arthur (www.clintarthur.tv)is a graduate of the Wharton School of Business. He is also the GKIC Infomarketer of the Year, a successful entrepreneur with fifteen years of experience running his own gourmet food company, and the number one best-selling author of *Break Through Your Upper Limits On TV*, *Break Through Your Fear Of Public Speaking On Local TV*, and *What They Teach You At The Wharton Business School*. His famous personal transformation experiences, keynote speeches, and frequent appearances on network TV, iTunes podcasts, and syndicated radio shows inspire millions of people to live larger, more intensely, and with more impact on the world.

BACKSTORY

"I made the biggest mistake that any entrepreneur can make: I tried to do something without being somebody special.

I know everybody is special in their own way, and we're each unique, but what I was trying to do was become a filmmaker and a movie star in Hollywood without being famous. That is tough to do. It's really tough to get cast for any parts, or get selected to do anything, or get investors to give you money for anything if you're nobody in Hollywood. That mistake cost me 13 years of my life pursuing the Hollywood dream. Six of those years, I was behind the wheel of a taxi, and what made it all the more difficult for me was I'm a graduate of the Wharton Business School."

"Ten years into this whole ordeal, I was out to dinner with my dad at a steakhouse in New York City. One of his best friends comes up to the table at this steakhouse, and goes, 'Look who it is, it's the Wharton taxi driver.' That was painful because I felt like I had not only let down my dad, but I had let down myself. The many years of hard work and struggle, and positioning that I had put myself through to get into the Wharton Business School, to get a 4.0 GPA in my Entrepreneurial Management major should have led to great opportunities in my life, and I felt I had thrown them all away pursuing the Hollywood dream."

"It all came to fruition on New Year's Eve of the millennium. I was driving a cab that night and made $513. I went back to my little boat in Marina Del Rey where I was living; no hot water, no running water, no toilet facilities, no electricity, and no heat. I'm in my bunk on the boat, shivering under my heavy down comforter, wearing all my clothes, and I just broke down crying. Because I felt like I was never going to be able to get out from the ditch that was my life.

That night I said, 'That's it. I can't take this anymore.' I quit writing screenplays. I focused on changing who I was and how I was going to show up in this world."

"I got into the gourmet food business and slowly started working my way into that business and changing my life. I had an advantage in that business, which is essential for every entrepreneur. I started this venture by saying, 'The number-one mistake to avoid is not being somebody special.' What does that really mean?"

"As an entrepreneur, the most important thing you can do is be different from everybody else and there are two ways to do that. The first way is to have a unique product. If you have a unique product that nobody else has, that makes you different. It's not that easy to have a unique product. Luckily for me, I had this super-gourmet butter from a little tiny farm in the middle of nowhere.

That was my gourmet food that I was selling, and it was actually an amazing product that was very difficult for people to get. People wanted it because it was so special. Unless you have a special product like that, it is very difficult to be successful as an entrepreneur."

"The other way to be different than everybody else is to be a celebrity. As difficult as that may sound, it's actually easier to be a celebrity than it is to have a unique product because a celebrity can be manufactured with an actual formula.

I have come up with a formula for creating celebrity by going on TV news and talk show interviews. It's amazingly easy once you know the formula. That's how I've been able to help about 500 authors, speakers, coaches, and entrepreneurs use my formula to create celebrity for their personal brand."

ON PERSONAL BRAND

"What does personal brand mean? That means, what do people think about when they think about you? When your name comes up in an email, do they delete it, or do they get excited and open it? You have to get them to be excited about opening your email. That's a good personal brand, and unless you have a good personal brand, you're not going to be successful as an entrepreneur."

"How do you do that? You have to become somebody special. The easiest way to become somebody special is to start going on TV news and talk show interviews about any topic, whatever topic. Get these people to start thinking of you as 'celebrity,' somebody who is famous; somebody who is a newsmaker. If you can do that, then the whole world starts opening up for you."

"That's been my journey. I started appearing on TV news and talk show interviews about five years ago. Since then, I've done more than 64 television appearances, including the *Today Show*, *CNN Headline News*, a whole bunch of shows, *NBC New York*, *CBS Los Angeles*, and *ABC Chicago*. I started out by going on small shows and I just worked my way up: the old-fashioned way; anybody can do it. That's the most important lesson I have to offer."

What was it about that New Year's Eve that made you say, "Enough is enough?"

"You have to look at your life in what Tony Roberts refers to as peak situations; when you're in a peak state. When you're in a peak state, you have a different perspective on the world. New Year's Eve provided very powerful perspective that clearly showed me what the hell was going on. When you're in the middle of a storm, it's very difficult to see what's going on. That's why, many times, my whole destiny became altered on a New Year's Eve and that was one of them."

"You're already dead; you just don't know it."

"Fast-forward to 2008. I was 'fat and happy.' I had been married for seven years and my marriage was on the rocks. My company was teetering because of the Great Recession. My body was in the worst shape of my life. I was 236 pounds, compared to my high school wrestling weight of 145 pounds. I didn't even realize how obese I was. All I knew was I could barely bend over to tie my shoes. That's when I was at a men's self-help campfire, and the shaman on the other side of the campfire pointed at me and goes, 'You don't even know it yet, but you're already dead.' And I said 'What are you talking about, man? I'm the most successful guy on this team. Eight years ago, I was driving a taxi. Now I'm a millionaire. I was living on a little boat. Now I live in a mansion.' He goes, 'You're already dead, and you just don't know it.'"

"I thought about what the shaman said for months until New Year's Day 2009 when I decided, if this was going to be the last year of my life, what would I want to accomplish? Once I started living my life as if it was going to be the last year of my life, that's when I was able to make the change."

"If you're thinking about changing your life, try living your life as if you were going to die at the end of the year."

"See what happens for you. That was such a powerful experience for me. I've done it four times. I've written a book about it called *The Last Year of Your Life*, which guides you through the whole process. It gives you all kinds of different exercises and experiences to try so that when you're living the last year of your life, you can get the full experience. I've done it four times, and I keep refining the process. It's a valuable and powerful experience. I'm not saying you should quit your job. I believe in straddling. Start a business on the side while you're still an employee, so you don't run out of money; and then you have to become a taxi driver, or a waiter. I don't advise anybody to quit their six-figure job. Keep your job and start something else on the side that you can get out of your job one day. Above all, ask yourself, 'If this was the last year of my life, what would I want to accomplish?' Make a list of 20 things that you'd want to do. The best times to do this are either when it's New Year's Eve, New Year's Day, or on your birthday."

What does creating celebrity for yourself actually involve?

"The celebrity that I'm talking about is manufactured. It's not easy to make it happen, especially if you don't know what you're doing. If you know my formula, and if you follow my strategy of starting in small markets like Reno, Nevada, or Fargo, North Dakota; those are good places to start because they're happy to have strangers from out of town come on to share their expertise.

When you talk about having a unique product, that product is you. *You* are providing a service to an employer, and the employer is buying your time, your labor, and your services. You're being paid based on their perception of what your value is, so the best way to invest your time and effort is to improve the perceived value of your main product, which is you."

"Once you've done 10 to 20 TV appearances, you'll be a different person. Once you've done 40, there's no stopping you and you'll have a different perception of yourself, a different perception of yourself in the marketplace, and what your real value is.

One time, I walked into a meeting and the person looked at me and said, 'Wow, I googled you and had no idea who you were.' I'm thinking to myself, 'Who am I? Why does this guy think I'm hot stuff?' Well, it's because of all the TV news and talk show interviews. At that point I had done 11 interviews, and the guy said that to me. To date, I've done another 53 appearances. The perception of me is way different."

"How do you do this? When you go on TV, you don't need a book and you don't need a product. It's better if you don't even have a product. You're much better off if it's all about one thing: delivering value to the audience. That's what this is all about. You want to go on a TV show, on a news or talk show, and you want to deliver three or four minutes of valuable information with a takeaway, something that the audience can take away from your appearance that day.

What do I mean by that? One of my clients is an auto mechanic and owner of an auto repair shop in Pittsburgh, Pennsylvania called Elizabeth Auto Care. He also coaches auto mechanics on how to make more money in their own auto repair shops. So, he's got two things going on. As an entrepreneur, you've got to have multiple things going on because sometimes one thing is hot, and another time something else is hot. That's the nature of commerce. Things change.

This mechanic, Dave Striegel, started out doing TV news and talk shows in small cities in Kentucky and Illinois and worked his way up to bigger markets like Las Vegas and Phoenix, and ultimately to Los Angeles. He did two TV appearances in L.A. All the while, his real goal was to become a speaker at a big auto mechanic conference, called the NAPA Auto Parts conference, in Las Vegas that's only held once every 10 years. During all these appearances he always mentioned NAPA, and he sent copies of these appearances on TV news and talk shows to NAPA executives.

Dave distinguished himself from other auto repair coaches who also wanted to speak at this conference. Subsequently, he got four breakout sessions, each one with 450 attendees. He participated in a three-minute presentation on the main stage in front of 12,000 prime prospects."

"So, in one year, my auto mechanic client Dave Striegel was able to do 12 TV appearances, and use those appearances to leverage himself into a prime speaking position in front of thousands and thousands of prime prospects for his coaching services. His whole world was transformed. He became one of the most famous auto mechanics in America in a year. That enabled him to accomplish amazing feats for his coaching business."

TV publicity serves two purposes: One is to create celebrity for you, by going on any TV show because it really creates a special luster and celebrity for your personal brand. The second reason is to help you get on *bigger* TV shows down the line. The more TV you do, the more TV you *will* do.

What do TV networks gain if you don't have a book or some kind of celebrity status? How is it that they become interested in you as a person?

"You have to be positioned as a credible guest. For example, the garage mechanic, he didn't have a book, but he was an auto repair mechanic. He talked about three mistakes to avoid when you bring your car in to have it serviced by a mechanic.

Listen, these spots are three minutes tops, and it's not like you're trying to cure cancer. Very often, the simpler your topic, the better off you are.

The book is created to give you more credibility. For example, if you're a professor of economics at a major university, you don't need a book. You're a PhD in economics. You go on to talk about economics, and they say, 'Here today, to explain why the Fed did not raise the interest rates, is economics professor from Cal Davis, Mr. Joe Smith.' That's the way they would introduce you. They try to put a person on TV who the audience is going to want to watch and they do that with their introduction, with the anchor or host saying, 'Here today, is the number-one selling, platinum recording artist Faith Hill!' They try to make you sound exciting.

Let's say you wrote a 2000-word book called *The Fine Art of Walking Dogs* and you published it. Your introduction would be something like, 'Here today, to talk to us about the mistakes to avoid when you're walking your dog, is the author of the new book, *The Fine Art of Walking Dogs*, which just came out on Amazon today!'"

Publishing a Book Creates Credibility, Not Money

"The only reason we have books is to add credibility. You don't make money off your book.

For example, one time I was at a conference. I spend a lot of money going to conferences, or, let me rephrase that the way one of my mentors—believe me, I invested a lot of money on mentorship. One of my mentors always says, 'it's not spending money, it's investing money in your education.'

I've invested a lot of money in education by going to seminars, conferences, and events. One of them I was at, it was a five-thousand-dollar weekend conference. I spent five grand to go to this conference for the weekend. A big part of why I'm there is to meet other people who are five-thousand-dollar conference attendees; and I go out to dinner with a bunch of guys, and I'm telling them what I do about creating celebrity. The next morning, I get a text from one of these guys. He goes, 'can we get together for brunch.' Sure.

I meet him in the café in the hotel. I walk in, he's got his iPad in his hand. I sit down at the table, he goes, 'look what I'm reading.' He's reading my book, *Break Through Your Upper Limits On TV*. Thirty minutes later, he had signed my consulting agreement to be an eighteen thousand dollar per year consulting client. That's the value of a book."

ZB: I guess the book is not necessarily to make money at all. You might make a few hundred bucks here, maybe a thousand bucks here or there, but the book is leading to such bigger things.

CONTACT INFO:

- Email: clintarthur.tv

ERLEND BAKKE
Never Work Again

Erlend Bakke (www.erlendbakke.com) is a Norwegian serial entrepreneur, speaker and number-one international bestselling author. He currently owns the following three companies: Mr. Outsource, 360 and 360 Factory. He speaks on the topics of entrepreneurship with a focus on how to automate and outsource your business to avoid the trap of becoming a business prisoner. He spends most of his time between London, Oslo and the Philippines, but speaks all over the world.

BACKSTORY

"My entrepreneurial journey started when I was fired in London and was figuring out what to do. I tried to answer difficult questions like, 'what do I want to do? What is the meaning of my life?' and so on. I reached out to friends and asked them what they thought I should do and also spoke to the people who had influenced me in my life. One of those guys was an entrepreneur and he was always different from everybody else at dinner parties. He always asked unique questions that had the element of why? Why do you want to do that? He persisted in digging to just understand. He was definitely an inspiration to me.

One of my friends started 360 Photography that allowed you to turn things around online. He got a massive contract and I took him out for lunch. I said, 'You're so creative. How about I come in and take care of the operations, secure some sales and then we can build this company together.' After a year, I left to start a similar company in Norway."

BUSINESS OWNER = FREEDOM

"For most people, we grow up without entrepreneurial parents. It's just a different world. The school system doesn't teach you how the world is built up, because society favors business owners, people that create wealth in the world. There are different rules for people that own companies and employ people. You can have companies in different countries. You can transfer money in between. You can invest money through your company. You can lend money to the company and back to yourself. There are many things as a business owner that you cannot do as an employee."

"My dad pays 55% in tax. Then after that he pays 25% VAT on everything he buys. He's effectively paying 75-80% tax on everything he earns. When you have your own business, you can decide how much you want to pay yourself, and how much the government is going to take. It gives you a much greater sense of freedom. I've traveled all over the world and that's been a business expense. So, I've been saving 55%, because it's a business expense.

What qualifies a business expense? That's a good question. As long as you can justify it, it's a business expense."

"I've started making Bucket List videos. I say, 'where do I want to go? I want to go to the South Pole. I'll go to the South Pole and make a video about going to the South Pole.' Hence, it's a marketing expense. I can put all the costs on the company which makes it a 55% saving versus somebody that's employed that wants to do the same. They have to make a lot more money to have the same amount of freedom."

"Starting a company is about long-term gain."

"Most businesses fail, as much as 9 times out of 10 in the first five years. It's only after between three and five years that businesses start seeing a profit. That's because business is counter intuitive. We're all accustomed to instant gratification, whilst in business, it's long term gratification. You need to be in it for the long haul.

A lot of the people start a business with a short-term mindset. Many of my coaching clients believe they're going to replace their income in three months. That may be possible, but it depends on the type of business and your contacts. If you already work as a consultant for a company and you're starting a consulting business, you've already established a good network. In that case, you could replace your salary or double it because you don't have the cost of your employer, but there's also risks involved."

LIFESTYLE BUSINESS VERSUS PERFORMANCE LEVEL BUSINESS

"Things are always changing and there will always be waves of trends that you want to surf. It's important to understand that there are two types of businesses: lifestyle business and performance business. A lifestyle business is typically 12 people in an office turning over $300,000 up to a couple of million. The business owner can live a good life leveraging the perks afforded by owning a business. If you want to take a lifestyle business to the performance level, it's a very treacherous journey where you make a lot of investments. You get multiple J-curves, (A J-curve is when you invest your money and you don't see a profit right away, but then it goes back up and you realize a return on investment.) I'm a coach for people that have or want a lifestyle business."

What does it take to beat the odds of business failure?

"Perseverance is key. To stay in the game for the long-haul is where personal development comes in. The following are what I consider the big four habits in personal development:

1. You've got to sleep.
2. You've got to exercise.
3. You've got to eat right.
4. You've got to train your brain.

The fourth habit, training your brain by listening to podcasts & reading books, is to get you to think differently. I started outsourcing because I managed to get this big contract and I'd been working 30 straight hours. My arms weren't working anymore from editing all these images by myself. It got to a point where I couldn't do it anymore. A friend of mine had started outsourcing to the Philippines and he had suggested I try it."

"The reality is it's difficult when you don't have the money to pay for people. That's where you have to get creative. Imagine you are Richard Branson. The first company that Richard Branson started was a student magazine. The guy is dyslexic, so he knew he couldn't write anything for this magazine. But he's brilliant at two things. He's good at the vision. Most people want to be part of something bigger than ourselves. If you can be a person who projects a big vision for your business, you are far more likely to attract great people. Vision and people are Richard Branson's exceptional skill sets.

He has this ability to do things, inspire people and attract A-players. You want to have A-players on your dream team. The irony is the beginning of the entrepreneurial journey is like a reversed Super Mario where instead of starting at the easy level, you're starting at the most difficult level."

"Again, our school system doesn't teach you how to make money; it teaches you how to become an employee and have an employee mindset. It's interesting how programmed we are. In school you are told to sit down and shut up and do the work yourself. If you decide to collaborate with somebody else, that's cheating. If you decide to model somebody else's work, that's cheating. All these things that are good in business, schools just train right out of you.

There may be more collaboration in group work now, but the problem now with group work in school is that people want different things. You need to have a leader in a group. How do you choose the leader in the group where some people want an A and some people don't care? Role-playing that doesn't work."

"To make it as an entrepreneur, it is about learning new things, acquiring a new skill set and framing your mind around being in it for the long-haul. Figuring out, okay if I save $1000 a month in index funds and different investments, then I can be a multi-millionaire in 20 years. Again, most people don't think about these things. We think about what's for dinner or how much we want that candy bar."

About *The Compound Effect* by Darren Hardy

"The reason why *The Compound Effect* is very good is because every little action in the present matters. A smoker goes, 'I'm just going to have this cigarette.' Then they have that cigarette and a few hours go by and they tell themselves the same thing. What they don't recognize is if they have three cigarettes a day, that's 1000 cigarettes a year and 10,000 cigarettes in 10 years, etc. I encourage people that want to start a business to get into shape, read books and prepare themselves before they start a business, because I just jumped straight in. In retrospect, I wish there was a 12-month training course where every week you could train and then when you launch your business, you're mentally and physically ready to go the course. Building a business requires ingraining positive habits."

ON CREATING VALUE

"Three elements that add value to your business are:
1. Attracting great people.
2. Creating efficiencies with technology.
3. Understanding how to keep money in the business and then invest it wisely."

OUTSOURCING

"There's a global talent pool out there that we have access to through the internet. You have access to talented programmers and graphic designers. The great thing with outsourcing is that these people are quite hungry for the work and/or they're hungry to learn and grow. That's the beauty of outsourcing is that you can connect with somebody on the other side of the world. I'm constantly sharing educational and motivational stuff with my team in the Philippines, because I want them to become better people and do better. People are willing to work for less money, if they believe in your vision and you as a person."

AUTOMATION

"For most small businesses, an Excel spreadsheet and a virtual assistant goes a long way. It's easy to get stuck in this pursuit of automation and forget the minimum viable thing you need. One of the things that I think about every single day is what is one big thing that I need to do today?

A Harvard professor called Bob Pozen who used to be the CEO of Fidelity, the bank – I asked him how he accomplished all of this in his life. He said that every day, he would sit down for 15 minutes and would think about what was important. And then he would do what was important. He would leave everything else. That is very easy to hear and very difficult to do."

"With automation, you need to understand what it is that needs to be automated. When defining what you need to automate, divide your company into project-based tasks and daily habits. A project-based task is like launching your book while a habit is invoicing clients and customer service. Everything that's a daily, weekly or monthly thing for you or your business is a habit. I would always start with, if you're going to employ somebody, you need to have habits. If not, you end up doing a lot of the work and when you start delegating, people aren't happy because they don't have the skillset to do the work."

"If it's a habit, it's worth spending time training somebody to potentially give you back 25 hours of your week. People always ask me why I outsource everything, except the things that I must do. Business is all about understanding numbers and identifying key metrics. If I'm doing anything in the business, I'm doing sales and marketing. That's typically what the entrepreneur should be doing."

About *Never Work Again*

"It is my entrepreneurial story and also there's a lot about outsourcing and automation. The philosophy behind the book is about freedom. Once they attain freedom, a lot of people notice that there's this massive void. But they're not hanging out in restaurants in the middle of the day, not doing nothing. People are active. I realized that freedom is just boring in the really traditional sense. What does freedom really mean? What is it that we're searching for when we say, we need freedom or want freedom? Why do we not like having to go to work? Why is it important that we understand why we want to be free?"

KEY TAKEAWAYS

- Society favors business owners
- Think long term gratification
- Perseverance is key
- Building a business requires ingraining positive habits
- It's worth training somebody to give you back 25 hours of your week

CONTACT INFO:

- Website: erlendbakke.com

RILEY TEMPLE
The Millenial Mindset

Riley Temple (www.rileytemple.com) backpacked around the world with his family when he was 16, visiting 24 countries and participating in over 26 volunteer opportunities. This not only ignited a passion for learning and service, but also helped him develop a new mindset around education which he shares and speaks with students to this day. At 18, his exploration led him to the tech world of Silicon Valley where he helped found a financial education incorporation for millennials. A lifestyle entrepreneur, Riley values genuine connection over all else, recognizes the potential in every moment, and has been coloring outside the lines since kindergarten.

BACKSTORY

"I'm blessed with a family that presented me an opportunity. I've always been a little bit of an explorer. I love pushing things and poking things as a lot of entrepreneurs do. Being in a public school wasn't benefitting me, so when this opportunity was presented, I couldn't turn down an adventure. We took nine months and backpacked around the world and here I am today, with the travel bug alive and well because I'm ready to hit the road again."

At 16, how did your family approach you and did you decide that this was an opportunity of a lifetime?

"It was a gradual thing, so when we took off it wasn't spontaneous. My mom was working with an individual who took her family around the word in the '80s. That profoundly impacted my mom to the point where she would mention it over dinner and ask us if you would want to go anywhere in the world, where would it be? That conversation slowly evolved into, 'What if we took nine months and backpacked the world together as a family?'"

"At first, it was laughable because we'd come home from our routines, me and my sister from school, my parents from work school. We'd all joke, 'What if we took off?' because we had a mundane day that day. Let's spice it up and leave. Slowly that started percolating and building until my little sister started homeschooling and then my parents took their businesses home as well. I was the last holdout being a sophomore in a public high school. And then, I just had one of those days.

The power went out at my school and we weren't able to learn things that we were supposed to learn that day. It was just one of those catalysts for me to ask, 'Where is my time being spent and is this truly a value to me?' I went home that day and said, 'Let's do it. Let's take that nine-month trip and let's not look back.' I didn't go back to public school the rest of that year. I started homeschooling doing online school in preparation for this trip, and six months later we were on the road."

"I'm from Portland, Oregon and we didn't just want to do the typical resort route. We called it high-adventure, low-budget. Before the trip we bought this big map in which we'd put on one of our walls here, and we were able to put thumbtacks in the places we wanted to go, and we'd have little votes as a family to decide where we wanted to go. We had a general itinerary for the direction which we were headed, but no specifics whatsoever because we'd sit in hostels, and we'd talk to the locals, and we'd talk to other fellow travelers and say, 'Hey, we're trying to head in this direction, we got two weeks, what would you recommend?'"

"It flowed organically from there and led to incredible conversations with individuals we would have never been in contact with before and gave us unique experiences that you couldn't recreate because they were that spontaneous. That kind of traveling kept us in the present and I can't describe to you what it's like arriving in a town and not knowing where you're going to sleep, what you're going to eat, but feeling like, 'I'm okay. I got everything I need on my back and let's see where this day takes us.' Every day was that way for nine months and it was such a blessing to live in that zone. We ended up visiting 24 countries, 85 cities did 26 service projects."

What was your favorite place?

"It's a toss-up between Cambodia and Peru for two different reasons. I'm a scuba diver so I love being in the water, and in Cambodia we spent a week on an island off the coast that was called Koh Rong. Every morning I got up and went scuba diving. I'd eat fresh fish on the beach for lunch, talking with people from around the world, and at night I went out to meet even more incredible people, explore the island, look at the incredible stars, and go swimming at night. It's unbelievable. I lost track of what day it was, what time it was, and I didn't have to worry about anything. There were so many incredible people on that island that I was able to come in contact with. I would milk every day and every minute if I could go again. I'm excited to get back there."

"Peru is a kick because it was a profound place for me because I felt spiritually connected. There was this energy behind Cusco, Peru where everything just felt right. Everything felt aligned and I felt invigorated and very much alive. A lot of cool travelers there as well."

Did you ever experience anything that was radically different from what you're used to?

"During the nine months of travel, we were robbed only once and that was a cell phone. A couple of burned cell phones were stolen and a camera, which surprised us quite a bit because I was traveling with my computer to do online courses. We were really surprised that we just didn't run into that issue as often as we anticipated."

"Other than being extremely uncomfortable, like there were a couple of sketch bus rides, especially through the mountains of Ecuador where I was outside of my comfort zone and safety was top of mind. Just seeing how people lived internationally. We didn't go to resorts. We tried to stay at the local spots and get a feel for the culture and, on top of that, through volunteering, we saw certain areas of countries that tourists wouldn't see. It was a humbling experience to meet locals who profoundly impacted us by how they lived. I'd have to say that was something I didn't expect to hit me that profoundly."

Who was the person that left Portland and who was that person that returned home nine months later?

"I was your stereotypical teenager,16 years old, had my select friend group that I stayed exclusive to. I did love to explore and poke like entrepreneurs do, but it wasn't channeled in the right direction; I realize that now looking back. I was poking things that weren't best to poke and, on top of that, I didn't really consider myself a learner of life. I had a different view of education because I didn't respect the formal system when I was in it and, therefore, they didn't respect everything that I brought to the table. It was this constant feedback loop between me and the public-school system because I didn't really vibe with it and I didn't find the information that was presented relevant."

"The biggest transformation for me was I discovered I am a passionate learner and I'm a lifelong learner as well. I just wasn't in the right space to fully and effectively discover that and learn in the way which was most beneficial for me. For example, I was taking a comparative theology course while traveling through Southeast Asia. I could get through online courses at my own pace.

I'd spent the afternoon going to Buddhist monasteries. I'd spend days at a Hindu village, and I'd see the relevance of information that was being presented in this course. Slowly, the cogs started turning and I started seeing it's being able to apply information that motivates me the most. I'm always wanting to learn. I'm always wanting to meet new people and see what I can pull from every opportunity and every experience. That was the biggest profound impact that the trip had on me."

What would you tell parents who have the ability to give their children this opportunity?

"I've been asked this question multiple times and I'm still trying to develop a satisfactory answer. Just realizing that kids don't all learn the same, kids have different passions and cultivating a space for kids to explore their own passions is key. Don't push them into a specific direction at such a young age, especially at the high school demographic. That's what breaks kids down when they're not able to explore. I was still in the public-school system, I was still in that consistent groove, I would have never found peace with learning.
It's about letting kids truly explore and having fun in the space that they're in and just being a supporter of them discovering themselves is the biggest thing. Not pushing your own view of what a successful student or a successful child is, but letting them find their own relevance."

At the end of this trip, when did you guys decide it was time to go home?

"We had specific places that we needed to be. Prior to leaving, we had a documentary team ask us if they could do a little number on what we were doing, the volunteering, and all. We had specific places we needed to be, and we knew we needed back in nine months. Having specific places gave us a little structure and a bit of insight into where we were going to be during specific months of the year.

Nine months was our projection and we ended up going to South America. We weren't even anticipating heading down there and we extended it to 16 days longer, and made our way up through Central America, and walked across the Tijuana Border, but we had no specific date to come back. It was pretty broad."

"As long as we were showing up in the manner in which we promised ourselves, things would happen, and incredible things would happen. We call them magic and miracles. People would show up and experiences would take place that we would never even anticipate if we were holding out a goal or had a specific mindset in how things should happen. It was a lot of fun to see things flow in that manner."

What happened when you got home?

"That was the toughest part of the trip. Before leaving for the trip, my excitement outweighed my nervousness. I was excited about the unknown, what was going to take place, and that excitement for the unknown carried to the end of the trip until we came back. When we got back, I was more nervous because I knew what I was headed into as opposed to the excitement of the unknown. I went back to my public high school and, at first, had a hard time because I wanted to hold the mindset that I had throughout the trip and be this completely changed person. I was trying to push that too much. That took me out of the present and away from the opportunities in which I could make the most of high school."

"It's rough to go from backpacking the world with our family to now a 17-year-old in public high school and trying to fit into the mold. It wasn't until I started applying that education mindset that I was able to make the most of the situation. I thought, 'Hey, this is my last year in high school. This is where I'm able to explore the things that fascinate me. There are resources and there are tools in which I could grab hold of and make the most of.' I ended up trying out for a musical in my school because I figured why not? This had never been on my radar before. My experiences traveling and then trying out for the talent show and putting myself out there made my senior year incredible. I started pushing myself in ways I would have never pushed myself in the past. It was fun to start applying that mindset in that manner as opposed to wanting to hold onto my own individual mindset as being in the trip."

How did you get into the tech world?

"I had an incredible year where first I was planning on backpacking South America for two years. I had a gig lined up playing music in a bar, and I was working at a hostel, and backpacked around South America as the money permitted. I've always been an entrepreneur. I grew up in that lifestyle and I was like, 'Why not? I'll just move down to California, see what I can do to make something happen down there.' Two weeks before moving to L.A., I had this intuition and I was like, 'Hey man, you're in love with the end goal but you're not in love with the process.'

'Where would you know that you could vibe?' I was like, 'You know what, I've been to San Francisco twice when I was 12. Why not just move there? There's a lot happening down there.'"

"So, in August of 2014, I moved to San Francisco and lived out of my car for four months, couch-surfing between various friends and acquaintances. It was there that I started tapping into the tech world, figuring things out. I received a couple of internships working at some corporations down there and eventually ended up getting a scholarship to Draper University which is an entrepreneurial university based out at Silicon Valley. That's where the ball started rolling for me on the whole tech side of things.

My entrepreneurial insights started coming into play. I met some incredible passionate individuals. I was subjected to startups and the world of venture capital and it was another experience that I didn't even see coming. I was anticipating being in California for two months and then heading to South America, but I ended up spending a year in San Francisco because there was potential and growth there for me as well. That's how I found myself in the tech world."

What role does finance play in your life?

"I learned so much living down in San Francisco, gaining insight into the whole startup world. When I came back up here to Portland, I saw a benefit. I just love talking to people and hearing their passions and how they're applying it to business. I said, 'I'll open the door for some strategy consulting work. I'll just open the conversation. Most people want to talk about their startup. I can provide some insight there.'

So, I started chatting with people, I started going to networking events, and I started getting clients here and there. I'm in the marketing space helping people outline social media campaigns and doing some random things around the same kind of vibe of the startup world. Through that, I was able to network my way into the travel industry. I was introduced to a startup called TripGrid that's building an app that will revolutionize the travel-planning industry. They're launching in February."

"Back to the monetary side of things, they hired me on to be brand ambassador for them and I'm able to the travel on behalf of them over to Southeast Asia for my first month of traveling where I'll be doing market validation, coming up with marketing concepts, and just chatting up the brand, talking to people. I'm blessed to have the guys at TripGrid helping me out. This is the dream end for me. I just want to chat with people and travel the world and that's exactly what I'm getting to do. Building upon that and building relationships where we can find mutual benefit is what I'm all about."

ON REDEFINING WHAT IT MEANS TO WORK

"These generation gaps are interesting when you look at what's ensued as result of the environment in which these generations were raised. There was almost a hierarchical sense of information coming from the CEO and working its way down the corporation, or in religion, or in the educational system. Now with the internet and everyone being so connected, this information paradox has been shattered. The power no longer lies in who has access to information, but it's what you do with that information is what counts. It's the entrepreneurs, it's the millennials who were able to connect those dots because we grew up with intro to learning computers and experiencing these technological advances, and subsequently creating new jobs left and right. Gen Z is coming up and they're a lot more refined in what they're learning because they're able to access information and technology.

It's rad to see all of these generations coming together and bringing their own respective perspectives about how things could be done. The old mold is completely shifting. Holding multiple gigs and doing freelance work is becoming the new norm. People are doing things that they love doing because they can access the information to make it happen."

WORDS OF WISDOM

"Find your relevance in relationships, in experiences, and in information. Dive into and follow your passions. See what intrigues you, but then see how it relates to you. You're not just blindly following your passions, there has to be some balance and reflection there. Find your relevance in the relationships you have with others, in the information that's being presented to you, and in how you can apply it."

KEY TAKEAWAYS

- Where is my time being spent and is this truly a value to me?
- Fall in love with the process
- Networking opens up opportunities
- Build relationships that are mutually beneficial

CONTACT INFO:

- Website: rileytemple.com

JOSEPH RANSETH
How to Start a Movement

Joseph Ranseth (www.JosephRanseth.com) has been helping individuals and organizations start movements for over 15 years. He's a featured expert on national television including Fox News, CBS, CTB, CBC, and more. Leading industry publications such as *Advertising Age* and *The Huffington Post* have recognized him for using social media to inspire the world. Whether in his best-selling book, on the TEDx stage, as a keynote speaker or a boardroom consultant, Joseph passionately and powerfully shares the principles of purpose-driven marketing and transformational leadership in the digital age.

BACKSTORY

"It starts with the little whisper inside of all of us and saying that there's just more. It isn't necessarily that everyone has a call to become an entrepreneur; it isn't that necessarily everyone has a calling to start a movement the way that Gandhi or Dr. King did. But I do believe that there is that whisper that says to us that we're meant to have a bigger impact than we're already having, that we're meant to fully express who we are and that's just nature.

Nature is always growing and expanding. For us, we have that drive. It's part of our human nature to want to do something meaningful, to want to have an impact. For some, we anchor that to money. Others anchor that to philanthropy or giving back. I don't think it necessarily matters exactly how we do it as long as we are giving voice to the best that's inside of us."

"That's how I got into the work that I had to do. In 1999, I started in internet marketing and I had this mental and physical ping-pong game between what I did to make money and what I did to find meaning. I'd do a big marketing campaign, make a bunch of money and then go and volunteer for a couple of months. I realized, 'Oh I need to go back for money.' So, I flip-flopped back and forth between those."

"One of my earliest mentors was Dr. Stephen Covey who wrote *7 Habits of Highly Effective People*. He gave advice that rattled my brain and changed the course of my life. He said, 'If you want to be successful, you need to learn to integrate the spiritual with the secular.' It spoke to me because I had that ping-pong thing and I also knew that by spiritual, he was referring to purpose. To that call in each of us to do something meaningful. I often think of the parable of the stone quarry where an old traveler is journeying, and he comes across a stone quarry and he sees three men working in the quarry and asks them the same question. To the first he asks, 'What are you doing?' That man, without taking his eyes off his hammer, grumbles, 'I'm cutting stones and I'm getting blisters on my hands.' He asks the same question to the second man, 'What are you doing?' That man stops and looks the traveler in the eye and says, 'I'm earning an honest day's wage to support my family whom I love.' To the third, he asks the exact same question, 'What are you doing?' That man puts down his tools, lifts his gaze high into the sky and in a beaming voice, says, 'I am building a cathedral to glorify the Most High.'"

"Each man was doing the same action outwardly but driven by a different purpose. What we do matters, but not near as much as why we do it. I would venture to guess that the third man was experiencing a much higher level of satisfaction in his work. He was going home happier. He probably had more energy and could probably be a better husband, and father because of how he felt about his job.

Even though it was the same job as the other two. I would also venture to guess that that third man was experiencing a lot more miracles; those small synchronicities that whisper to us, 'You're in the right place' and that say, 'I'm onto something.' I bet he was experiencing those an awful lot more than the other two if they were experiencing those at all."

"Conflict doesn't happen between people; conflict happens within people."

"If there's conflict in a situation, it's happening within the first person. It's not going to be happening between that first person and the third person. The first person maybe has jealousy, envy, or anger toward the person who's getting a higher level of satisfaction out of the same work. They may feel that they're a victim. The reality is the only difference was the state.

When we're envious of others, it's not necessarily because of their position or their possessions, it's because of the state that we see them in. That they are what we perceived to be happier in a better space. We think it's their money, the fancy car or the big house. But when we think of why we want those things, it all comes back to we want those things because of how we think it'll make us feel, the state that will put us in."

ZB: I'm curious to hear from you, in this idea of creating a movement, how much does this require as to be present and aware of what's going on around us?

JR: "You hit on a couple of things that are extremely important there. One of them is staying present, but the other is choosing our beliefs. You could've seen that number and just dismissed it, but you chose an empowering belief that that moment to say, 'I take this as a sign that things are in flow right now. I'm choosing to interpret this in my favor.' That's what purpose-driven people do."

"Studies have shown that people who think they're lucky end up having far more lucky experiences, end up happier, and have more opportunities."

"Often, we look for the perfect circumstance to empower us when the reality is it's our belief, that empowers us. It can help us make the most of a situation and it doesn't matter if our beliefs are necessarily true. What matters is that they empower us."

"We choose our beliefs."

"I'm not saying that we should believe in things that are patently not true, but I'm saying that when we choose our beliefs, so we need to look at things and say, 'Does this belief empower me?' When I was a kid, I played on a basketball team and I would generate this belief that I was Michael Jordan. Now, that wasn't necessarily true, but it put me in a peak state, and it helped me to play the game at a higher level and to just stay and flow. We can adapt that same principle. That personal work is critical to starting a movement. We have to not only do the right things; we have to be in a certain space if we're going to make things happen."

What prevents people from starting movements?

"There are two main things: One is fear, and fear will come up in a couple of ways. Fear that we'll fail and look bad or fear that we'll succeed and have to deal with everything that success brings. Ego and/or selfishness is the other roadblock that prevents people from succeeding. I'll explain that a little bit more after we go into the blueprint. When people are full of ambition or inspiring dreams and things fall apart, it's because they've got fear or they're selfish."

ON STARTING A MOVEMENT

"If you look at all of the great leaders throughout history who have started significant movements, you'll find they had three things in common:

A Big Idea

First, they all had a big idea. By big idea, I mean, it transcends the individual level. What also makes a big idea is, if necessary, we're willing to give our lives for. If you examine these ideas, there are elements that unite people who would have otherwise been divided and they still celebrate their differences. A big idea is one that recognizes that our differences make us unique and it should be celebrated.

At a deep level, these big ideas are all an expression of the universal truth that we are all connected.

You look at any of the great movements and the common thread is people will come together to labor for something much bigger than themselves.

A Clear, Compelling Message

The second commonality among great movements is they all have a clear message. We all know the picture of Dr. King where he's delivering a speech, with his arm extended, before 300,000 people. And we know he's saying, 'I have a dream.' We all know that that's the heart of the message. Any movement or even any great marketing campaign has a clear, compelling message that when you share it, people get it, understand it, and are moved by it.

An Evangelist and an Army of Advocates

On that hot summer day, 300,000 people showed up because Dr. King's big idea spoke to them in a way that compelled them to adapt it as their own big idea."

What differentiates these leaders from others who have shared their own big ideas that never caught on?

"What's interesting about that is it requires a tremendous amount of inner courage and inner strength both to lead as well as to join a movement and we have to be willing to labor without receiving credit. It takes tremendous inner conviction to say, 'I'm going to labor for this big cause and I'm okay if I don't get the credit.' It also takes a lot for someone to say, 'I'm going to join this even though it wasn't my idea. I'm going to assign my name to this and labor under it even though I didn't start that company, or I didn't start that cause or message.' The big idea must be that compelling and that requires a certain type of person who isn't in it for personal gain."

ZB: To achieve that takes a lot of inner work and growth because we live in a generation of people who want credit for the things we're doing. I look at social media and it's a giant scrap of, 'Look at all the things that I did.' I'd imagine that's conflicting with how we live our lives now and maybe that's another aspect as to why people aren't creating movements because we really want that confirmation of, 'I did some good and everybody knows it.'

JR: "You just hit on it here because a while ago, I was just having this conversation with my business manager. For years, as a keynote speaker and consultant, I've been sharing this blueprint of how to start a movement and so my business manager said, 'If it's so easy, why doesn't everyone do it?' I said, 'Well, element zero is actually a fourth component, but it's not really a fourth because it comes first.' My business manager said, 'Element zero? The fourth element to the blueprint but it's not the fourth, it's the first. What are you talking about? That doesn't make sense. That is not a clear message.' As a marketer, I'm looking at that through this branding lens and saying, 'That doesn't say what it's all about. It wasn't meaningful, but there's something about that that I like.'"

"It's about that personal growth and power that Gandhi and Dr. King possessed that enabled them to become a vessel worthy of carrying that message. Less than 24 hours later, I was doing more research and came across this story of when Gandhi went to Britain to meet with the monarchy about India's liberation. A journalist asked Gandhi, 'What is your secret?' How does this little 90-pound guy in homespun loincloths come to meet with the monarchy and how is it that he's crippling the largest empire on the planet?' His answer was, 'I make myself zero.' He was saying, 'This isn't about me. I'm waking up every day and I'm getting rid of the little me, so that I can work for the welfare of others.' That element zero that, fourth one is not only the power we develop personally, but also the purpose of letting go of selfishness, of arriving at a place that we're filled with love and motivated only by love for others so that we completely abandon our personal desires.

We're committed to doing this for the well-being of others. That was what allowed him to develop the powerful conviction to overcome the challenges in order to see it through."

ZB: That's such a tough place to get to. What are good examples of self-work to put us on the path of increased awareness and enable us to give ourselves to others?

JR: "You can't fill up anyone else's cup unless your cup is full. The dichotomy of that is that we get a lot from giving. We need to always be in that space of service but also remember that we need to come from a place of being full; they go hand-in-hand. We can't focus solely on filling up our cup without serving others. We also can't completely give ourselves to others without doing the required self-care."

"A great tool that helps illustrate that point is meditation. This is when you first start your day where you sit, close your eyes, get into a comfortable meditative state, and imagine this light of pure love either coming into you or springing from within you.

See it start in your heart and fill that up and expand out through your whole body then slowly visualize it expand into the room and watch it go into the rooms of those that you love, watch it going across your city into the houses of the other family members or friends.

Watch it expanding going into the homes and the hearts of your clients and those you serve and slowly, removing your gaze further away and watching yourself shift higher and higher and seeing it expand out over your state then the country and the globe and filling the whole world with this light of love. That is such a great way to put yourself in a beautiful state of love and mindfulness for others. It's also a great way to anchor that throughout the day as we walk around and we're now thinking, 'How can I share love? How can I give it?' It sounds overly simple, but it's powerful. As you're going through the day, count how many times you can ask the question, 'How can I serve others today?'

The simple exercise of trying to count how many times you can repeat that to yourself will be a profound spiritual realization of how often your mind goes to worrying about work or thinking about what you're going to eat for lunch. The point is to shift your mind from being preoccupied with ourselves to saying, 'How can I serve others?' This simple exercise serves us on both an intellectual and physiological level; it can profoundly transform us."

FINAL WORDS OF WISDOM

"Start taking action and if you're still trying to find out what you love, try a bunch of different things. Often, we have this idea of what we think we love, that 'My life would be great if this happened. When I graduate and do this job, I'll feel great.' At best, that's speculation. We need to do something that we *know* makes us feel great and we *know* that when we're in the moment with it.

Find things. Get in the moment. Get busy. Listen for those little nudges and confirmations that say, 'This feels good, doesn't it?' Maybe you're in the right place."

KEY TAKEAWAYS

- We're meant to express who we are
- What we do matters, but not as much as why we do it
- Choosing your beliefs will impact your outcome
- People will come together to labor for something much bigger than themselves
- Let go of selfishness
- Ask yourself, "How can I serve others?"

CONTACT INFO:

- Website: JosephRanseth.com
- Twitter: @JosephRanseth

ROB SCOTT
Hijack Your Mindset

Rob Scott (www.robrob.com) is known for hijacking people's minds, rewiring their limited beliefs, and leaving them completely transformed. He is a master-level coach who creates digital products and training programs for the world that make them break through their deepest limits. After working with Rob, people become incredibly effective, more successful and deeply fulfilled. His flagship product, called the Identity Shifting Mask, reprograms people's mindsets, and connects them to their deepest purpose.

BACKSTORY

"Today, my life is exceptional. I'm deeply living my purpose and I'm financially doing incredibly well with somebody I love. Things are amazing, but it certainly wasn't always like that. I had a very abusive upbringing, I was being raped repeatedly for years as a young child, and it left me really unable to trust and it created a mountain of shame in me, I didn't have the safe emotional, mental and physical upbringing that people assume you've had."

"I was doing drugs at an obscenely young age of 7. I was a kind of mascot for these older college kids in the neighborhood and I'd do anything they sent my way. My childhood was skewed and that led to major dysfunction. Later, I became seriously addicted to stuff and that led to homelessness and in and out of institutions, halfway houses, and rehabs. I was living on the streets, and then something changed."

"I woke up and realized that nobody was literally or figuratively punching me anymore. I had carried a major chip on my shoulders and to deal with that, I was both a tough guy and a victim. I looked at everything I'd been through and realized none of that was serving me. It was as if I was dragging this crappy past like a ball and chain, continuing to live in it, and dragging it into my future. This was a fundamental shift in my world view. It shattered everything I knew.

It was so incredibly profound that it triggered dramatic change in my life. I went from being homeless and a temp in the basement of a business, being diagnosed with an aggressive cancer to a few short years later of becoming Vice President of Technology, and building a large, complex software company and then selling that company into a much larger company. That allowed me to exit in a positive way because there was nowhere else to go in that corporate environment."

"I started to do a podcast and I was sharing ideas about how we can evolve our mentality. Do we evolve our consciousness to become the next version of ourselves? What is it to shift our identities into something profoundly new, and what is hypnosis? I started to get global listeners that requested coaching from me. I didn't think that was my jam at first, and then a friend was like, 'I'd hire you right now.' I tried it and immediately realized that that is what I've been best at my whole life.

As a little child, I pretty much coached my parents to getting along, and see things differently. I definitely have an ability here, but I have also spent many, many years honing it. I've been getting phenomenal results out of people for the last decade, and I love what I do. My office is a lab where I'm hacking people's consciousness to allow them to get extraordinary results."

ON THE CORRELATION BETWEEN STRESS AND ILLNESS

"There is a lot of evidence that our mentality changes how neurons and neuron bundles are formed and fired in our mind, which completely informs the hormone balance of the body and the levels of cortisol, serotonin, and dopamine. We tend to separate the mental and physical connection because it makes it easier to address. But we are holistic; we are one complex system."

"I firmly believe that mentality or a history of stress 100% influences health."

"One of the differences between a rock and an animal is that the animal can react to its environment. Sight fires neurons in the basal part of the brain that affects the nervous system and that may result in a faster heartbeat and the emotion of fear. If we were *only* reacting to that environment at that very base level, we'd be much more instinctual and reactive to other animals. That's because we have this big extra part of our brain that sits on top, which allows modelling, imagination, memory, and all these things."

"What we know now, is not only what I see influences that neuronal bundle, but also what I'm remembering, what I'm imagining, and how I'm thinking can change how we feel at any moment."

ON THE CORRELATION BETWEEN THOUGHTS AND SUCCESS

"If I'm about to go on stage and deliver a presentation, what I make of the meaning in that moment controls my anxiety and/or confidence. There are a variety of studies that show this, all the way down to dying. Studies show that people who live a life full of anxiety, that believe anxiety is bad for them, die much sooner than people who have anxiety, but consider it normal, edgy or exciting.

We now know that what we make of how we're feeling goes down to a base level of self-love. Without self-love, stress levels are higher in our body, which makes us oxidize faster and we literally die sooner. How you think affects your body. No doubt. And it certainly affects your motivation and your results."

"I identify those thinking patterns that create an identity that lead to self-limiting beliefs. The reason this is rampant is because it keeps us safe by not taking that risk, not breaching your comfort zone. What I do is get clients to master how they are making meaning and how they think, taking someone who wants to be an entrepreneur, but they're not there yet because they have yet to learn something, or they can't do sales calls because they are not good enough *yet*.

If my client frames their identity to, 'I am an entrepreneur and an entrepreneur makes sales calls, an entrepreneur gets it done, an entrepreneur hires the right people,' you'll see a whole different set of behaviors that come with that different identity. All of our identities are changing all the time, but we are not doing it consciously, and that change is based on fear and resistance. So, instead of consciously going, 'Wait who do I really want to be? What does that look like? And how do I step into that?' I'm interested in helping people master that."

ZB: This reminds me about when I first started writing my book. I had always wanted to write a book and I joined this coaching program, and we'd figured out the outline, the title, what we wanted to write about, they were like, "Alright, now you are going to get the book cover designed," and I'm like, "What?! Why am I designing the cover? The book's not written!" And it was amazing what happened once we did this. As soon as I saw that cover design, it solidified to me, "I am going to write a book!" I had these ideas, but I had no clue how they were all going to tie in together, and when I saw the book cover design, I knew exactly how it was going to happen.

Zephan cutting in here for a quick moment – the book I'm referring to here is *Life Re-Scripted: Find Your Purpose and Design Your Dream Life Before the Curtains Close.*

130

I released it in 2015 and we sold over 4000 copies in the first month rocketing it to #1 bestseller on Amazon in three different categories. Feel free to grab a copy if you'd like! Admittedly it was my first book so you'll find proof that I'm not perfect, but it was a big accomplishment that I'm really proud of; If one person pulls one golden nugget out of it then I did my job. End shameless promotion.

RS: "So, what happened was, there was a difference in belief of 'Will it happen or not?' to 'This is really happening.' It's clarity on where you are going. A lot of what I do is to help people shape their belief systems – not political or religious – but what we believe about life. So much of our life is about what we believe will happen or can happen and most of us have these incessant limiting beliefs, that we take on as truth, right? 'I'll never be rich.' 'I'll only ever live in this size house.' 'My business could be $100,000 a year, but it will never be ten-million a year.'

This is happening in the background and they may not even be 100% believed, but they're little unconscious whispers revealing our limits, showing us where we fit in the scheme. And to have a profound change, you need to go in and edit that belief structure. And that happened to you once you saw the cover of your book."

AWARENESS

"Awareness is a game-changer. If you can shift your awareness in a fundamental way, it changes the whole game, not just in this moment, but it iterates throughout other challenges, in your life."

"Awareness is a new level of consciousness."

"If you think about how in the East, there is a deep history of meditation and being. What does it mean to be fulfilled and happy in the moment? And here in the West, we are so good at doing, we're good at succeeding. It's almost like there's this science of success that we want to understand. How do we get to Mars and colonize it? How do we build nuclear technology? And that's great, but we're not as good at *just* being and being present.

If you go back to the East, somebody who is good at sitting, being present, happy and fulfilled, they might not be as powerful in the world. Right outside that theatre of managing their own emotions, they may not be causing change. And if another villager comes to burn down all your houses, they may not be ready to deal with that. So, we're not just trying to feel good, and we're not just trying to succeed."

"It comes down to mastering, being and doing."

"The worst-case scenario is if you master success but never feel great about it, when you make the million and now it's ten million, because you've gotten good at reaching goals, you're never satisfied in it. When you have mastered awareness and success, I call it stillness and motion. It's bringing this present quality to our actions, where we live a life full of purpose, connection, and wonder. In any moment, we can either be hating what is going on, or we can be appreciating what is amazing. As we slow down, we'll realize that the universe is giving us a message all the time, but we are being too loud in our thinking to feel it."

"Imagine going to the best masseuse in the world. Two different people are going to go in, and the first person is laying down getting the massage, but the whole time they are thinking about their late taxes, the mismanagement of their company, and who they have to hire right. They miss the whole massage. They never brought their attention to be with this beautiful massage.

Another person goes in, pushes all the other stuff aside, and focuses on their breath and the feeling of the massage. They have put their attention on where they are, and when that happens, it is beautiful."

ON CHANGE

"Mastery is a stage of evolution where the stages are beginner, intermediate and advanced. You can enjoy the stage you're at; you don't have to be a master before you feel amazing about your life. It's about just going in the right direction. Somebody who is overweight, as soon as they start showing up for themselves, even in the first few days going to the gym and eating differently, they feel so much better.

Your state, how you feel, your happiness and your fulfilment can be affected almost immediately, and sustained you continue towards your goals, towards the mastery. Fast and profound change can be much more immediate than people think when you rewire how you make meaning, how you show up for yourself and the world."

What's the one thing someone can do to change their lives?

"It's about shifting your level of awareness to understand how you see. Most of us are unaware that we're looking through a lens that skews our view of the world. Training and understanding to become self-aware will shift how you carry self-limitation. And once you systematically challenge your limits and drop them, and develop a new way of thinking, you control so much more of your life. This is a level of enlightenment that replaces fears, fighting back, and feeling less than with growth, success, sustainability, and gratitude."

"The loudest sound bite is you control way more of this than you think and the first step is becoming aware."

KEY TAKEAWAYS

- What you make of meaning in the moment controls your anxiety and confidence
- How you think affects your body, motivation, and results
- Our identities are changing all the time, we are not doing it consciously
- To have profound change, you need to change your belief structure
- It comes down to mastering, being and doing
- Put your attention on where you are

CONTACT INFO:

- Website: identityshifting.com
- Blog: robscott.com

BRYAN & JEN DANGER
One VW Bus and the Open Road

Bryan and Jen Danger (www.thedangerz.com) quit their jobs and left normal society to drive their '67 Volkswagen bus through Mexico and Central America. They thought that they'd probably end up living on a beach and never coming back. They just did. As it turns out, they realized that their home in Portland where their tribe is, was just as important to them as traveling. They spent the last few years creating a home based in Portland and trying to ensure that they never again have to take jobs that they dislike.

Jen: "When we meet people who say, 'I love my job,' it fills us with joy because you don't hear that very often."

ZB: What types of jobs were you guys working before all this went down? Where were you in life and what led to this decision to leave?

Bryan: "We're both working pretty corporate North American jobs. Jobs that the average person would say we should have been happy to have. We were working 60 hours a week under fluorescent lights. I was traveling a ton for work, but not the type of travel that you can get excited about, more like a new state every day, a new rental car, a new hotel, just seeing the same old thing. Jen wasn't able to join me for it. We tried to make it fit to just say, there's got to be a way we can do this like 'normal people.' It never fit. We couldn't force ourselves; a case of a square peg/round hole."

Jen: "I worked for different sporting goods companies and different outdoor brands. I worked on the product team, but in numbers, so I was crunching numbers and forecasting future sales and things like that. Bryan was in a consulting firm. Their main focus was education. We had great jobs. They just didn't suit us because we were thinking there's got to be more to our everyday existence."

ZB: Did you guys have travel experiences before then?

Bryan: "We always tried to optimize the two-weeks of vacation we got every year. We'd go and scuba dive, hit the islands, take a trip to Thailand, one or two international trips over a course of 14 years. It's not that we didn't know the world was out there, but it seemed like we were so far removed from it."

Jen: "Every time we traveled; it was for 10 days to two weeks. Once you get there, a quarter of the way through that vacation, you already start thinking about your jobs and your to-do list. It just never felt like it was long enough, or that we were able to release enough from that daily life."

ZB: Who was the first person to come home and say, "All right. We've got to do this?"

Bryan: "Jen, for sure. She often gets upset by the way I describe it. For the better part of a decade, she was just pulling and tugging, and saying, 'Let's drop it all and leave.' I thought that was crazy hippie talk. There's a reason we're working. What about our 401(k) and our retirement? All these things that we spent our life trying to do. It took me a long time.

She has no fear in the world about this type of thing. I couldn't let go of the normalcy and the fear. My consolation was, 'Let's not leave today, but let's spend the next few years downsizing, purging, downsizing more, and saving money, to at least make sure we have enough of a travel fund to be gone for a while and that we could come back and have enough padding if we had to go back and find another job, so that coming back wasn't suddenly more stressful than before we left."

ZB: It seems like things have changed for the better, that you haven't had to go back to that style of job.

Bryan: "No, far from it."

Jen: "I always felt like, 'Let's go take a year or two, be wild and crazy, and do something completely different. Maybe we will choose that lifestyle again. Maybe we want to go back to a company where we're trying to help optimize their sales and bring success to them, something that would bring us joy, and be a part of that normal society path."

Bryan: "That hasn't happened."

Jen: "That hasn't happened; the opposite. In fact, Bryan sometimes says, 'Oh no, we're broken because now we can never go back to normalcy.'"

ZB: Where was the turning point for you Bryan? Where was it, "All right, it's time to do this?"

Bryan: "I just had a routine checkup after work one day and walked in to the doctor. He literally was like, 'Anybody ever tell you, you might have high blood pressure? We have to do some more tests to be sure. You should be on medication right now.'"

Jen: "You're in your early 30s."

Bryan: "I got quiet and went home, and I was like, 'I'm in.' That was the point when we said, 'Okay, what would it take? Let's look at some blogs and see how much people spend when they're on the road.' It's still important for me to have that foundation of a security blanket. I was pretty committed, but don't get me wrong because this was right around the housing crash. We had moments of terror where we aborted and postponed, and then came back at it. It still wasn't an easy thing. So, every day after that appointment, I was committed to making it work."

Jen: "We had two good friends who lost their jobs during the time we were still working but thinking about leaving. That spoke to us too, 'Are we being careless? Should we be more appreciative to have the work?' So, when it came down to checking in with ourselves and listening to our hearts, we had to keep moving forward and follow those voices."

ON THE TRADITIONAL MODEL OF WORKING FOR AN EMPLOYER FOR YOUR ENTIRE CAREER, RETIRING AND MOVING TO FLORIDA

Bryan: "Doesn't do you any good if you're not here to enjoy it. I come from a family that had all of those same underlying premises. I remember every single month, every single year listening to my parents talk about how when they retire, they're going to move into their camper and travel the United States. They've now been retired for 15 years and have yet to take more than a trip a state away, because things come up. It's difficult to do. In all reality, if I had stayed at my last job, I would have had my first heart attack by now. The stress was just that high. It's fair to think about that other side."

"It's also fair to say that since we left, it's eye-opening to me how opportunities create themselves if you look for them, identify them, and take advantage of them."

"When we were working our jobs, I don't doubt that opportunities came and went all the time. We were exhausted. We didn't have the ability to reach out and grab them. I refer to this feeling like walking through a dark forest with a dim flashlight. Everything is horrifying because you couldn't see a few steps in front of you. If you trust that it's going to work out, with every step you take, you get farther along, and your eyes start to adjust to the darkness. Even your flashlight suddenly seems stronger than it did before.

You keep seeing new paths ahead of you. We don't have all the answers. I believe that this is actually possible, that there are paths out there. We're still figuring out the nuances, but we're so impossibly happy that there's no way I would try to pull us back the other way."

ZB: It's one of those things that you can never tell looking into the future what it's going to look like. You have to keep moving towards it. You guys got a VW bus, what was the reasoning behind that? Maybe share a little bit about how long ago that original trip started and where that took you guys?

Bryan: "We left our jobs in 2012. We had started outfitting the van, I don't know, a year or two before that. If we're going to go live on the road, we need a vehicle. We need something we can sleep in. Our car didn't allow that. We started looking at taco trucks that would blend in. Box trucks that we could put some delivery name on the side up. We looked at everything. The more I read about, the more I kept stumbling upon this thing that in Mexico and Central America, the old school VW bus with none of the technology can be fixed by anybody. It's an easy way to make sure you can stay on the road. Then we went into it at Westphalia. We looked at a few different VWs. Then we made the mistake of climbing into a split window. The visual artist in me fell in love with it. from the second we saw one, there was never going to be another choice."

"We finally found one that was a decent price. We outfitted the inside as a camper. It actually was the perfect vehicle for that road trip. I don't know if it's necessarily because of what I thought is that it would be on the road all the time, because we broke down every three days on average. It also helps. It set its own schedule."

"We couldn't decide to be somewhere on a certain day. We couldn't keep a certain pace. We couldn't even keep up with other travelers. Somehow, I don't know. It helped us. Those first few months, I don't think we'll ever forget those first few months in Baja. We left an odd time of the year. There literally were no other travelers. There's nobody that spoke English, the hottest places which is why there was nobody there."

"Our vehicle kept breaking down every few days. Somehow sitting on a beach until we had enough things fixed to move to the next beach, it allowed us to decompress and realize that we were in a different place, and start to open our eyes and embrace that newness as opposed to — it took a good couple of months before we finally realized we didn't have a call that we had to be on the next day."

Jen: "After years and years of deadlines, and structure, and routine, and racing around trying to be on time for everything, and juggling all of that, it was opposite to be driving a Volkswagen bus that you never had any idea when it was going to break down. You're in the middle of nowhere. You don't speak the language fluently.

We knew a little bit. But we learned to roll with it. That made a big difference in our psyches."

ZB: It's got to be different from here. My first thought, if my car breaks down is call AAA. Get somebody here right away, pull the phone out, figure this out, and get me out of here. Now, I don't necessarily have beaches as close to me on the East Coast right now where I'm at. If I broke down, I'd probably want to be able to say 'we're on the beach. Let's make a fire and hang out for a little bit.'

Jen: "We were always 'Before we took off for a drive, do we have water? Do we have dog food? Do we have food for ourselves, and do we have tequila? We're good to go.' Because if we break down, we have all the necessities."

ZB: You're living in relatively close quarters. You probably learned way more about repairing vehicles than you ever expected. Do you have any tips or advice for living in such a small space? I have a townhouse right now. I've got some roommates. There's a lot of space here. A lot of stuff. I couldn't pack everything I have in my house into my car right now, despite having an SUV. What have you guys learned from having a small space. I'm sure you downsized before you left, but you probably ditched a bunch of things on the road too that you didn't need?

Bryan: "The underlying tip is to get rid of it, all of it. If anything, now, we've become experts at minimal and small living. Even now that we're back, the place that we converted into our 'perfect home,' basically a home base when we're not traveling is 480 square feet. It feels like a mansion to us. We recently did another project that's over 200 square feet and it still feels great. Compared to the van, it's enormous."

ZB: The 60-square-foot van.

Bryan: "We're now embarking upon another camper and it seems huge. It's all relative. In the same way that a lifestyle is different than another, the amount of things and the amount of space that you live in is all relative. We used to live in a five plus bedroom house. Every bedroom and the attic, and the basement, and the garage was full. We couldn't put anything else in it. "

"We call that our forever house. We're going to live there forever. It all started with one move away. We're trying to move. We moved out of state and we're trying to mix things up. By the time we came back, it seems ridiculous. We had no desire to live in anything that big ever again. A few moves later and a few purges later, it's funny. We now share with our clients that it's the Sleep Number Bed except for some square footage. Everybody has their number. There's a certain size space that's perfect for you. For most people it's far smaller than what society has pushed us towards living in."

ZB: I could see that. I missed the days of—when I was in college, I was even at a point where with my apartment there, I could have packed everything into my car within an hour, and had everything I needed. Minus my mattress probably wouldn't fit in the car, but I had a sleeping bag. That and everything else, I could squeeze into the car. I really missed that. That's one of the things that I love about traveling. I have my one bag with my stuff in it and that's it.

Jen: "There's a real freedom with that."

Bryan: "It also takes a concerted effort and decision. For us, that decision was to collect experiences rather than stuff."

ZB: Right. That's not something where you say, I'm going to go sleep tonight. Tomorrow I'll wake up ready to do that.

Bryan: "Now, there's a system for sure. For us, the system was — it changed over time. The more comfortable you get, the easier it becomes to push things to the curb. In the beginning, we would pack bins with stuff that was questionable and put it away. If we didn't need it, or touch it for a month or two, then we had a rule that it went. It would get pushed out to the curb and be — a free sign put on it, or it goes straight to Goodwill because if you open that bin, you're going to pull something back out. There's always that knee-jerk reaction ', I'm going to need that later.' If you can put away for awhile and you don't need it, chances are you actually don't need it."

Jen: "Somebody else does."

Bryan: "Somebody else might."

ZB: How long have you guys been home and what have you guys been up to since you got home?

Bryan: "We're three and a half years without jobs at this point; amazing."

Jen: "Our trip is about a year. We came back to Portland in June of 2013."

Bryan: "We thought that was a quick trip. We were still loving life on the road, but things were less impactful and uninspiring than they were before. It was time to change things up. Then we Skyped with dear friends of ours who had had a child while we were gone. We met him over Skype. We both broke into tears afterwards. 'It's time to go home and see friends.'"
"We came back and thought it was a quick trip. We actually left the Volkswagen in Costa Rica, flew home. Then darted around from friend's room, to friend's basement, to renting an apartment. It slowly became apparent that we were going to stay here longer. We still had our house. It had been rented the whole time we were gone, but the lease was coming due. Were we willing to bite the bullet and move back into the three-bedroom house?' We hated the idea of taking roommates. We didn't have enough stuff to fill three bedrooms."

Jen: "We didn't want to pay the full mortgage. That would require jobs."

Bryan: "We finally realized that there was this garage that was sitting unused. We converted the garage into our house so that we could continue renting the house. It immediately changed everything in terms of our trajectory because that allowed us to continue having the mortgage paid, to live essentially free month to month except for what it takes for us to eat and drink, and now of course to travel.

This is the flashlight story. Never could have seen it, but once you're in that spot, all you have to find is enough to eat and drink. Suddenly it takes all the pressure off of finding the perfect job. It takes all the pressure off of how hard you have to work. It gave me enough at least to create the freedom to say 'Wow! What do I want to do? Do I want to do anything?'"

Jen: "One thing, it's obvious now that was a big lesson was when we were working we had all this money, but we didn't have any freedom. We don't have any time. We couldn't go and travel a bunch. Then phase two, we find ourselves with all this time but not a ton of money. That's where we are right now. We're trying to solve that, find that perfect balance. We want to keep our freedom and time. We want to keep our schedules flexible. We also want to have a little bit more money so that we can go to any exotic vacations that our friends throw out, go scuba diving, go to the most pristine beaches of the world."

Bryan: "I know a lot of people solved that. I'm sure if you interview travelers all the time, the common story we hear is 'We're going to go home and work for two years. Save a lot of money and then we're going to take off and travel for a year or two.' Which is a great response. The idea of going back and working for two years sounds as horrible as going back and working for 20 more years. We're hanging on to this idea that there is a gray zone in the middle ground where we can actually find a balance of both."

ZB: You're in the garage that's next to the house currently? Does that make money or is that a break-even type thing?

Bryan: "A funny thing happened after we moved in. Again, the idea was to let somebody else pay the mortgage. Then we had to find a way to pay off the construction cost of it because we spent the remainder of our travel funds on the construction cost. On renovation.

One of our neighbors actually recommended it. We still had to go back and get our bus back from Costa Rica. Last winter, one of our neighbors recommended that we put it on Airbnb while we travel. It was another light that went on. We had never considered that someone might want to pay money to stay in our place. If anything, we thought, we were going to have to pay someone to watch it.

When we took off for Costa Rica, we actually had several people stay in our place and essentially funded the flight and some of the gas on the way back.

Over the course of the last year as we've been trying to further, and further this idea of living this way, we've been Airbnb-ing different portions throughout the year. Last summer, we would put it on Airbnb for a month. Somebody would book a week, and then we'd close out the other three weeks. That would be the week we would go backpack and see the northwest."

Jen: "That was fun because we would look at each other and say 'where do you want to go during that week? Do you want to go to Vancouver, BC? Do you want to go backpacking? Do you want to go to wine country? Where should we go?'"

Bryan: "Hit the coast and surf."

Jen: "Vegas."

Bryan: "Again, we'd find ourselves 'back home' for now. More nomadic than we were when we were on the road, because we're at other people's whims. It's proven to be great for us because we've lived in the northwest for a long time. Every year, we feel we didn't take advantage of it. We didn't see enough of it. We didn't explore and backpack enough of it. The year since we've been back from our trip where we actually feel we're doing those things."

ZB: It makes me want to go renovate my garage because we have a garage in the townhouse and Airbnb out the house. My three roommates would be a little upset about that.

Zephan hopping in here – at the time I was renting my parent's townhouse with some friends. I'm married now, and own a four-bedroom house so I need to be transparent on that front. I still dream of being minimalist at times and I think it's certainly a possibility in the future. I dream of building a tiny house someday but for the meantime while I build a family I didn't think it would be fair to force everyone to live as simply as I do and having a 90" movie theater screen in the basement is a nice luxury from time to time.

Bryan: "That happens. It's funny because Portland is leading the charge on a movement that seems to be evolving in tiny housing whether it be wood, or 180-square-foot houses on wheels, or whether it be accessory dwelling units which is formally what our garage is now called. It's interesting to see the number of people that are gravitating towards this movement while others are still building larger and larger homes to collect more and more stuff."

ZB: We're not talking you're living in a box. There are some nice, tiny homes out there and accommodating to the comforts that some people still wish to retain.

Bryan: "We wake every morning feeling like we're in a spa. Our garage, everybody seems to have this vision of living in a damp, cold, space. After the renovation we did, we wake up feeling like we're in a resort somewhere."

Jen: "The beauty is that you design the space to be your perfect home. What are all the things you want to accomplish in it? Do you want to be able to have 20 people over for a party? Do you want to be able to have 10 people for dinner? Even if it's 300, 400 square feet, there's creative solutions to be able to have everything you want. You don't have to deprive yourself with anything."

ZB: That's great. To look forward into the future, having been on this journey and been home for a little while to see friends, what do you guys see to round everything off for the future?

Bryan: "If there's one thing that we've realized we're poor at, it's planning. It's hard for us to say where we're going to be in a week, less a month, or a few years. The trajectory seems right. Again, at this point it's all about balance. I feel we're living that right now, but we've been spending maybe too much time getting the projects done.

It's nice that we're moving in to our freedom point on that. We are not rowing in the money. Let's be clear. We seemed to be finding ourselves with enough to comfortably eat and drink, and go hang out with friends. We're starting to talk about where we want to travel. That was the goal.

The next few years, we're going to see more travel. We're outfitting another camper right now that we'll be excited to hit the road a little more and not worry about breaking down as often. The goal seems to be that if you can be as excited to get on a plane, or get in the van, and drive back home as you are to leave home for your trip, that's a pretty good place to be."

Jen: "We have a super-sweet dog. Our travel for the next three to five years while she's still part of our tribe is going to be road based because we don't want to check her up with our friends and take off for two months to Asia. We'd rather drive up to Alaska and camp, or drive down to Mexico, or do some local Pacific Northwest stuff with her. That's our short term. Then longer term, we're going to sail. I don't know how we're going to afford the sailboat, but we are going to buy a catamaran, learn how to sail, and we're going to scuba dive, and snorkel, and catch lobster. We're going to do all that."

Bryan: "Not only do we not know how are we going to afford the sailboat, we also don't know how to sail. There's a lot of unknowns here. Technicalities."

WORDS OF ADVICE

"There's a quote by Mary Oliver we've got hung up on the wall of our garage. It says, *'Tell me, what is it you plan to do with your one wild and precious life?'* We use that as a conversation starter when people come over. It's a way to focus in on what's truly important to you and how you want to get there.

If anybody wants to talk about these things, give us a ring or come on over for happy-hour. These are the conversations that light us up and keep us going. If all we did all day was talk about freedom, dreams, goals, and how to achieve them, we'd be in a pretty happy place."

KEY TAKEAWAYS

- If you're unhappy in your job, plan a way out
- The less you own, the easier it is to pack up and leave
- There are creative ways to cover housing expenses

CONTACT INFO:

- Blog: thedangerz.com

JON NASTOR
Hack the Entrepreneur

Jon Nastor (HTEbook.com, hacktheentrepreneur.com) has been an entrepreneur for the past 13 years and it was only in 2011 when he became obsessed with doing business on the internet. By 2012, he was running a successful software company from his laptop while traveling the world with his family and playing drums in a punk rock band. He hosts *Hack the Entrepreneur* where he's conducted 200 interviews and received 1.4 million downloads. He's in partnership with Copyblogger Media and Rainmaker FM, where he's the co-host of *The Showrunner* podcast. He's just released his first book, *Hack the Entrepreneur: How to Stop Procrastinating, Build a Business, and Do Work that Matters.*

"Life is creating things, producing cool stuff I really want to die with."

ENTREPRENEURIAL LESSONS FROM BEING A PUNK ROCKER

"Being in bands from an early age, I learned this whole do-it-yourself thing – living out of a van, putting on shows, making and selling t-shirts, if you want something done, you have to just do it yourself. Bands don't have resources; you just have to make things work. You can't wait for other people to hand you things. It's just creating something out of nothing and if you can then turn that something into an exchange of money back to you, you can continue this whole game we call entrepreneurship."

OFFLINE TO ONLINE

ZB: How does one go from running businesses to discovering the internet and saying, "Wow, I can run with this and just be a punk rocker and travel the world?"

JN: "Before my daughter was born, time didn't matter to me – it was one big blur. And then my daughter was born 10 years ago, and time started to matter. At the end of the second year of her life I was like, 'This is crazy. I have to be somewhere closer to what I ultimately want to be doing,' which was more freedom to be able to travel with my family as my daughter aged. And I couldn't do that with an offline business. I sold my business and had enough money to take a year and a half to figure out the internet as a business. That was five years ago, and I haven't looked back."

What Advice Would You Give to Somebody Who's Right on the Cusp of Something Great Only They're Worn Out and also on the Cusp of Quitting?

"A lot of people quit when they're tired, you should quit when you're done. You quit when somebody told you that you should quit. You quit when you didn't think that you were quite good enough to do it. You won't regret the extra work, the extra hours, the extra sweat, the extra blood, the extra tears that you put into it, but you will regret when you look back on that very moment in time when you felt that spark that you were on the cusp of something and you quit."

What About Doing Something Different When the Going Gets Tough Financially?

"When that happened to me, I had to work at a job that I didn't want to continue doing. I worked all day, came home and worked four to seven hours a night for eight months and I was like, 'I'm focused now. This is crazy that I did this to myself, but I will never do this to myself again.' You have to be willing to do the work and you have to change your mindset from a consumer to a producer and you have to start to produce things. You don't spend three or four hours a night watching Netflix. Somebody's living a really good life because they are a producer and you are the consumer. Switching your mindset is absolutely essential to anyone's growth and success."

Between the Podcast, the Book and Other Projects, How do You Know the Next Right Move?

"Two years ago, I went to a think tank with 24 really smart podcasters. That was the initial push for me to do a new show by myself. I had this list of 30 brilliant business people that I wanted to interview. It was early July when I did my first interview and I launched my podcast September 5th. Seven or eight weeks into launching, when I thought it would fizzle because I talked to everyone I wanted to talk to, I had that spark where I felt like I was on the cusp of something, now it's time to go all in. I went from two days a week to three days a week and I really focused on my show, making it better and pushing it."

As if that wasn't enough, Jon wrote for *Copyblogger* to promote his show because he didn't want to regret not pushing it to the max. His interview of Brian Clark with *Copyblogger* led to *Rainmaker* and that led to *The Showrunner*. And the rest is history.

TAKEAWAYS

"I don't think I'm a good interviewer. I've done 200 over the last year and a half, but at the beginning of that 200, I had never interviewed anybody in my life."

"I hate the sound of my voice, but somehow I'm a podcaster."

"I still don't quite know where a comma goes in a sentence, but I just released a book that ended up as a bestseller on Amazon."

"What if I just do it and get good along the way? Then maybe things will happen."

"Business should be created to create the lifestyle you want."

ABOUT HIS BOOK, *HACK THE ENTREPRENEUR: HOW TO STOP PROCRASTINATING, BUILD A BUSINESS, AND DO WORK THAT MATTERS*

"The best way I can explain the book is it's a giant boot that will kick you in the ass and make you live the life that really is available to you with the internet. I've discovered this internet as a business and wish everybody would because we live in an amazing period that has never existed before where you can scale and reach the whole world from your own home. That's brilliant and should be taken advantage of by way more people."

KEY TAKEAWAYS

- You can't wait for other people to hand you things
- Don't quit when you're tired, quit when you're done.
- You have to be willing to do the work, change your mindset from a consumer to a producer
- Sometimes you don't have to be good at something to be successful at it

---

CONTACT INFO:

- HTEBook.com
- hacktheentrepreneur.com

MITCH MATTHEWS
Dream Think Do

Mitch Matthews (www. mitchmatthews.com) is a keynote speaker, success coach and bestselling author. He speaks to student, corporate, nonprofit, and association audiences around the world on the power of DREAM THINK DO. In 2006, Mitch started something he called the Big Dream Gathering. Originally, it was supposed to be something his friends and family could do for a few hours to get clear on their dreams, but this simple concept became a movement that hasn't stopped since. Thousands of dreams have been launched as a result.

He's become a respected thought leader on coaching and workplace mentoring, plus he's created a coach-training program that has been utilized around the globe. You can listen to Mitch on his popular weekly podcast called *DREAM THINK DO*. Mitch proudly lives a highly caffeinated lifestyle in Des Moines, Iowa.

BACKSTORY

"I've been weird from an early age, a bit of an extreme personality. At about 10 or 11, I fell in love with bikes, and my dream job was to own a bike shop. I grew up in a small town in Iowa with a hole-in-the-wall bike shop next to the Goodwill store and in front of the strip club. The summer I was 12, I rode my bike up to the shop, sometimes spending up to seven hours hanging out and helping with chores like wiping down the counters and taking out the trash. At the end of that summer they decided to hire me, and at the age of 13 I had my first dream job. At 14 they took me to a sales seminar, and the concept of professional sales intrigued me and expanded my dream."

"There's often a misconception that there's only one dream job."

"If you ask somebody about their dream job, they often lock up because they think they've got to pick one that's going to be their one thing. I've conducted over a hundred interviews with people who have achieved what they would call their dream job. We identified their dream job as doing work that they love for the season and giving themselves permission to explore and experiment with that, while also continuing to stay open for the next dream job."

"It's not about changing jobs every six months, but it's about being on a course of discovery and a journey of continuing to uncover those opportunities."

"What's amazing is that even through the low times, you continue to dig, propelled by the marriage of your passion and talents and fueled by a crystal-clear purpose. That's when everything else falls into place."

ON WORKING "TRADITIONAL" JOBS

"I've had some peaks and valleys. I've had what I call 'bridge jobs,' which are those jobs that get you from one place to the next, but it's not home. You wouldn't want to live on or under a bridge.

When you're in those bridge jobs, you want to focus on what you can learn, what you can earn, and who you can meet. I was in the pharmaceutical industry, and a number of opportunities were great fits, but one in particular was a very bad fit. However, I used that as an incentive to get me on this course of starting my first organization. Although the job was a bad fit, I appreciated that I could sit there with a big goofy grin on my face and deliver excellence, while at the same time, knowing I was taking care of my family and had flexibility to do what I wanted to do on the side."

EMBRACE THE "SUCK"

"One of my favorite interviews from *DREAM THINK DO* was an extreme swimmer named Kevin Hawe. He's a corporate attorney and very good at what he does, but his true passion is extreme swimming. You can't make money off of extreme swimming, but I'll give you an idea of what this guy does. Kevin lives in San Francisco and without a wetsuit and from a dock, Kevin swims out to Alcatraz, around Alcatraz, and then swims back. I'm talking about waters of 40-50-60 degrees. He loves it. He swims several times a week.

Part of the reason his current job is his dream job is because it allows him to do the extreme swimming! Listen, every job has a 'suck factor,' that's 20% of the job. So, 20% or less of what you do is not your favorite, you're probably in a dream job. It's something you could put up with because you're able to do those things you love either in or outside of the work."

"Another thing that happens frequently is when people hear the concept of a dream job they want to poo-poo it. I have a grumpy uncle who guffaws and rolls his eyes at all those things. It's sad because we all should be aspiring to this concept.

We were put here for a reason, to do amazing things that would equate to a dream job. And sometimes, when people start to attain it, they think it isn't their dream job yet because they don't love *everything* about it. My suck factor is taxes. I hate it. That's why I've got a great accountant. It still bothers me, but it's in the less than 20% category."

"Gratitude is the body's great antidepressant."

"When I'm in those moments, I have to think gratitude and latitude. A lot of people talk about the power of gratitude as an antidote for worry, and stress, and all of those low points. To be able to look around and find something that you're grateful for, whether it's a relationship whether or whether it's just being in the moment.

If you really want to move the needle, before you list those things that you're grateful for, take a moment to feel the gratitude. Your body will release serotonin and dopamine, your body's way of triggering pleasure, happiness, creativity and even improving memory."

"The latitude part is about getting yourself to a higher-envisioning point going from where you're at now to allowing that 30,000-foot view, to both remind yourself, 'Hey! I put myself in this situation.' There were times that I was building our business on the side, working really late, and/or only sleeping a couple of hours, and I found myself almost putting my grumpy pants on, because I was tired! But I'd remind myself, 'I'm doing this for a reason.'

So, it's looking at the vision and also looking forward and being able to say, 'What am I looking forward to?' Just as gratitude is powerful, with latitude, our anticipation is a powerful emotion that produces positive chemical reactions in your body which allows you to create a vision that will propel you forward. Combining gratitude and latitude will get you through the inevitable lows."

"Give yourself permission to feel gratitude."

"In those moments, you have to give yourself permission to feel gratitude because part of your brain is going to fight going there. Your brain has a pretty good B.S. monitor; it's always looking for crap that it can throw out and that's why a lot of people believe in affirmations.

There's some power in affirmations, there's no doubt, but the challenge with affirmations is if you're in a challenging situation and you say, 'I'm happy, I'm healthy, I'm here, I'm happy, I'm healthy, I'm here,' your internal brain B.S. monitor is going to go, 'Nope! I can give you a thousand reasons why I'm not happy, why I'm not healthy, and why I'm not here!' But if you give yourself that permission to even look for, 'What's something I'm grateful for in this moment?' your brain has that powerful B.S. monitor that says, 'Nope, that's crap, I don't believe that.' But if you give your brain a question, your brain almost can't help to start to digging in."

ABOUT DREAM THINK DO

"*DREAM THINK DO* is the name of my podcast, and I've been wildly blessed with an incredible list of people I've interviewed. I've been able to interview people like Brandon Burchard, Louis Howes, and Jeff Goins who was recently on the show.

What's exciting about having a podcast it gives you an excuse to reach out to your heroes. For example, someone shot me a TED talk said, 'You're going to love this.' I watch it and it's fascinating and has a few million views. After I enjoy something like that, I think, 'I'm going to invite them to be on *DREAM THINK DO*!' I sent an email to England and invited them. Their team member got back to me and said, 'Margaret would love to be on!' So, I'm really going to be interviewing this person. I love having that excuse."

"*DREAM THINK DO* is all about helping people dream bigger, think better, and do more of what they were put on the planet to do. *DREAM THINK DO* is hopefully a bit of a catch-phrase, but it's also something I stole, which I feel really good about. I stole it from the scientific method.

As a recovering perfectionist, I love the scientific method because you build a hypothesis, you think through a plan, you make a best guess on how something's going to go, and then you experiment. You learn from that experiment, and then you adjust and evaluate. That's *DREAM THINK DO.*

The dreaming is to say, 'What is it that I want to do, achieve, or experience?' Then the thinking is, 'What's my plan? How do I want to go about it?' I strongly believe in separating plan and process because we often start planning too early and stifle what we've created.

The Wright brothers owned a bike shop, and if they would have said, 'We want to fly!' too early, they wouldn't have had enough money to make it happen. *DREAM THINK DO*, to be able to dream first, think second, and then take action, start to experiment."

KEY TAKEAWAYS

- There's often a misconception that there's only one dream job.
- it's about being on a course of discovery and a journey of continuing to uncover those opportunities
- what you can learn, what you can earn, and who you can meet
- 20% or less of what you do is not your favorite, you're probably in a dream job
- look around and find something that you're grateful fo
- Combining gratitude and latitude will get you through the inevitable lows

CONTACT INFO:

- Websites:
  mitchmatthews.com
  dreamthinkdo.com
  mitchmatthews.com/itunes
- Podcast: *DREAM THINK DO*

STEPHAN SPENCER
Reboot Your Life

Stephan Spencer (www.marketingspeak.com) is a three-time O'Reilly published author of *Google Power Search: Social Ecommerce, and the Art of SEO*. He's an SEO consultant, search engine optimization consultant, he knows a ton about Google, how it works, and how to reverse-engineer the algorithms to get your website to the top of search results.

BACKSTORY

"In 1994, I was studying for a PhD in biochemistry just when the internet was heating up. I met one of the guys from Netscape when everyone was still using the mosaic browser and I met Rob McCool, the inventor of Apache. I got starry-eyed and decided to quit my PhD, take a part-time job and start an agency.

Within a couple of months, my agency took off and four years in, I moved to New Zealand with my family, and came back eight years later, sold my agency two years after that, and followed Tony Robbins around for a few years as a platinum partner, which was amazing and life-changing."

ON TONY ROBBINS

"Tony changed my life for sure, in the first event that I attended, doing the fire-walk on the 2000-degree hot coals and realizing I could completely reboot my life. I was literally unrecognizable from the guy I was previously. People would not recognize me at conferences. It was fun."

"It's been amazing for me to expand my horizons, to think differently, to change my mindset, and obliterate limiting beliefs. It's really been transformational for me. I went through all these changes over the next 10 months, and became the person that you see, the picture on optimizedgeek.com, which is my podcast show called *The Optimized Geek*."

"Then, I'm working on a self-help book about personal transformation, which will have the same title. I was so inspired by Tony to make all these changes to my life that I thought, 'I better share this with the world, and see who else can change too.' Because Tony doesn't appeal to everybody. I didn't know anything about him, you know, some people said, 'He's that guy with big teeth and big hands, just a celebrity motivational speaker, and shallow.' But they don't really know the content of what he teaches until they do a deep-dive, even if you just listen to one of his CDs, you don't really get the full immersion until you go to one of his live events."

"To take it the next level, I started following him around the world on these amazing trips where we went to India, to Varanasi, where they burn bodies found on the shore of the Ganges river, and we went to Udayapur, and he brought in these wondrous monks, and we received these wondrous blessings called Dichas. It's stuff that I would never have been exposed to otherwise. I did a platinum partnership for three years and I met incredible people.

I have a new peer group of people who not only are very successful, but who are very contribution focused, growth-focused, and I'll tell you, the peer group is everything. You are the average of the five people you hang out with the most, and you change your peer group, you change your life."

Tell us about the person you were in that 2007 image.

"From the outside looking in, you'd think, this guy has it made. He's in a part of the world that most people only dream about living, which is New Zealand, up to middle of 2007, and I had a wonderful family. I was married with three daughters and a stepdaughter, and I could take time off if I wanted to because I was not shackled to my business.

At one point, a few years earlier, I was able to take a full six-month Sabbatical. So, on the outside, you'd say, 'Hey, this guy has got it made! He's got the total digital lifestyle where he can live anywhere, he can come and go and do what he pleases, and he can take time off.' Sounds great, but I was not fulfilled. I was not living up to my full potential, and I was in an unhappy marriage.

In 2008, when my wife told me the marriage was over, I felt devastated, lost, and depressed. I didn't have a roadmap or structure to fall back on, to say, 'Okay, here's what I need to do to fix my life and take it to the next level.'"

"I was in a mastermind with Neil Strauss who taught all sorts of stuff about how to project a more confident, better you. Neil Strauss is a bestselling author of *The Game, The Truth, Emergency*, all these great books, and this whole new world opened up to me. But the *before* version of myself was holding me back, and it was all subconscious, and I was just sleepwalking in many respects. Showing up to do my thing, and then not really dreaming of what's possible and about why I'm here on this earth. That was something that unlocked through this process of self-development seminars."

"I'm an avid learner, I soak this stuff up like a sponge. It's the external changes that you'd literally say, 'This guy is the living embodiment of the *Benjamin Button* movie.' I look 20 years older in a picture that was from eight years ago. How does that work?"

ZB: How can you go about building a business that allows you to invest in yourself to learn and grow in ways you otherwise may not have been able to do?

SS: "Let me set the record straight here that the ROI of self-development is unimaginable. You can equate real dollars to these different seminars, masterminds, books, and home-study courses. It's a process that takes time.

You don't invest all of it at once, you just work through various milestones. But as far as cash, the cash ROI of being a platinum partner for me was probably 2:1."

"But let's break it down and see how somebody could start with a minimal investment of $50. Start with getting a book, a CD, or a DVD. If Tony's not really your thing, there are plenty of other self-development folks that you could learn a ton from like Brian Tracy, Wayne Dyer, Luis Haye, and Mary-Ann Williamson. Read one of their books – not just interesting reading at bedtime – but start applying it in your life. For $20, you start making changes. You could go to Tony's entry-level event, Unleash the Power Within, which is $800, and you get to bring your friend. It's affordable and it's a great starting point for your journey. For me, that was the tipping point where I knew that I was going to change my life because I had the power, the drive, and the passion to do that.

When I wanted to take it to the next level, I couldn't afford it because it was a business mastery event that was $10,000. I wasn't in the right place in my personal life to afford it and I certainly couldn't pull it out of the company coffers."

"You'll get better answers if you ask yourself better questions."

"So, I asked the question: 'How can I go to this seminar for free?' When you ask a better question, it forces you to think outside the box. It wasn't that hard! An industry colleague kept asking me to come and train his team on SEO. I kept saying no, because I didn't do client work myself, that was all done by my staff. I was out there speaking at conferences, writing books, writing articles for thought leadership matters. So, I called him and said, 'I've got a deal for you. You've been asking me to do this training for ages. I'm willing to do it if you pay for my travel expenses and buy me a $10,000 ticket to Business Mastery. I'll come in and train your team.' He said, 'Done!'"

"This can work at any level. Listen, when I started my business in 1995, all I had was student loan debt; I was completely broke. I was two months into running my business, I didn't have any clients yet, and there was a $2000 conference I wanted to go to called 'How to Market on the Internet.' I could not afford it, but I got in for free as a mic runner. And there's a bit of an embarrassing story here, but it shows my drive and desire."

"As the mic runner, you've got the mic in your hand a lot of the time. So, I was hearing these panelists and speakers saying the stupidest things about how to market on the internet. I was like, 'Oh my god. This is terrible advice!' So, when I had the mic and people asked questions, I just chimed in. I was 23 at the time and didn't know any better. I'll tell you what though, I got a ton of business cards by the end of the day, people coming up and saying, 'You were so much smarter than those guys up on stage!'

Jim O'Donnell, founder of Modem Media, was angry at me because I was not invited back for day two. That threw me off-guard but being cheeky, chiming-in, and upstaging the panelists resulted in my first two big accounts worth a half-million dollars. They were essentially my angel investors, so I didn't have to go out and give away a piece of my company. You have to be resourceful."

How do we know what a better question is?

"Start asking the other half of your brain to chime in on areas that you may not see where the opportunity lies, or where you may not see the path forward. We're not tapping into the right hemisphere as much as we could be. I interviewed Bill Donias on *The Optimized Geek*, and he walked us through his process.

Get into a meditative state, ask your right brain to chime in to help you solve whatever the problem is, and write the solution with your non-dominant hand. It works! The goal is to think differently and start coming up with new approaches."

"All growth happens outside of your comfort zone."

"If you're doing the same thing, day in and day out, how are you going to grow? How are you going to see new opportunities right in front of you?"

FINAL WORDS OF WISDOM

"The book *Think and Grow Rich* by Napoleon Hill is the one book that everybody must read. It was written almost a century ago and it's just as applicable today as it was back then. Napoleon Hill studied all these huge giants of industry back in the day like Rockefeller and wrote this set of strategies that each one of these folks all have in common. Apply those habits in your life, and things like being part of Masterminds is one of the thirteen principles that will change your life. Think outside the box as far as your vision for what could be possible."

"For me, living in New Zealand was a pie-in-the-sky idea, I'd never even been there, and I decided that supposedly this internet thing allows you to do this from anywhere, so let's just go through the motions and see where it leads. I applied for residency, and I got in. Then I went and made a trip to find a place to live, rent a furnished house in a neighborhood that had nice schools. The following month, we moved our whole lives to New Zealand."

"My thought was: no risk, no reward. The risk was maintaining a U.S.-based business. If the business falls apart because of this move halfway across the world, I'm maintaining a U.S.-based business halfway across the world and the risk was that clients could leave because of that. Be willing to live outside your comfort zone and take calculated risks, nothing crazy or stupid. Try to live outside your comfort zone, because that's where all the growth happens."

KEY TAKEAWAYS

- Change your peer group, change your life
- The ROI of self-development is unimaginable
- If you want better answers, ask yourself better questions
- Be resourceful
- Live outside your comfort zone

CONTACT INFO:

- Websites:
  optimizedgeek.com
  marketingspeak.com
  stuffandspencer.com
- Podcasts: *Marketing Speak, Optimized Geek*
- Recommended Reading: *Think and Grow Rich* by Napoleon Hill

NICK UNSWORTH
Life on Fire

Nick Unsworth (www.lifeonfire.com) hosts the podcast, *Life on Fire*, that covers everything from marketing to time management, motivation, and interviewing awesome people. Nick offers awesome free content to help you live your best life.

BACKSTORY

"Ever since I was a little kid, I always knew exactly where I wanted to be, I was always the dreamer. I was always fixated on this thought of living a Life on Fire: where I love what I do for work, where I was making a difference helping people, making a great living.

What sucked is that for many years there were many challenges along the way. Things weren't easy, and it was constantly battling through challenges. I had failed multiple times, near bankruptcy twice, but it was the thing that continued to propel me through everything was never losing sight of the dream. Every time when people were 'Man, why don't you quit?' or 'Why don't you be more like your brother?' or 'get a job.' I allowed that stuff to fire me up and fuel me, and I always knew that."

"After reading enough books, every entrepreneur has a story, and every entrepreneur has to fail at X amount of businesses. For some, the X value may be zero. Some people hit it out of the park in the beginning, they built this big tech company or something. For me, I had to fail at eleven businesses. I knew that eventually I would make it. I had enough belief in myself knowing that—I hope it's not when I'm forty. I knew eventually I would make it, and, in my head, I was fixated on selling a business by thirty-years-old.

For years, I always wanted to do that, and, sure enough, it happened by that time. I wish I picked twenty-three-years-old, what do I mean? It was always knowing that I had to basically fail forward fast, and get through enough of these failures. Then eventually, I would find my rhythm and find what I'm here, meant to do."

ZB: I like what you said about using what people said as fuel for the fire. It reminds me of this time we were out boating on a family vacation. There's this huge cliff, maybe fifty, sixty feet up, and we see people jumping off of it. My dad turns to me, and I'm fifteen, sixteen, whatever, he says, "I bet you won't do that."

I'm one of those people where if you say I can't do something, watch me.
I was out of the boat without a life jacket before he even finished his sentence, climbing up, jumped off the cliff. First time I've ever gone cliff jumping.
I think that is such a great tool. Use the haters and use the naysayers and the people talking under their own limitations to fuel your own fire.

Nick: "It's the you won't do it— when someone says 'You won't do it.' It's 'I'll jump off that cliff,' or 'I'll find a way to succeed.' That concept of —as entrepreneurs, we have to find ways to motivate us, which is why all this—I was actually more driven to prove people wrong than I was to prove myself. It's pretty wild that sometimes we have to know what fuels us. One of the hardest things for most entrepreneurs is actually finding the deep-rooted motivation to do the things necessary to actually be successful.

Because when you look at most entrepreneurs and you look at what they're doing, and why don't they have the dream that they want to have, or why are they still working fifteen-hour workdays, and they're not where they want to be. It's because they're not actually doing the things necessary, the proper producing activities, to get them to where they want to go. And why not is because, they want to be an entrepreneur, they dreamed about it. They have all these thoughts and visions, but they're not truly connected with their deeper purpose that's pulling them through.
What I find interesting is that—until you have that deeper sense of motivation, it's you're pushing and pushing and pushing as an entrepreneur. You're relying on discipline, stamina, and willpower, go, go, go versus when you connect to your entire business to a greater purpose that's bigger than you. It's Tony Robbins always says 'That will literally pull you through.' Pull you through the challenges; pull you through all the things that you have to do."

ZB: It's almost like when you jump on a surfboard and you've got to paddle out through waves, and the waves keep crashing into you. Once you figure out that meaning behind it, you've turned around, you've stood up on the board and the wave carries you where you want to go.

Nick: "That's good! I like that."

ZB: It's true. Once you open yourself up to this possibility of where you want to go because many people are thinking "I can never do that, but that's what I want to do." Once you realize that, when you ask the world for this, it's going to give it to you. Man, that's where that wave carries you. I've seen it in my own life.
I started a business at sixteen. It was a crappy computer repair business. My mom and dad had to drive me around to people's houses to fix computers. Of course, it failed because I wasn't in it.

I started my video business two years ago, and most entrepreneurs fail within the first year, and I made it through the first year. Most who make it past the first year, fail in the second year!

Nick: "What I love about you is you got a coach, and you invested in yourself, and now look at where things are going. That's the one thing, if I could change anything, it's —I got a coach when I hit thirty.

I sold a business by thirty, but I was completely unhappy and unfulfilled because it's not all about the money. I knew it wasn't about the money, but that was spent, invested all of my twenties. I sacrificed so much: vacations, relationships, you name it. By the time I actually did it, it was sweet. I have a view; I've got a beautiful place; I've got nice stuff. But I was single. The business had no meaning at that point, and— then I got the coach, and when I think about your story for you getting the coach, that will help you see things on a bigger level and then grow much faster. And not be one of the 5% that actually makes it. It's getting into—instead of 95% fail, it's —with a coach, you flip the script."

ZB: It's interesting to hear how transparent you are in your story that it took eleven businesses. This is not something that happens overnight despite what many people see because they see our on-line presence. They find our website. They are 'man, this guy woke up one day, and it worked.' It didn't. That's not how it works. I'm curious to hear from you—what was, maybe, your hardest point in leading up to thirty? What was the biggest obstacle that hit you, and caught you off guard?

Nick: "I have a lot of train-wreck, bad business things that I kept screwing up. I had a pattern of feeling I needed a business partner. I had gotten taken advantage of many different times, where I was the workhorse, I was the idea guy, but I always felt that I needed someone else. I never had the full confidence to do it all on my own, and every single time I got screwed. I did all the work, and then I reaped very little of the benefits. Every time the partner somehow would end up screwing things up, and that was a constant pattern. Finally, I created a business called the New Perks card.

This was after the real estate crash. I was in real estate — I literally got into real estate as it crashed. Imagine this timing. I moved to San Diego to get into real estate, to work on a big project with a friend, and two weeks after I get to San Diego, that's when the meltdown happened in the economy. think of that timing! And that project ended up being awful."

"I come back to Connecticut, and I was thinking, 'I need to do something on my own, no partners, and I need to do something that's going to be meaningful, that's going to help people.' I come up with this concept where there is a card that was the size, of a business card size, and it was called the New Perks card. It folded out an accordion, think of a business card that folds out, it had a couple of different flaps to it. That card had discounts to about forty-five local businesses in the town that I lived in, in West Hartford, Connecticut.

Imagine how tough it is to go into a business and get them to give you half off a bottle of wine every Tuesday for the next twelve months when someone shows this card. Because they are like 'Who are you? Why would I put that discount on the card?' I had to create the vision of the New Perks card. We are going to have forty-five businesses in West Hartford. When someone buys the card for twenty dollars, ten is going to go to charity. You are being a part of something that's charitable, and then the other ten is going to go to advertising."

"My marketing plan included on-line marketing, and I had this whole platform. And I said 'We will literally have thousands of these cards in circulation. For the restaurants, I was telling them, listen 'Are you busy on Mondays and Tuesdays?' 'No.' I'm ', perfect. If we get foot traffic on Mondays and Tuesdays, and they come in with the New Perks card, and they get half off of a bottle of wine, you think they are going to buy appetizers and food?'

What I had attached to is the fact that if I could get thousands of these cards in circulation, and then when someone buys a card for twenty bucks, half the money would go to charity, but the thing was, it wasn't my charity. It wasn't what I was passionate about. Do you ever see people that do the walk for breast cancer? They do the walk for whatever cause."

"People are always asking their friends for money, but there's not a value exchange."

"It's more of a 'do you mind giving money for this cause because I have a family member that's ill.' Now, of course we all feel we want to support our friends. We feel awful about whatever they're going through, but I was like there has to be a better way. What if there's a value exchange?

Instead of saying 'friends and family, would you support this cause that's important to me. Would you support this cause, but here's this new perks card that you'll save hundreds of dollars throughout the year. Whether it be at a restaurant, grocery store, dry cleaning, jewelry store.'"

"The thing is that people loved it. People wanted to buy it, and it got them thinking about giving because they had to choose where the donation would go to. Now, it wasn't what I was making them donate to, it was their choice. I negotiated with all these big non-profits: Heart Associations, Make a Wish. These organizations, I was trying to give them money, but they were all skeptical. It took me months to allow me to give you money. I mean, crazy. I couldn't use their logos on the site, nothing. They didn't want to have anything to do with me. But I said 'Can I send you a check?' I'm going to put you in a drop-down menu when they check out. 'No logo, I want to give you money.'"

"Long story short, I create this whole business, and my vision was that this would help me build my brand. What's in it for me is I would build my brand. I would do something good, and I was a realtor at the time, I would be the person that everyone would know. Imagine in your town, you walk down the main street with all the restaurants, and there's this diamond that says 'We proudly support the new perks cards of West Hartford.' I had these decals made for all windows and then it took off.

Everyone was loving it. I'm on TV. I'm in all the papers. This was a business in a box. I was going to take it and then sell little mini franchises to realtors throughout Keller Williams real estate across the country. It's taking off. I've become a top producing realtor. Everyone's thinking 'Holy crap! Unsworth finally is doing it. He's finally made it.' Sure enough, everything is going good, and then all the sudden people start saying things like 'You've got to go to the next level. You've got to hire an advertising agency. You've got something here. You struck gold!' All the local business says 'You've got to go to this one particular company.'"

"I went there, and I had my marketing plan written out, it's about eight pages or so. I go in there with it, and it's all grass roots. It's all word of mouth. It's all gorilla marketing and online marketing. Now that I had some money I could put into ads. They say—they literally took it. Imagine in a swivel chair, the guy we sit face-to-face, and the guy spins around, and dumps it in the trash, literally. 'We won't be needing this anymore.' I'm like 'What a-hole does that? 'You didn't even read it.' He says 'We know what to do, and you need to do TV commercials.'
Long story short. They say that that's the only way. You've got to do TV commercials, and advertise at the six-o'clock spot where the news is, and I'm thinking 'This is crazy.' Isn't it expensive for TV commercials? Isn't it not targeted? whose ever is sitting in front of the TV."

"Six o'clock news—think of the demographics. Six o'clock evening news, that's anybody could be in front of that. At least for a show, if you were to advertise to someone that's watching the X-Games, you could market energy drinks. The news is anybody! Except for kids. That doesn't seem targeted. I was like 'Why would we advertise to the entire state of Connecticut? My card is only good in West Hartford.' People aren't going to drive two hours to save 10% on their dry cleaning. They are not going drive two hours for a free appetizer.

It didn't make sense. I didn't trust my gut. They were saying 'we have your best interest in mind.' I said 'What? Maybe this is why I've been failing. Maybe I need to get out of my own way. Maybe I need to let the pros do it.' I decided to do it. I spent ten thousand dollars for a fifteen-second animated commercial. You would die if you saw this thing. It's fifteen seconds, and it's a little animation. It's ten thousand dollars. You would think now we could probably make that on Fiverr for five bucks."

"I do that, and I have this whole party. I've got people at my place. I'm living in a dump: no kitchen cabinets, old yellow nasty looking counter tops, a rugged area of town. Have people over. Popping bottles of wine. We're all excited. The commercial is coming. It's 5:57. Three more minutes, it's coming. Watch the commercial, fifteen seconds go by, and I'm thinking 'This is going to be great!' I go to my authorized.net merchant account. Wait a few minutes. Nothing. Go back an hour later. Nothing. I'm freaking out. It must be broken. It has to be broken. Has to be.

Because the ad set cost me ten grand a week, and I'm thinking I'm going to bring in thousands. Sure enough, it's not broken. Out of a total investment of thirty thousand dollars, guess how much money I made back? In card—total gross card sales."

ZB: I don't even think you broke even. From what I heard.

Nick: "Breakeven would be, let's say thirty grand. I had gross sales of two hundred and eighty bucks. Half of that money went to charity. A hundred and forty dollars was my money back, and it was devastating. I put so much into the business. I didn't have money to build it, I had some credit card debt going on. That pounded me into credit card debt, and it was devastating."

"I'm freaking out with the advertising company. 'Turn it off! Turn it off!' They're like 'We never had someone quit this fast.' I'm like 'Dude! I can't blow thirty grand and make a hundred and forty dollars. That's insane.' They were like 'You need to do it more. It's about frequency and branding.'

I kill that. Then what was wild is the traffic kept coming, and I'm freaking out. Saying 'I thought I said to turn it off. Why are you still advertising?' They assured me that they weren't. A few days later, I found out that I had actually ranked on the first page of Google, unexpectedly. While it wasn't converting because it's marketing all over the state, it only made sense in my town, but what percentage of people were in my town? What was happening is I was getting all this traffic, but it wasn't relevant. The offer wasn't relevant.

Long story short is because I ran ads, and this is back in 2008, Google's algorithm proceeded to be valuable because of all the traffic. Then I actually got it to rank in the first page of Google, accidentally. Think of how that awful situation, instead of it being this is going to ruin my life, it was like, 'What's the positive?' Every single time I've failed, I always took it in stride. I always was excited. Now I know not to do that, and now I know every single challenge I always pulled out the positive, the positive was 'Holy crap! Look at what happens on Google. Look at what happens with this traffic that I paid thirty grand for. It's not converting, but imagine if I had an offer that was."

"Fast forward and people are still loving the cards. I go into my real estate office, and I get this letter. I've got the West Hartford news coming in for a meeting in the morning, and that's my first meeting of the day. I open up this package, and open the package, it's a freaking lawsuit. It's a cease and desist from a big national eight-figure business, eight or even nine-figure business that said I had ripped off their trademark. I was obviously devastated from that too."

"I get this package. I got the West Hartford news in the office, and I'm like 'oh my god! How am I going to put on a happy face now?' Then I call them up, and long story short, they are coming after me with full legal team. They said 'Mister Unsworth, we need to speak to your legal department.' Legal department!
I'm twenty-six at the time. I'm so far in debt now, I don't have a nickel you can take. This is to benefit charity. Give me a little slack. Why? There's nothing—this is a little small concept in one town, and they did employee benefits for corporations. They came after me full-fledged, and what stunk about it is that I asked my attorney to do a name search, which he did incorrectly. Because he was my real estate attorney, we didn't have an agreement, I had no recourse."

"Think about who you hire, and getting stuff for free is not always the best. That advice from him ruined me. Then the advertising company that I asked about trademarking, they said 'No, wait until you prove the concept.' I learned a big lesson about trademarking, and I'll never forget it, and that lesson—I always, no matter what your name is, it's USPTO.gov, you have to search trademarks because you can build a business, and it could be gone like that.

That business got destroyed because of that. Within two weeks, the website was gone. If I had distributed anything, I was going to be sued to the fullest damages, everything."

"I said 'There's got to be a better way.' I went another twenty grand into debt learning online marketing, Facebook advertising, and I said 'What if I become someone that goes back to these same businesses and says 'Do you think that these guys are good? They lost all of my money. What if I could help you create advertising that made you money? If you put in a thousand bucks, what if you made four thousand back?' That was revolutionary.

No one was making that, and that's what I built my entire business on. That would have never happened if I wasn't failing forward fast, turning over stones. When you always have that mentality to look for the positive, you can always find your next move, and it only takes a handful of those moves to where you finally get into that sweet spot where you love what you do. Then money attracts to you much easier."

ZB: It's amazing to see where you are now because I love what you do. I'm very passionate about the changes that you're creating in the world. I guess I have to ask you, what does Life on Fire mean to you? Because many people think they're living. Until they sit back and ask what is my life? That's what I had to do. I had to literally script out what does my life look like, and what is it that I want? I'm curious to hear your perspective on what is Life On Fire?

Nick: "What I love is that the definition can be unique to every single person in what's important to them, but to me a Life On Fire is a life where I love what I'm doing for work every single day. If you think about it, we spend more time working than any other task. More than time with your family, more than time with friends, more time than you sleep. That's what defines us. That's the legacy that we're building, for me it's—to love what I do for work, but if my work can impact others and make a difference, and if I can leverage my business to create cash flow that I can give back, I can make a difference in this world.

Now, the best part is if I can build up a business that gives back, and that if I can inspire other entrepreneurs to build a business and give back, I'm creating this massive ripple effect. Let's say I donate ten million bucks in my lifetime, and that creates schools and orphanages and all kinds of stuff. But if I inspire a hundred entrepreneurs over my lifetime, where they each maybe give back a million dollars, you can see how that starts to impact more people."
"It's every single person that I work with, part of what defines who we work with is based around the values of Life On Fire, which is making your money matter, making a difference with how you work, and I call it prospering with purpose because when you have purpose behind your business, that's bigger than you, you're going to be motivated, you're going to excel, you're going to attract people to the business.

Plus, what I realized is I made a bunch of money when I sold my business, but for what? It didn't matter. As soon as you have the mentality that you're going to have a for-purpose business, everything shifts. Life On Fire is building that movement, and creating that tribe of clients that are out making a difference, but that's one piece. That's my career."

"Outside of that, my Life on Fire is waking up next to the woman of my dreams. To be able to wake up with her, pray, meditate, go walk on the beach for an hour before we start our day. To own my life. To be madly in love. To have fun. To be able to do weekend getaway trips and not have to feel I'm chained to a job, I've got a level of time freedom where—as entrepreneurs it's our choice on how we live. A lot of entrepreneurs, they build themselves a job. They build themselves so many walls where it's 'I've got to work fourteen hours a day.' No, you don't.

If you've ever been on vacation, how much do you get done before that vacation? I challenge my clients and I challenge everybody right now to take an extra day off. I don't schedule anything on Fridays. Fridays are additional days that I have off. You find a way to get more done in less time, it's about having that enjoyment, and when you think about it, that the old way of thinking, in my opinion, is to spend all your time and energy working towards this end destination. That's what I did before when I sold the business at thirty."

"What I realized is that it's about the destination, it's about loving what you do every single day. That's what drives meaning and happiness and fulfillment. The people who have regret in life are the ones that spent all energy working towards retirement. Then they retire and they have no purpose. Or someone that wants to sell the business and make money, then they do, and they have no purpose. It's when you love what you do every day, you have meaning, and then if you create abundance in your business, you can take that. You can give back. You can have time freedom. Have time for friends, family, and love and all that good stuff. I think of it as living to the fullest to your potential, and looking fear in the face, going straight at it, each and every single day."

KEY TAKEAWAYS

- Never lose sight of the dream
- Fail forward
- Use naysayers to fuel your own fire
- Invest in yourself
- Love what you do every day

CONTACT INFO:

- Website: lifeonfire.com
- Podcast: *Life on Fire*

JORDAN HARBINGER
The Art of Charm

Jordan Harbinger (www.theartofcharm.com) started coaching other people how to date and network. He and co-host AJ Harbinger (who uses Jordan Harbinger's last name as a pseudonym) started *The PickUp Podcast*. When Harbinger graduated in 2006, he moved to New York. Around that time, he formed a company called "The Art of Charm" to turn his coaching into a business.

By that time his podcast had gained traction, and he started focusing full-time on the coaching business. In 2010 an app was launched, and by 2011, Harbinger had a radio talk show called *Game On* on both Sirius and XM Satellite that aired on Friday nights. By 2011, Harbinger had relocated to Los Angeles. By that time the company offered week-long "boot camps," and offered other options like coaching over the phone.

ON ENTREPRENEURSHIP

"The entrepreneurship thing is wrongfully trendy. I love the fact that more people are becoming entrepreneurs, don't get me wrong there, but the pendulum has kind of swung too far. Whereas before it was like, 'Get a job. Get the 9 to 5.' However, the pendulum has swung way too far where there are a lot of people being like, 'You're in the 9 to 5, you're a sucker. You're just creating wealth for someone else. You're a sheep,' and it's like, 'No, there are a lot of people who need those jobs and are better suited to those jobs.'"

"And frankly as an entrepreneur, I would rather have a 9 to 5 if I could be satisfied with one, but I'm way too ADD/hyper/control-freak. I couldn't ever do it. I would be a terrible employee and I have been a terrible employee. The only time I can stay focused on stuff is when it's very flexible, when it's my own thing, when I can work on my own stuff. I need to be able to jump gears a lot. I've actually hired my own boss here at Art of Charm many times in the past because I need my own boss to keep me focused. I need to also *not* be under that boss's thumb, where I'm like, 'Can I take a day off and go to the beach?' and have him be like, 'No! You used all of your days off.' I can't have that part, but I need the part where somebody cracks the whip and says 'Hey, remember that thing you said you were going to do? We need that now.'"

"I've got systems in place to be productive and to maintain focus, but I do need someone to help me prioritize. I need somebody else who's kind of steering the ship, and I need to be able to steer the brand, which are two different things."

ON SCHEDULING AND PRODUCTIVITY

"My calendar is insane. Fifteen minutes is the lowest amount of time you can schedule without manually editing manually in BusyCal or iCal. I've got the whole day from 8 am to 8 pm scheduled out. People say, 'That's terrible.' I've got Starbucks in there, checking email, all the little tasks that people don't put on their calendar, it's all in there. That's been a huge productivity hack for me because I think a lot of people put things on their calendar like, 'Call with Jordan at 4 pm,' and that's the only thing on their calendar. Before 4 pm they're 'working,' but nothing is really prioritized. Some of that stuff is in their head. Meanwhile they're like, 'Ah, I better check my social media' they get sucked down all these little rabbit holes. I don't care how focused you are."

Zephan butting in here for a moment – this is exactly what I do. My wife makes fun of me for it but if you were to open the calendar on my phone right now you'd see scheduled in is every hour of the day from travel time to when I'm going to do the laundry or eat lunch. The schedule is fluid but I use it as a checklist so that I can see everything I need to accomplish in the day and plan accordingly. Looking back, I think Jordan is where I got this strategy from. I know that everyone has their own system but if you're looking for a better way to stay organized this might be one to try out. Ok – back to the good stuff...

"I'm not checking email instead of handling social media. I'm not checking my Facebook instead of doing something in our CRM. I'm not checking Twitter instead of handling a call or being late because of that. All of these things are delegated to someone else or they're scheduled out on my calendar and they get done. Then at the end of the week I don't go, 'I never even got to this, and I didn't get to that.' They get done."

"You've got to be very careful with your time. The way to do that is to block it off in your calendar. If somebody calls 20 minutes early or 10 minutes early because they had a minute, don't answer the phone. You've got something else during that time. Right now, I've got you on this list to do this show. If my mom calls during this time, I'll call her back in half an hour when we're done. People say, 'I never have time to go to the gym' because they didn't put it on the calendar just like phone calls and emails or they didn't build any flex-time in case something else ran late and now you don't get to go to the gym all week."

"I don't even know what's happening later, but I don't have to. It doesn't take up any psychological space because it's been planned out for two weeks."

What are your thoughts on the word 'entrepreneur?'

"For me, the word 'entrepreneur' is super-pretentious, and it just sounds grandiose. The other problem is, it's getting worse actually. If you say, 'I run a small business with some friends,' that doesn't sound as cool as, 'I'm an entrepreneur. I run 17,000 different businesses.' It's weird because all of these things are trendy right now, so everybody wants to do that. Like I said before, if you're not doing them, you're some kind of loser, according to all the marketers that want to sell you entrepreneurship plans and products. The problem is, not only is this bad for people who are in their regular job and perfectly happy doing it, they get this weird 'FOMO', fear of missing out.

If you're not running your own business, you're working for the man. It's causing a lot of people to start – I know I'm going to take heat for this – but there are people who are starting businesses that shouldn't be. The problem is, you don't know who those people are until they've tried it for three years or more. Anybody who saw me running Art of Charm with A.J. seven years ago, would've been like, 'Guys, don't quit your day jobs. Oh, you did? Good luck.'

There are a lot of people who don't need to be entrepreneurs. They just aren't doing what they are cut-out for work-wise, and they have no business trying to start their own niche. One of the flags that I see from this are a lot of the things that are built up to be cool and grandiose by the entrepreneurship, aka, the internet marketer community is trying to sell people products on running businesses. One of the flags is they're all clones of each other. You read an ebook on how to make money online? Here's what I think about that: Insert expletive here and blur out my hand, because that's what I think about that."

"One of the major red flags that causes me to say, 'This guy is full of shit,' is they run two or three businesses, but they've only been in business a short time. It is so f-ing hard to run one business, do it right and bring it to seven and then eight figures. It is difficult to do that when you have no experience doing it. Once you've got one business off the ground, you can bring other businesses up. It's like, 'Holy crap. That took me five years the first time and now it took me three months."

What can people do right now who are searching for a more meaningful or purposeful life?

"That's a good question. I'll wrap that thought with a last issue I have with entrepreneurship which is most people are focused on the entrepreneurship stuff from the angle of 'Wait. I can quit my job that I hate and have a bunch of stress and start this new life. I can work from anywhere.' There are pictures of laptops on the beach and what that says to most people is 'Wow, I can work from the beach.' What that says to me is, 'You have to bring your laptop on vacation,' because that's what real 'entrepreneurship' is. You have your laptop on the beach because you have 3,000 emails that you've neglected. Not because you can.

The problem is, most people are focused on the escapist mindset of entrepreneurship. They're focused on, 'I can quit this job and leave and then I'm in control of my destiny.' They don't think about the fact that now you're responsible and the buck stops with you."

"People should be looking for ways to contribute more value at work. They should be looking for ways to develop more relationships in their industry or switch industries. Believe it or not, contrary to what the sales letter says for the latest entrepreneurship product, there's plenty of people that are in their 9 to 5 that love what they do and that's totally okay."

"You can start a business on the side, but you should not quit your job until you're at the point at which the only thing that's required for you to scale your business is more of your time."

"The mistake I see people make is they'll quit their job and then they fart around on social media trying to get their Twitter engagement up for six hours a day and they're writing blog posts that no one will read and things like that. They should've stayed in their 9 to 5, focused on learning different skill sets, maybe switched industries or switched jobs, and then scaled their business by hiring as many people as they needed to get things done, not using their own time. Worked on this thing on their own time. If you're running a successful business or a business that has legs, you can hire team members to do a lot of things for you. You don't necessarily need to be there working on it 24/7.

You will eventually need to quit in order to scale. That's totally legit, but I think people are in a rush to quit and then they quit, and they go 'Okay. Now I've got to fill all this time that I have with business stuff.' What happens unfortunately, is they go, 'Oh my God. I have no income now. This new business needs to take shortcuts to get income to pay me the salary that I just lost.' That's a dangerous place to be because now you're not playing the long game anymore, you're playing the 'Oh my God. How do I pay my rent?' game. That's not good for business."

ZB: So, you're recommending that entrepreneurship can still be an option, but it needs to be something that you think critically about as opposed to just following what everyone's selling you, this whole, "Quit your job tomorrow and next week everything's fine and peachy."

JH: "That whole laptop on the beach thing is a freaking fantasy. If you're doing something that makes you $7,000 a month so that you can live off-grid in Thailand, cool. You can do that. If you're building a real business that's going to sustain you and your family, it's going to work in the long-term, it's branded you're managing a team, and it starts to get scalable, none of that stuff is going to be real for you for years. You're going to be grinding it out 80 hours a week. It's just reality. I don't know anybody that's successful that doesn't do that, or that didn't have a phase where that happened. I literally can't name one person, when you get down to the non-B.S. part. There's a lot of people who sell products that teach you how to do that, but I know those people and they work harder than anyone."

ZB: I've seen it first-hand, having left to start my own business, thinking, "Replace the 40 hours a week that I was working, and this will be fine." Now, if you look at my calendar, I'm getting up and working from essentially 8:00 in the morning until 11:00 pm or midnight. I'm pulling 16-hour days constantly and sometimes if that means staying awake for two days straight, then that's what I have to do to get it done. How do we make sure that we're at least happy in what we're doing?

JH: "When I first started The Art of Charm with the guys, I still worked on Wall Street, A.J. still worked in the cancer lab, Johnny got a bar job in New York instead of North Carolina, where he came from. We were busting our tails off. Then eventually, A.J. quit his lab job and moved out to New York. Johnny still had the bar job for a long time. I still worked on Wall Street for a while. Eventually I left the Wall Street gig. Johnny kept his bar gig for a while until we needed him to coach more programs that were all sold out. We were able to do that and give him a raise. He quit the other job. That was how it worked. We had those other jobs for a long time. Then we worked 80 hours a week and we still do. It's just that now we really enjoy it, and it's lucrative. There's no more, 'If we do this and it doesn't work... this just sucks.'"

"For years, I woke up several times a week and I was like, 'I should just work at the post office. I bet it's less stressful.' I didn't sleep for eight months one year. It was awful. I would be walking down the road or driving, and I would see construction worker and I would be like, 'I bet those guys don't have to worry about anything. They may go home exhausted, but they don't worry about anything compared to what I'm worried about.'"

"I got to a point where I couldn't sustain the anxiety for very much longer and went to see a therapist. We looked at all these different ways to lower the anxiety in other areas of life by getting a trainer, eating better, getting sunshine, returning phone calls

171

on walks instead of sitting in the office all day, getting a standing desk instead of sitting on a bed, which I did for literally two years. I worked from a bed. Sitting on the edge of a bed because I didn't have an office. There were a lot of little things that I was doing wrong that added up."

"Once I implemented those suggestions, my performance in the business increased and got to the point where I didn't have to worry about putting food in the mouths of myself and the whole team and selling programs and all the rest. Now it seems like, 'Wow, it's so easy now.' There's still a ton of work, but we made it through that curve. That's why this is not for everyone. People think, 'I'm going to set up this automation thing where I make money online.' For very few people at low amounts of money, that's feasible. It's not necessarily going to be sustainable. It's not necessarily going to feed your family, and it's certainly not going to build a real scalable business."

WORDS OF ENCOURAGEMENT

"This is my weird way of teaching stuff, but what I just said is encouraging if you look at it this way: I love what I'm doing, and I wouldn't trade it for the world. If you're in a hole full of you know what, you can largely persevere and get through it if you have the fortitude. If you're working right now and you're thinking about starting a business, don't even think about quitting your job and starting a business at the same time. Start the business small, scale it up, make tons of mistakes while it's a hobby and not the way that you're going to provide for yourself and your family. You learn stuff along the way."

"What it comes down to is mental fortitude. There's a lot of work ethic involved and crucial systems to ensure that you're productive. They're all learn-able. I'm uber-ADHD. I barely made it through college. Then I went to law school and started to crush because they had these systems in place and I was willing to outwork everyone."

"If you think people are smarter, more creative or harder working than you, work on your weaknesses and leverage your strengths and you'll be fine."

"Don't be married to your idea because you may need to pivot. If you're doing your business right now and you think, 'Wow, I used to love it, but now I hate it.' You don't necessarily have to quit what you're doing, but you can outsource the stuff that you don't like. You should start to consider how you can be flexible. I can't count on my hands how many times in the past decade I've said, 'I hate this business. I've got to get out of it.' Now, I love it. I wouldn't trade it for the world. The dip wasn't a month, it wasn't a year, it was half a decade for us. If you're willing to slog it out, you can be successful."

KEY TAKEAWAYS

- Not everyone is meant to be an entrepreneur, some people thrive in a 9-5 work place
- Be very careful with your time
- You're responsible for your success, the buck stops with you
- Don't be in a rush to quit, start small, scale up, make mistakes while it's a hobby
- Be prepared to grind 80 hours a week
- Work on your weaknesses and leverage your strength

CONTACT INFO:

- Website: theartofcharm.com
- Podcast: *The Art of Charm*

JEFFREY SHAW
Forget the Focus

Jeffrey Shaw (www.joinwarriors.com) is the guy who spent 30 years bringing life into focus as one of the country's most sought-after portrait photographers and is now inspiring creative entrepreneurs to leverage their so-called lack of focus.

Business coach and speaker Jeffrey Shaw encourages entrepreneurs to use their natural creative strengths to build businesses that are profitable and fulfilling, so that they can make a living doing what they love. He's also the host of the popular business podcast, *Creative Warriors*.

"Some of the clients that I'm closest to are ones where I made a mistake, but then recovered."

BACKSTORY

"The thing that intrigued me about photography initially was the science of it. At the end of the day, I realized in life that everything that appeals to me is both an art and a science. I've studied landscape design, I love to cook, and of course, there's photography. I realize the common denominator was I love the interplay between the left and right brain.

I seem to be drawn to things that are both a science and an art. For me, photography—originally, it was the science of it. It was being in the darkroom in the day and watching photographs develop. I liked screwing with the chemicals to see what

174

would go wrong. Eventually I ran out of things to print, so I needed some things to photograph and then I picked up a camera.

Coincidentally, by the way, we had a darkroom in the house I grew up in. My father kind of dabbled in it at one point as a hobby. I picked up a camera. Photography itself, the camera, even being in a studio and in the darkroom, it was all an escape for me because I was a shy kid—it enabled me to survive high school. I never would have made it through high school if it wasn't for photography and being able to hide out in the darkroom.

Same thing while you're out shooting. There's always glass between you and the people you're photographing. There's a box between you and the street that you're photographing on. That was always the biggest protection for me. The ultimate irony is you pick up these things in life that you do to escape something and then you wind up being good at it and everybody notices.

Then it's like, 'Holy crap. Now what?' I wound up being good at photography and getting all these awards in high school and going on a national tour with a group of artists. I went off to photography school and I was 'Best in Class' and I had to speak at graduation. The irony was that which was my escape from life wound up putting me center stage in the movie of my own life, if you will, to use your own book title (Life Re-Scripted). That propelled me into a way of being in business that I didn't expect, for sure."

ZB: Now we live in a world where we have a pane of glass that's in front of us most of the time now. It's just called an iPhone. Are we missing out by not really seeing what the camera sees?

JS: "There's a lot of criticism about people missing life because they're staring down at their phones. I was at a concert the other night to see Madonna here in Miami. We were in the front row, the first elevated section. You look down and it was kind of amazing to look at the number of cell phones lit up. This is before the concert even started, so it wasn't just the picture-taking. It was so fascinating. I get the question, but you know what? It's not going to change.

I don't criticize my kids for being on the phone too much. First of all, I'm more guilty than they are. I just think it's a reality. I don't think it has to mean that we're missing life. In fact, I treasure the fact that everything's photographed. My kids and myself included, we don't let a moment of life go by that we don't capture it. We share those moments."

"As much as these devices and these panes of glass might be keeping us out of the moment, on the other hand, there's an appreciation for the moment that has never been there before. What is interesting is the popularity now of Snapchat, Periscope and Meerkat which are temporary mediums. I'm fascinated by the temporary because that's a whole other statement; it's now. We don't even care about holding onto it.

I have three kids. My son's 23. Being in that millennial generation, there's something of value about the 'not wanting to hang onto' mentality and saying, 'I'm acknowledging this moment, but I'm not hung-up on hanging onto it.' So, there's a paradox. There's a way in which these panes of glass and devices keep us out of the moment, and they are a way that they put us in the moment, therefore it balances out and I'm okay with it."

What is your take on the ongoing debate that smartphones with cameras are putting photographers out of business?

"I realize my clients run around with their own iPhones capturing every moment. I don't mind them taking pictures while I'm photographing their family. I also provide images for them to share. There's a difference. What we want to do is educate people to the difference between capturing the moment and preserving the moment; they are two different things. Digital's not permanent and to rely on anything digital is just crazy. I'm a proponent as a photographer for printing out portraits and creating albums like you used to, because nobody sits down and flips through their vacation photographs on a computer. Build an album of the experience or relive it. Have portraits displayed in your home. They're different concepts that I don't think one has to stop the other. You can enjoy the moment and the sharing of your life while still knowing there are ways in which you need to preserve those moments."

Talk about how you don't have many photographs of your childhood.

"I have one photograph of my childhood. I was the youngest of three boys. My parents were in a different financial position by the time I came along. I was the third child, which must have been boring, nothing exciting here. Being a shy kid, I probably kept so much to myself that I wasn't in life. I don't know, but there's literally one photograph. When that was brought to my attention, through a coaching experience, I realized that it was more than just wanting to make sure other children were photographed. It was bigger than that.

The way I naturally built my business as a photographer was to take care of my clients in a way that they would never have expected to be taken care of. I did more than just serve them in the moment that they hired me. I was always thinking for them. I realized I fought so hard to make sure that they were responsible to their children. I made sure that my clients photographed all their kids at the same age. I would call them and remind them like, 'Hey, you know what? We need to photograph Johnny because we photographed Susie at the same age.' I would call them and remind them to do their annual holiday card photograph."

"By recognizing I only had this one photograph, the bigger lesson in it for me was that I was making sure that their children didn't feel the pain that I did."

"It was truly a turning point in my career because then I amped that. I'm like, 'Okay. If this is my core skill in life, my core skill is that I'm able to help people, without them asking, to be more responsible in their lives.' I upped the game. I started doing more things and little touches that would constantly help my clients guarantee that their family was photographed in a responsible and predictable manner, so that their kids never felt the way I did."

How do we discover, at our core, what it is that we truly believe in?

"It is a process. Being a lover of the left and the right brain, it is a mix of both. The pattern is you've got to do the inside work first. This is one of the distinctions that makes being in business as a creative person different than if you own a mini-market and you're selling groceries, you don't have to do a whole lot of inner work, so it's a linear path to success. If you're marketing yourself and your talent, you have to be in business in a different way. That's my skill set as a coach and those are the people I support, the creative warriors. Creative warriors are in business marketing themselves and their talent. I can help them with that because I get what needs to be done differently.

One of the key distinctions is that when people are hiring you, you are your brand and they're hiring *you*."

"The more you can magnify and clarify what you stand for, the easier it is for people to know whether you're the right fit for them and to know what you stand for."

"You have to do the inner work first and that means diving in, finding out why you are compelled to do this work, what's the story behind it, and is the story true? That's a step I take that I don't think a lot of coaches do. I like proof. Creative people can present dramatic stories and that's great, but it's only marketable if it's true. You'll only stick with the hard road for 30 years if your purpose is proven. That's the sustainability. If you don't really get that in your bones, you're not going to stick with it.

Personal growth is organic, and you're never done; you're always seeking. I lived my life as a photographer for 31 years believing that's why I was put here on earth. Now, I'm even more committed to how I can help creatives in business by being a coach, a speaker and an online coaching program. I'm more committed than I've ever been to anything in my life in part because I'm 50 and I don't feel like I have forever to get the work done. I'm going for it in such a strong way and that calls into question, do we have just one purpose?

I thought being a photographer was my purpose. Now, I feel like helping creatives in business is my purpose, but then again, there is commonality in both things. Maybe there is a core purpose and it shows up in different mediums in the way that we have an artistic style, but we can express that style in oil paints and pastels. I can't say I have a definitive answer to that. It's one worth exploring."

ON FOCUS

"I'm tired of living in a world that tells us creative thinkers to focus. I am vehemently opposed to the idea that we have to focus. It stifles creativity. There's a huge advantage for our so-called lack of focus when harnessed correctly. One of the ways it can benefit us as creatives is that we can have a diverse business model."

"My favorite quote of my own is, 'When you know your core purpose, you can wear many hats and they'll hang on one hook.'"

"The hook is what you want to stand for and your job is to understand the hook. What's your unique differentiator in business and in life? What is it that you have to bring differently to this time on earth? There's your hook. Now, go out and express it freely and build a business model that allows you to do a lot of different things."

"Stop following traditional business advice that tells us to focus, to find a niche, and not to multitask. Those are all things that we need to do to encourage the creativity."

"There's a practical side of business where you have to know your numbers, but none of that means anything until you know what you stand for and build a clear brand."

"The turning point in being successful in business is when you can identify that uniqueness."

ZB: Who's going to tell a photographer to be out of focus?

JS: "There's an irony to the fact that I spent 30 years focusing life, making sure that my images were sharp, and bringing families together. That's the irony. The paradox is I was successful as a photographer in business because I didn't focus on one thing. I built a business model that became more diverse. Over a 30-year span, I witnessed this business trend going from generalized to specialized to now diversified. That doesn't mean that we're jacks of all trades; we're just good at many things."

KEY TAKEAWAYS

- Small details and little touches for clients help you stand out
- When people are hiring you, you are your brand. They're hiring you
- Clarify what you stand for
- Harness your lack of focus for creative thinking
- Identify your uniqueness

CONTACT INFO:

- Website: joinwarriors.com
- Podcast: *Creative Warriors*

JAMES LAWRENCE
The Iron Cowboy

James Lawrence (www.rodsracing.org), also known as the Iron Cowboy, is a proud husband, father of four daughters and a son. He is an extreme endurance athlete and currently holds the world record for the most (140.6) official races in a year, and recently accomplished the seemingly impossible, the 50/50/50 which I'll have him explain in just a moment.

BACKSTORY

"Kid James loved to play, loved wrestling. I wrestled for eleven years. It was just a massive passion of mine, then just found my way to Utah as an adult and found my wife, and have set up a life here. As an adult, I wanted to have those same competitive outlets that I did as a kid in wrestling. I found that in endurance racing and triathlon."
"In 2010, I was raising money in a quiet way, building dams in Africa. The charity was also responsible for setting up women's groups and orphan feeding centers. They do a lot of really great work and I wanted to be involved with that charity and try to make an impact. I just set out to do as many races as I could. It turned out to be a world record that year, which I happened to set almost as a bi-product of what I was trying to do for the charity. And it really wasn't about the world record."
"Then I thought, if that was obtainable, let's see what the mind and body is capable of doing. In 2012, I intentionally tried to set out and break the world record for the most full Ironman's in a year. We did 30 full official events through 11 countries in one calendar year."

ABOUT IRONMAN

"A triathlon consists of swimming, biking, and running. There are four distinct distances: The shortest distance is a sprint, the Olympic distance, the Half Ironman and then the Full Ironman is a 2.4-mile swim followed by a 112-mile bike ride, and then after you've done that, you just follow it up with a 26.2 standard marathon run. It totals 140.6 miles and you've got to cover all that distance by yourself."

ZB: I did a Tough-Mudder and that was maybe 12 miles and I thought I was going to die. I can't even imagine what it's like to push your body for all that time. What's a decent time in completing a race like this? How much time are you investing during the race and then what do you do leading up to this? How are you preparing yourself for that?

JL: "Anybody that finishes any distance of race has to use discipline and apply certain concepts to be able to accomplish it. Finishing an Ironman is a massive accomplishment. Your fastest, most elite athletes are going to be right around the eight-hour mark. These are the professionals and that's their livelihood. You get all the way up to 17 hours to complete it and you have from 7:00 am to midnight to complete it. During the 30 in one year, I averaged under 12 hours for all of those events and 12 hours is a great benchmark for people that are progressing through the sport. First it's, 'I want to finish an Ironman. I want to break 14. I want to break 12,' and then you want to break 10. For someone that's really striving to push their limits and have an athletic aspiration beyond completing an Ironman, pushing your limits to get into that nine-hour range is something that will push a lot of people."

What does your training look like?

"I coach Ironman athletes. You cannot cram for an Ironman. It's not a test that you can flippantly prepare for. There's a lot of elements that go into it: mentally, physically, and nutritionally. It has an extremely steep learning curve. Most people can go out and wing a 5K, 10K, or a sprint triathlon once they get over the hurdle of the water, but an Ironman is a different beast."

"An Ironman takes intense sacrifice mentally, physically, and emotionally. If you have a spouse and children, you want to make sure that they're on board with what you're doing. It needs to be a group decision. People don't give it enough respect. They're like, 'I can swim 2.4 miles, so I can do an Ironman.' Or, 'I can bike 112 miles, so I can do an Ironman.' It's totally different when you start to string all of these together and go beyond 8 to 11 hours of physical activity and trying to stay mentally sharp throughout that entire time and not give up. There's a difference between going through the motions of an Ironman and then racing and pushing the pace of an Ironman and trying to bring out your best self. That's a different mental game altogether."

ON CHARITY

"Every time I do one of these events, we always attach a charitable aspect to it. It's one of the huge goals, but at the same time there's always a personal journey along the way in what we're trying to accomplish. It's a beautiful mix of trying to make yourself better, to push your limits and figure out where you are mentally and physically, and at the same time, helping others, bringing people together, motivating, empowering, and inspiring. It's just this great collaboration of a lot of cool things that come together and the opportunity to do something on so many levels is rewarding."

What in the world is going through your mind for 8 or 12 hours during the Ironman?

"Doing an Ironman race is about the journey to get to the starting line because that's where you learn the most. The day of an Ironman, that's a celebration of the hard work and sacrifice where you get rewarded. If you've included your spouse and kids during the whole journey, it's a day for them as well. Ironman racing is a challenging day for the spectators. They're there to celebrate the day of the person doing it. They're also there to celebrate their own sacrifice and efforts, so the whole day is for everybody."

"When you're in the midst of doing an Ironman, there's a lot of self-talk and grinding away. Despite all the alone-time, you can sense your family's energy and excitement. Then it's a big celebration when you come back together and see them a few times throughout the day. A good Ironman course will be spectator-friendly. There's a point when you come out of the water and you can see them and hopefully they catch your voice. Then the biggest spectating portion is the the marathon, where they line the streets and you can embrace your loved ones as you're progressing through your adventure and think about what that means to you. At the finish line, you have full access to them and it's just an amazing moment when that all comes together and the right people are there supporting you."

Talk about 50/50/50 – 50 Ironmans in 50 days in 50 different states

"We set out to really push the mind and the body to a point that every single person said it was impossible. Then we set out to raise money for Childhood Obesity. We did a 5K every single day at the end of my Ironman where the public participated with us. It was just amazing to see the country come out and support us and be part of this."

"The prep for this was unbelievable. We had no idea or any way of anticipating how challenging those 50 days would be. We literally did an Ironman every single day in every state. We were sleep deprived. We had to figure out the logistics of getting everywhere, raise the funds, and include the public in what we were doing. It was just a massive struggle but the highest of highs upon successful completion."

How did the idea for 50/50/50 come about?

"Everything happened organically and it felt like the next natural progression for me. I'd done the half's, I'd done 30 full's in a year, but I was like, 'Man, this isn't it. There's more. I haven't accomplished what I've set to do. I haven't pushed myself mentally or physically.' It just came to me, 50/50/50. This is something we're doing. It was outlandish and outrageous that it wasn't received well. Once I committed to it fully, got the support of my family and we started working towards that goal, the more involved we got, the more confident we got that we could do it. There was no question. It was just a matter of figuring out how to keep moving. We didn't give ourselves and out or an excuse. It was like, 'No. This is what we're doing. We just need to figure out how we're going to do it.'"

Was there ever a point where you wanted to quit?

"There were speed bumps that we had to endure and counter, but there wasn't a defining moment where I said, 'Okay guys, I'm done.' We never had to have that pep talk. There were definite moments where it was like, 'Okay, James needs a minute. He needs to regroup,' but it wasn't a matter of quitting or not."

"Plan A was 50 Ironmans, 50 days, 50 states, but we didn't know what that would look like. We had a general idea of how to get there, but we never had a Plan B or a Plan C because the moment something goes wrong, you would adjust your goal and go to Plan B or Plan C. To execute Plan A was just a matter of creativity, intelligence and flexibility to keep us moving forward. We figured out obstacles as a team and kept pushing towards the ultimate goal."

Is this something that's teachable?

"Absolutely. It's teachable to someone that isn't entitled and wants instant gratification. You've got to have patience. You know, my mental preparation stemmed all the way back to when I was in 7th grade and I lost my first wrestling match. I started to develop a skill set to improve my mental strength. I got better and better at developing it. I put myself in a lot of situations to where I was able to strengthen my mental fortitude and get stronger as an individual and as an athlete. Every single one of those experiences and challenges added up. At a certain point in time, I was ready to do it."

"There is no goal that's not obtainable. You need a sufficient time frame associated with such big goals and be willing to do the <u>right things consistently over a long period of time</u>."

"That's what I mean by people having entitlement. They want it right now and they're not willing to be consistent. They're not willing to work towards it. This goes for any big goal, whether it's business, financial or family-related. Any super-successful person has a massive back story that led them to the point where they became the superstar. You're only seeing the arrival. You're only seeing the part of that journey where they made it. Most individuals that we see in the spotlight, they got there because of consistency and hard work over a *lifetime* of experiences."

What's the biggest mistake people make when they're pushing their limits?

"They try to make everything happen too fast and they try to fit a square into a round circle. There's a fine line between forcing something to happen and pushing your limits. You don't want to force it so that it fails and is too quick, but you want to push that envelope and progress at a reasonable rate."

Who do you admire?

"I love the MMA, Mixed Martial Arts, world. Georges St. Pierre was a great guy that exhibited patience, discipline and respect in the sport and did nothing but hard work. Then you look at iconic people like Wayne Gretzky, Michael Jordan, and LeBron James, and all of these people that are just unbelievable at what they do. I look up and follow all those guys as an example as far as their discipline, or the way they approach things methodically and how laid out everything is. Then just patience, patience, patience. It goes all the way back to the simplest of concepts and that's doing something consistently for a long period of time."

"The secret to success is action."

"Action and work, but individuals aren't willing to do the work. I get emails every single day with concepts and ideas and I've yet to see any of them come to fruition or anybody actually take the action and put it into play. There are so many amazing ideas out there. But it's about taking action and doing what you say you're going to do."

What's next for the Iron Cowboy?

"I thought once I reached the 50 and I was approaching the finish line that it was going to be my finish. I realized it wasn't. It was simply a milestone. It was simply a launching platform to whatever direction I wanted to go next. That's the way life should be. We should try to achieve milestones and see what's next. For us, we've got an incredible opportunity to help and empower people to reach their limits and their potentials. I've launched a new program where we can take this to another level. I speak at corporations, clubs, teams and schools spreading the message of doing the hard things, putting in the work, and applying principles and patience to achieve greatness."

"The reality is fear is in everything and it is what is holding most people back. A better 'you' is on the other side of fear."

'Stop talking about it. Just go do it and take that first step.'

KEY TAKEAWAYS

- Strengthen your mental fortitude, get stronger as an individual
- Do the right things consistently over a long period of time
- Most people in the spotlight exhibit consistency and hard work over a lifetime of experiences
- The secret to success is action

CONTACT INFO:

- Websites:
    rodsracing.org
    teamironcowboy.com

JAMES MILLER
Lifeology

James Miller (www.jamesmillerlifeology.com) is a licensed psychotherapist and piano composer who resides in West Palm Beach, Florida. He's been in the mental health field for 20 years working in all types of settings from prisons to residential treatment centers, outpatient clinics, universities and many, many others. He was most recently in a private practice in Washington DC for the last 10 years.

James was not feeling fulfilled in his practice and knew there was a next step of growth and development in his own path. He started to create an augmented version of who you wanted to be based on the idea of being location-independent. He formulated his dreams around the concept and was able to actualize the plan by creating James Miller Lifeology. Instead of continuing psychotherapy for individuals and couples, he felt he wanted to focus on areas in peoples' lives that are already going well and making them even better.

BACKSTORY

"I started voice lessons when I was three-years-old and when I was in third-grade, I started piano lessons. I was going to be a geneticist when I went into undergrad. Then it changed. I got a huge music scholarship, so I changed to vocal and piano performance and then switched from that to psychology with a Spanish major. I was all over the place. Like many people, I have very divergent interests and was blessed to be good at some of those."

"I wanted to be in the film industry and all those things but thought I should at least get my master's degree in counseling and then if things change, I'll go back and do something different. It never happened. I was very successful in the psychotherapy world and that became bigger and bigger. With that, my dream was to still compose music. I hadn't composed for about five or six years. Some transformations were happening in my life and I literally sat down one day and started composing. It flowed out of me in such a wonderful way and with that, my first album was released. It was ten original compositions. If you listen to it, it's more like a movie soundtrack."

"I've been very successful in one thing and now this whole transformation for me coming down to West Palm Beach and doing something that I really enjoy. A lot of the times, mediocrity is something that we all feel and experience, but I was able to say I've been successful in what I was doing. Now it's time for something different. That's when I created the whole concept of Lifeology and was able to actualize it with my whole plan of being location-independent. I didn't want to be centralized in an office. I want to be able to go anywhere in the world and do what I'm doing. That's how everything came about. I chose West Palm Beach, told myself I'll be here for a year and then we'll see what happens after that."

Talk about being successful and then changing course.

"My practice was flourishing, and I would see about 30 clients a week, but there was something inside of me that said, 'I enjoy what I'm doing, and I'm helping everybody else but I'm not growing internally.' And then I thought about how I wanted to develop. I wanted to create things for myself where I was being fulfilled in all areas of my life. I was successful and flourishing financially, but my own creative side was not flourishing. I created a graph that looks at all the different areas of my life and broke it down into categories like time with friends, relationships, finances, and health and wellness. Then I rated each category from one to ten and that gave me a good snapshot of where I'm being fulfilled. When I did that, I discovered that I was not being fulfilled in some of these areas of my life. I was really surprised by that because when you're good at something, you think that everything is going well. That snapshot revealed that the things that are important to me aren't flourishing. How could I make that different?"

"That's when I started to reformulate the plan for myself. In the psychology world, we tend to focus on things that are not going well in someone's life. So, someone would come see me in my practice and would tell me everything that's going wrong and I would reframe it to say, what is really going on? When someone is overwhelmed, it's hard for them to reframe what that looks like. You take a coin and the closer you bring it to your eye, that's all you're going to see. Things weren't going bad in my life, but I was so consumed with everyone else's struggles and difficulties that I really wasn't growing in the personal areas of my own development."

"Lifeology is about working with people who are already successful and making them even more successful, by finding those things that are going well and making them even better. That's why I'm really my own client when it comes to that, as it's helping to reframe a situation and building on those things that are already going well."

ZB: What would you recommend for people who are stuck in a job, living paycheck to paycheck and they want to make that leap, but fear comes in because they still have to pay the bills?

JM: "I started my plan a year-and-a-half before executing it. Many people have an idea of what they want to do, but they don't fully map it out. I don't mean that you have to think about every nuance of what's going to happen, but you need to roll out steps. We think the information-gathering stage means action. 'If I get this information, I will have to make a decision now,' and then fear kicks in and we'll execute a plan without thinking it through and trying to get as much information as possible. Let's say you're in an accounting job, but you want to really help people for a living. On the weekend, you can invest at least half an hour in something that is in the direction you want to go and slowly, it starts to take on a life of its own. But many times, people have a concept of what they want to do and take a huge leap without doing the due diligence to practice and plan and that's when people fail."

ON THE THREE-SECOND RULE

"We're made up of three parts: our spirit, mind and body. I don't mean that in a religious sense. Our bodies are a corporal part of us that we work on every day, our diet and exercise. Our mind is a logical component that gives us reasoning and logic. The spiritual part of us gives us hope – it's that cheerleader, that encourager. A three-second rule is, if you allow logic to overtake something within three seconds, all of a sudden, you don't hear the spiritual part that says, 'Yes, James, this is the time to make this difference.' The logical piece will always kick in, that part of us that plays it safe. Well-meaning people in your life will say, 'You should stay in this job because this is what makes sense, this is what you went to school for, therefore you should do it.' The three-second rule is, if you don't catch it within three seconds and say, just let me look at this in a different way: How would I be able to reframe this, put the logic aside, and then help myself? The part of us that always wants to stay safe, is the part that will always prevent us from flourishing."

"Let's say that you have a New Year's resolution to get up at 5 am to go to the gym. So, your alarm goes off at 5 am and if you don't get up within three seconds, you'll hit that snooze button and you'll go back to sleep. The point is, anything that we want to do differently, we have to prepare for it. It goes back to planning. If you're going to go to the gym at five in the morning, then your clothes need to be ready the night before. If you're going to make a career change, you need to do all your research because in order to do something, your logic will always kick in within three seconds. You have to make a very conscious decision to be aware of how you can self-sabotage within that three seconds."

SELF-ACTUALIZATION

"Self-actualization is a fancy term to say what's happening inside of you. I teach people how to have a random check-in. You create an alarm on your phone and when the alarm goes off, on a scale of one to ten, with ten meaning you're doing well and one meaning you're not doing well. When this random alarm goes off, that's when you check in with yourself to say, 'How am I doing emotionally? How am I doing physically? How am I doing spiritually?' When you create that snapshot, it then becomes part of who you are and then you can always self-monitor. If you find in the moment that you're not happy with something, or you find in the moment that you're perhaps overreacting to your situation, when you have that internal awareness, you can change it."

"Many times, people are so caught up in their daily life that they become very reactive and don't even realize that they have the ability to change the situation, and/or they have the ability to change their perspective about something. We often live a very reactive as opposed to a proactive life. A proactive life is choosing to feel a certain way, choosing to do something different when you have that awareness by simply creating these little check-ins."

ON REFRAMING

"Did you realize that it takes doing something 66 times, not 21 times, before it becomes a habit? So, that's why it doesn't work when people try to change an aspect of their life for two or three weeks; they just didn't do it enough times to create a habit. We've heard the cliché that life is always teaching us lessons. And that's true. With everything we do, the main thing to ask ourselves is, 'What am I learning about myself right now?' Let's say you're in traffic and someone cuts you off. For some people, their immediate response is going to be road rage. You can stop and ask yourself, 'What am I learning about myself right now?' If I find an emotion that I don't really want to feel, like frustration or anger, look for its opposite, which would be patience. In that moment I say, 'All right, James, you're angry right now. The lesson this is teaching you right now is you're struggling with patience.' When I reframe the situation and say, 'Ah, this is a perfect time for me to practice patience,' it then puts the onus back on me to then say, 'Now that I'm aware of that, I can either stay angry, or I can practice this lesson of learning patience.'"

"Always ask yourself what am I learning about myself right now? That is something that will help you stop and think, to have that internal reflection, to say, 'I'm struggling with this thing here, I'm struggling with this over here. What do I want to learn about myself? What do I want to teach myself?' Once the situation happens again, you'll have already learned the lesson and it's not going to affect you the way that it did before."

"One thing I like to do with my clients is I hold up a book and I say, 'What do you see? Of course, they tell me what they see on the cover. Then I say, 'But you realize there's another side to it' and would show them the back cover or open the book and flip through different pages.' It's a very effective realization that in every situation, there are multiple sides to consider."

"The more information you have, the more your perception changes."

"Our perception or belief about a situation determines how we're going to feel. Our feelings then tell our body how to react. So, when you have more information about something, your belief is going to tilt slightly and you're going to view the situation with a different perspective. That's going to inform your emotions to have a little bit more emotions in this area, a little bit less in this area which triggers the appropriate chemical reactions like fight or flight. Ask yourself if you had more information, how would you react differently? You know, we often react in such a quick way with this whole concept of, I perceive; I do. When we can create that slight break to simply say, 'I perceive, but do I have enough information?' That can simply be with clarifying a situation. Every situation presents an opportunity to pause or hold off and ask if you have all the information and ask, for example, 'does this person really mean to hurt me this way?'"

"When we have to stop and think, it gives us the ability to say, 'Do I want to feel this way? Does this really matter? Am I investing too much time and energy in this?'"

"So, when you're able to catch that in the moment, you're not going to be as reactive and you'll be able to choose how you want to react overall."

ON CREATING POSITIVE CHANGE

"One of the biggest things to focus on is to simply do a check-in. Ask yourself, 'How am I feeling? Does it even make sense that I'm feeling this way?' Sometimes we have this agitation or frustration and we have no idea why. When we're able to stop and say, 'Do I want to feel this way anymore?' and if you don't, then consider what you need to do differently. It's not so much about processing why you're feeling this way, it's that you don't want to feel this way anymore. Create that awareness."

"We might have this idea of who we want to be, and we try to become that person *today*, but as we know, it's a process. You're growing and learning every moment, so you are not the same person you were 15 years ago. Sometimes you'll flourish and sometimes you'll not recognize what the lesson is in that moment, but you'll get to practice it again until you finally get it. When people can recognize that right this second, we have a choice to figure out how we want to feel. We have a choice to decide what's healthy for us. We don't have to worry about what's going to happen 10 minutes from now; we stay in the present moment and that gives us the ability to say, 'What I'm doing now will determine how I'm going to feel in ten minutes or how I want to feel tomorrow.' It helps us really focus on the moment and understand what that looks and feels like."

PARTING ADVICE

"One of the biggest things is to slow down. Simply slow down and get to know yourself, because you are the person that you're with all the time. When you understand the nuances of who you are, there's nothing that can stop you from being the person you want to be except for you."

KEY TAKEAWAYS

- Being good at something doesn't mean everything is going well
- Map out your idea
- The part of us that always wants to stay safe, is the part that will always prevent us from flourishing
- You have the ability to change the situation, or change your perspective
- Always ask yourself what am I learning about myself right now?

CONTACT INFO:

- Website: jamesmillerlifeology.com
- Albums: Consolation, Restoration

MICHAEL GRANDINETTI
Masters of Illusion

Michael Grandinetti (www.michaelgrandinetti.com) is not your ordinary magician. With performances on national and international television and stadiums, arenas, casinos and theaters around the country, with Oscar-winning composers and symphony orchestras for NFL halftime shows and major sporting events while surrounded by 70.000 people, for Fortune 500 companies and even at the White House, Michael has made a name for himself around the world as an extremely talented and innovative illusionist and entertainer. He's starred at NBC's *The World's Most Dangerous Magic* television special, the CW's *Masters of Illusion* series and Pop Network's *Don't Blink* series. Among many others, he's also been featured in FOX's *Bones* series and quite a few others. Michael's pioneered live magic in one of the most challenging environments imaginable, major league football stadiums, baseball stadiums and basketball arenas for the NFL and NBA halftime shows.

BACKSTORY

"I got a magic set when I was five and I'm so lucky to have found magic that young because it shaped my life. I would save up my allowance and every couple of weeks my dad would take me to the magic store where I would spend hours. I wanted to see everything they had in there. My dad was very patient and from that point on, I was off and running with magic".

Talk about your journey as a magician to performing during NFL halftime shows.

"It was a process, but it was a labor of love over many, many years. I'm lucky in that I found magic when I was very young, so I could take the time to really study it and to set goals. As I got older and older, I set little goals for myself to have to meet and eventually beat. I would always try to top myself. Throughout my early childhood, but particularly as I got in my teens and young adulthood, I was goal-driven with my magic. It helped me to create a path for myself to push forward in what is an undefined field. There's no real defined path in a lot of performance-based careers. You have to find your own way but being goal-driven was my technique for doing that."

Is there any single character trait that has allowed you to push for greater and for more?

"Persistence. Like I said, it's a labor of love. I spring out of bed every day, I'm excited to get to work, I love what I do. When you have that passion for your work, it fills you. But you must be persistent. There's no easy way to do it. Once I moved from Pittsburg to Los Angeles and started from zero in a new city, I spent a lot of years knocking on a lot of doors and meeting as many people as I could and making a lot of phone calls and sending out a lot of letters and always being persistent."

"I was very determined to move forward in my chosen career. People ask me what was your backup plan? What else would you have wanted to do? There was nothing else I wanted to do. It was always the case of I am going to do what it takes reach this goal. It was always about finding a way to achieve that goal. You have to be flexible and you have to adjust along the way. As you move forward down the path, you're going to find little roadblocks along the way. And *that's* where persistence is needed to push on through and to remain on the path."

"Persistence demanded I figure out a way to go around the roadblock and keep moving forward."

"I'm a firm believer that people can achieve anything they want to achieve. They have to go out there and do it and they have to be willing to work for it and also understand it's not going to happen instantly. I hear the term 'overnight success,' and I wonder if people really don't realize how much work was truly behind that 'overnight success.' Nothing truly happens like that. Most of the time, it takes a lot of work over a lot of years."

"I went to college and got a degree in marketing, which was my goal. It's showbusiness and I wanted to be armed with as much knowledge as possible. My business degree has been tremendously helpful in navigating the waters of showbusiness."

Did you ever get to any stage where there were any big misses where you wondered if you should keep going?

"It was never a question of should I keep going. As in anything, there were challenges, there were rejections, there were times of great success, there were times of challenges and that meant working harder and pushing forward. You will hear that from everybody because that happens at any stage of business and any stage of somebody's career. A popular misconception is that you've arrived, and you coast. I hear stories in LA of well-known actors still having to go audition for roles and read for roles. You're constantly having to continue pushing and continue to stay on top of your field. One of the things that I'm very proactive about is making sure I am always on top of what is going on in my field and making sure we're always doing the best that we possibly can at all times. There were no any major roadblocks, anything that made me doubt my path ever, but there were certainly challenges and bumps in the road along the way."

How do you create a path for a profession where there is no set path?

"The key is putting yourself, your personality into what you do. I've always said you can give ten different magicians the same piece of magic and you should see it performed ten different ways because they should put their own personal spin on it, their own personal style, their own personality into it. That's very important. That's a focus of what we do, and I say we because I have assistants and dancers that do our show; it's very much a team effort. It's making sure that it's a reflection of you as an individual and that'll help you stand out and help you not look like you are one of many. That's extremely important."

ZB: Is there a part of your personality that you see shines through in your performances that people would know if they see your show versus someone else?

MG: "A sincere love of magic and a sincere appreciation of the audience. I realized that in today's world, whether it's a television audience or a live audience, people have a million other things they could be doing with their time. They don't have to come to the theatre, they don't have to tune in their television show. If they've made a decision to do that, I truly, wholeheartedly appreciate that. that when the audience watches our show I would hope, I would hope that that's sincere appreciation for them and that passion for what I do comes across. people love to see other people loving what they're doing. When you watch somebody truly enjoy anything that they're doing, it pulls you in. If anything, that would be my hope is that those two things come across to the audience."

ZB: How does the magic spill over into the rest of your life and how do you balance if you're on the road doing shows or things like that? How do you make sure you're taking care of yourself too?

MG: "It's tough. I work 17 hours a day, seven days a week. Balance is a tricky thing. To be quite honest with you, I live and breathe my work. I'm married to my work. That's the balance that works for me. I don't recommend that for everybody unless it truly works for you."

"The key is everybody has to find their own balance that works for them."

"At this date, I love what I do so much. I really am very passionate about it, that there's not enough time in the day. The sun goes up and the sun comes down quickly and, wow, another day's over already. I didn't get done near as much as I wanted to. Even with that schedule, I try and stay healthy. I make sure I get rest and exercise. I'm in the gym five days a week for sixty to ninety minutes per day. I eat tremendously healthy, I'm so regimented on my body care and maintenance because if I'm not in good shape, I can't keep up the pace that I would like to keep up. That's basically the balance that I keep, and I make sure I stay healthy but push ahead very hard with work."

ON NFL HALFTIME SHOWS

"The halftime show's typically about seven minutes long which is not that long, but you walk off after that seven minutes and you feel like you've just run a marathon because you exert so much energy out there and it's so exciting out there, it's such an adrenaline rush. I don't care how many times you do it. Every time you walk out that field, you get the chills. It takes a lot out of you but what a wonderful experience."

What was your first experience like performing before a very large audience?

"There are so many little benchmarks that I can think of in relation to that question as far as different audiences over the years. Everything from my first audience when I performed for show-and-tell kindergarten, I remember that like it was yesterday. I was a really shy kid. From my first shows when I was still in high school, to the stadium shows we started 15 years ago, I don't get nervous, but it's an adrenaline rush. I get excited to get out there. Once we're out there, it's comfortable."

"A couple of months back, we did the Arizona Cardinals halftime show in the 60,000-seat stadium. So, we were rehearsing in this empty, vast place and I remember thinking that I should be nervous standing out there, but I was so calm because of the love of what I do and the excitement that comes with it. That's always been my experience. I always felt so good to walk out in front of audiences and share my magic with them. But the first time you walk out in front of a stadium audience, you get chills, it's absolutely amazing."

How has your show impacted others?

"I always appreciate and love hearing from people. The fact that somebody enjoys our show makes me incredibly happy. We were doing a show in Hawaii one time and a woman came up to me after the show and she was in tears and she said, 'It was so wonderful seeing someone love what they're doing up there. She expressed to me that she was in a job that she didn't exactly love at the time and seeing people doing what they love made her think about the importance of finding that for herself. I'll never forget that. I hope she found it. There's nothing better than seeing people happy and amazed after a show. That's why I do what I do. It's to let people forget about their daily lives and for 90 minutes, let go and have fun like you're watching a movie. That's worth all the work, it's worth all the traveling, it's worth all the rehearsing. Giving people that sense of amazement, seeing that look on their faces and knowing that you're giving people positive emotions, there's nothing better.

What would you say to those who are experiencing roadblocks in their lives?

"These sorts of roadblocks are self-imposed. Go out there and be excited for what you are, be appreciative for what you are and realize getting in front of 60,000 people is no less risky than getting up in front of one person. You're doing the same thing. Don't put the limitation in your mind that it's scary, the thing that you're meant to do. Go out there and do your thing and it's going to go great. As cliché as it sounds, keep the positive in your mind. Don't put those limitations in your own mind. It's so important."

"If there's something out there that you want to do, do it. Absolutely do it. Find your passion and follow it because you never want to say, what if? What if I would have tried this? That was my big motivation for moving from Pittsburg to Los Angeles, right outside of college. Now, you have to be smart in your planning. I was very careful with my planning and I tried to be detailed in what I was getting into. That said, if there's something that you want to do out there, absolutely go for it. If I can do it, you can do it. Everybody can do it. Especially in today's world where we're so connected that we can reach out and make connections all over the place. Don't hesitate to go after what you want to do, don't hesitate for a minute. Again, be smart about it, be very detailed in your plan, but go for it and be persistent. Even if you don't achieve exactly where you wanted to go, I guarantee you'll enjoy the journey and you'll be very thankful that you took the journey."

ADVICE ON MAKING THE NEXT MOVE

"You need to always be open to finding out what that passion is for you. I'm a firm believer that every individual has something that is their thing. My thing is magic, some people it's music, some people it's comedy, some people it's business, some people it's being great at sports. Everybody has their thing. *Be open to it and don't be in a rush.* It'll come to you, but don't be afraid to try different things. Enjoy the journey of all of it, and when you find it, you will know. There was never any doubt when I had found magic, there was no doubt, there was never, 'What if magic doesn't work out? I'm going to do this instead.' It was, 'This is what I'm going to do.' Find it and enjoy the process of exploring it. I'm telling you, even if you never do it as a career, having that in your life is tremendously rewarding."

KEY TAKEAWAYS

- Becoming successful is a process but a labor of love
- Set goals and then exceed them
- You might be one roadblock from your next success.
- Put your personality into everything you do
- Don't rush finding your passion

CONTACT INFO:

Website: michaelgrandinetti.com
TV Show: *Masters of Illusion*

GARY MANCUSO
How to Time Travel

Gary Mancuso (www.thelastplacesonearth.com) was introduced to me by Sean Dasani who was a guest on episode YOP 026, called *Born to Transform*. Gary was introduced to me by Sean and he was looking to basically take his book to the next level. He's got an awesome story. It's exactly why we wanted to bring him on the show and share his story with everybody.

BACKSTORY

"I was working as head of business development at a foreign exchange trading room at a large regional bank here in Los Angeles. There, I developed an automated payment service that outsourced the processing of certain types of payments for a particular company niche. It did very well. Nobody else was doing that and it was a fun journey. It gave me a lot of freedom to travel while I was working. As I was travelling, I started noticing that there was a lot of very sad things happening in many of the places I was visiting. I'd go to these supposedly pristine paradises like the South Pacific, and I would see that the island cultures and the environments were being degraded far more than most people will ever imagine."

"I would come back to work that I really enjoyed, I had a nice home right on the coast, I was happily married, had lots of friends, and frequent dinner parties. I certainly was enjoying myself, but I felt compelled to get out there and just experience the sort of the beauty and awesomeness of the world while it's still there. It's degrading so badly and so fast. There's a lot of good going on with modernization, but a lot that's also not good. I just dropped everything. I quit my career, sold my home, my then wife and I sold our cars, put everything else in storage and we set out on a long journey."

What were some of the fears or things going into that decision process of, we're going to get ready to travel the world?

"I was definitely taking a big risk by short-circuiting my career, which was on the fast-track and then to completely uproot and disconnect from what I was doing. I've always been pretty resourceful, and I'd had several periods of my life where I took off and did long journeys that were typically for months, not years. This was a different magnitude. I just felt that I *had* to do it. It was a dream of mine and I've always wanted to know and experience the world and have the freedom and time to do it. I also felt like if I didn't do it now, whatever the cost, it would be too late. Say I waited until the time was right, when I was set up for life or ready to retire, it'd be too late. The color and awesomeness that's left in the world and vestiges of the past, we could still see the way we were 15,000 years ago or the way we were back in the biblical times or the way we were back in what we call the Dark Ages or the Middle Ages. Time travel is still available to us, but it's all going to disappear. Even though I was taking a big financial risk, it was worth it. I'd just figure out how to get going again when I got back."

What is there for us to gain by learning from these other cultures and people who walked before us?

"Part of that would be personal interest. For me it was a fascination I've had since I was a kid. That curiosity with a sense of adventure to want to know things outside my daily realm. From a more universal standpoint, when you look at somebody and the way they lived, let's say, back to Neolithic ages or as close as approximation we could get to that today, we see ourselves. We see who we were at one time and how we thought and the myths that we developed in our minds and the ways that we structure our lives and our religions and our societies. What we do now is still very similar to what people did a long time ago. We build mythologies and we build religions around that, then we structure our societies around that."

"We can know ourselves better today by understanding who we were as primal people. On a personal level, I always wanted to understand people. When I'm talking to them, where are you coming from, who are you and if I see who you were 15,000 years ago, I can understand you better than I could otherwise. We can also learn a lot about philosophies and how people lived and what value systems were important. I don't want to sound cliché, but so much of that gets lost today in the race for whatever people think of is important today, making sure they're on the career fast-track, getting that promotion by a certain age, having a certain size house or certain amount of net worth. People are striving for things that are not of fundamental importance."

Talk about the transition from working full-time with all of the material trappings to the journey of your travels.

"The first big trip was to Papua New Guinea, the island of New Guinea which is off the northeast coast of Australia. I had been there once before, but that was on a diving trip. I made a few short land excursions while I was on that diving trip. The island of Papua New Guinea is a split island. You have Papua New Guinea on one side of the island and West Papua on the other side, which is owned by Indonesia. I was on this boat and went to shore for a few hours. Most of the divers were on a tour with local indigenous people living there. I didn't want to do the guided tourist thing; I wanted to do something on my own. I hiked up a hill and found this little cave that was overlooking the water, maybe, 800-feet high or something, it wasn't that high of an elevation, but it was a nice little walk. I peeked into the cave. It was a small dark room. It took me a while for my eyes to adjust to the darkness, but after a while I saw these shapes and finally it got clear what I was looking at. I was looking at a room full of skulls that were all stacked up in rows."

"Then I walked in a little bit and, it was a small place, about eight feet high and five-feet deep and six-feet wide. I started studying the skulls and I thought it was strange because they were all neatly stacked and every one of them had a hole, an inch in diameter, in similar spots. Later that evening, I asked the skipper of our boat about that and he explained to me that the hole in the skulls was from ritualistic cannibalism that took place in some parts of Papua New Guinea. When an older person died, they would take the skull and would puncture a hole in it and pass it around at a gathering and they would all consume a small piece of the brain of the ancestor and the idea was to imbibe the wisdom of those ancestors. That really interested me, and I knew I had to come back to this place. The skipper had been running dive expeditions for many years and told me interesting stories. That first trip started this long journey as I went to the island of New Guinea. I was there with my ex-wife and she was a real trooper because it was a tough place to travel, but a pretty amazing experience."

"At first, I went for three to six-month journeys. I used Thailand as a home base for the six years I was gone. It was a much easier deal getting from Thailand to my entry point in Africa for the various trips I made in the African continent. It was obviously very easy to go from there to almost anywhere in Asia and over the South Pacific. Typically, I would make three to six-month journeys. Then I would come back and stay in this little island called Koh Samui, down in southern Thailand and spend a couple of weeks reading, exercising, eating good food and if it was available, grabbing a good glass of wine. I'd also be preparing for my next set of journeys. Generally, that was the pattern. Once in a while, I'd come back to America for a week, see my family and friends, and take care of personal business."

On these trips, what did you do if you got sick?

"All my life I've had perfect teeth. The minute I'm in a remote place, I have this small crack in the back molar that was a huge pain. I was in the hills of Peru. I did the Inca trail up to Machu Picchu, which is a popular thing to do, and then I was in some other areas that are a little bit more remote. All of a sudden, I was in a situation of having to find a dentist. You just figure it out. I'm lucky because I'm strong from a health standpoint, mostly, I got through most of the years with only usually minor stuff. When I was in Cape Town, I did need surgery for a serious knee injury and, in that case, you just make do. I carried around my own medical kit which, for all intents and purposes, was fairly useless. What came in handy was carrying around antibiotics. Cipro was my best friend for the first couple of years. I'm not recommending that people go self-medicate, but periodically, a round of Cipro did wonders to recover from some major, very bad bouts of stomach illness."

What was it like being away from people and conveniences?

"I was accustomed to it in some ways because I had done a lot of travel into more remote places that were very different from what I was accustomed to. I had done that on and off all my life. The first six months of my journey, my ex-wife travelled with me. She was a great traveler. She was strong and she went for it. For various reasons, we ended up taking different paths, and after about the first six months, she went on and did something else. Then I became on my own. From a social standpoint, you learn how to become very social which, for me, is pretty natural anyhow, so that wasn't a big transition. You meet people everywhere you go. Generally, when you're in a place where it's very different from you, you're very different from them. Lots of people you run into are going to be curious about you. The more traditional, the more remote, the more tribal areas you get into, you can't go in there anonymous. You're going to have to meet somebody to help you get around because you can't speak the language. You can't just go stumbling into somebody else's territory. Often, you're entrusting your life to those people, especially if you're going into a conflict zone or post-conflict zones."

"As far as keeping up with the modern world, I was pretty plugged in. Before I left, I developed a tech-based, software-based service. I have a banking and finance background. I would download magazines, *The Economist* magazine, every week, whenever I had access to modern communications, I would get the latest issue of *The Economist* and read it cover to cover. I was always reading the news on the Internet whenever I was at a place where you had Internet access. I became an early paid subscriber to Skype, and called people from the strangest, remote places."

"The other interesting thing that you find when you're travelling is how much modern communications has already gotten into some of the most remote places. Even in tribal areas like the highlands of Papua New Guinea, there might be a missionary place and they would have an Internet connection via satellite. You could go in there and use it for a few minutes. There's always somewhere it seemed like, not always but often, there'd be things that you would not expect. I kept in touch with my friends at least every few months. I had to take care of my own financial affairs and investments which sometimes is a little rough to do because I would be out of touch for a long period of time."

KEY TAKEAWAYS

- Travel can take you back to the basics
- There are many unexpected places to keep in touch while travelling to remote places
- Travelling can introduce you to new and interesting people

CONTACT INFO:

- Website: thelastplacesonearth.com
- Book: *The Last Places on Earth: Journeys in our Disappearing World*

MINDIE KNISS
Heart Intelligence

Mindie Kniss (www.mindiekniss.com) is a high-end coach and creator of the Heart-Path Retreat series and Core Coach Training Academy. Her diverse background includes working in the wilderness as an adventure trip guide and in corporate America at a Fortune 100 company. Mindie is the recipient of the prestigious Global Health Fellowship in Nairobi, Kenya for her humanitarian work in developing countries. She holds an MFA in creative writing and is an author of the book *The Heart of Consciousness*.

ON DIFFERING WORTH ETHIC

"It's about understanding what works for you personally. I'll give you an example. My husband is extroverted and if he were to spend all his time at home and not get out and see his friends every now and again, he would go crazy. Me on the other hand, I'm a super-crazy introvert, so I am more motivated and energized by spending my time being quiet and alone in solitude. It comes down to what works best for you and then knowing and honoring that. Granted, I also need to get out of the house, too. I'm not saying that I have to spend every day inside but it's about understanding yourself and your own energies."

When people are lost and at a point where they don't know what to do, where do we even start?
"Pay attention to what I call the nudge. The nudge is, you can call it the universe or some higher power, whatever it is for you, that is urging you towards something different. I had a great job in corporate America – it was well-paying, not too

stressful, and I had my house and car and all this stuff, which was great. I should have been happy with all of that, but this subtle whisper got louder and louder and by the end, I was miserable there. It was unfortunate that it took me so long to realize, but I couldn't get myself around the idea of leaving everything and doing something completely unknown and I didn't know what that was going to look like. Pay attention to the nudge and start asking questions or figuring out what it is that you do want to do. Even if you're already on your path, it can be helpful to clarify where you're headed."

"Get out a piece of paper – don't do this on your computer – you have to write it down with a pen or pencil or markers, whatever you have, and create three different columns. The first two are standard in terms of what people would typically say. The first column is your skillsets. If you say you're good at video, are you passionate about video? I don't know. You would write down video and your skillsets, anything that you're naturally talented at, that goes on the list, even if it's baking or roller skating or something that you couldn't have any idea how that would impact a career, write it down. The second column is what are you passionate about? What do you like to do? What are the things that jazz you when you wake up in the morning? What would you be excited to go to work and work on? A lot of people say, just merge the two together and that's your career. However, there's a huge piece missing if you just do that. The third column is what are the needs of the world that resonate with you? People need to save the dolphin, hunger in children, illiteracy and everything else that's going on out there. What are the ones that pull at your heartstrings? Which are the ones that call you to want to make a difference in the world? Take those needs and look at how your skills and passions can fit into them, look for the puzzle piece that is the connecting point or the linchpin between all three of those, that's going to be the way that you should proceed."

"For me, I didn't know what that looked like because I love the wilderness and camping and leading trips and I love coaching and counseling and I love books and writing and all these things, so how in the heck am I going to create a career that can do all three or all of those various passions? I've created a high-end coaching practice that also leads retreats in Sedona, Arizona, where we get out into the wilderness and hike and connect to mother nature. I'm a writer, so I can combine all of those and the need that I'm focusing on is figuring out what you're here to do. What is the important work that only you have the ability, the skill, the passion and that desire for? And how can we get you motivated and working toward that thing?"

"One of the other things I did when I was looking at becoming a coach and leaving corporate America was, I created this fake schedule for myself. I had zero clients at the time. nobody even knew who I was or what I was wanting to do and I didn't have a website, nothing, and yet I put on my 'weekly schedule,' these different names of potential clients. There was Mary and John and Bob, these were not real people, but they were the people that I wanted, and I wanted to create my week, how I wanted it to be. For instance, I'll take Wednesdays off and I'll do this on this other day and

Mondays all go climb mountains or whatever it was. Since I started by coaching practice eight years ago, my schedule never once looked like that, but it keeps getting better all the time. That's the key: You can plan things and have goals and dreams, but not having the attachment to them, because if you're attached to that, then you just get that, instead of something potentially even more amazing."

What do you do when life throws a curveball at you that you didn't quite expect?

"What it comes down to is going with the flow and being willing to receive the best that life will offer. I was living in Portland, Oregon when I met my husband and he was living in Chicago. I was so career-focused, that I wasn't even interested. I met him in a business context, as a networking thing and he was not thinking that, he was thinking of more of a dating thing, but I had no thoughts about that because I wasn't looking for that. Yet, life presented me this opportunity, this guy, this relationship and if I would have said, no, I'm working on my plan, that would have been the most ridiculous thing that I could have said. I would have missed out on so much opportunity, so much growth because I have learned – sometimes the hard way – that relationships are the best personal growth program you could ever get. If you have a quality partner, you are called to the table to be your greatest and true self."

"Having a plan is only a plan. That doesn't mean that it needs to be the reality. It can be a great goal and I'm all for dreaming big. I'm all for doing the impossible and setting that as your goal. Yet, often life has something different planned for you. One of my favorite quotes is by a guy named Ed Townley, a reverend with Unity Church, and he says, 'The good is the enemy of the best.' What he means by that is that, you could be going along with good things in life, like I had what I thought to be a good thing with my career and my life in Portland, however, what was offered me was this whole other experience and if I would have stuck with what was good, I would have been negating the best thing coming into my life. 'The good is the enemy of the best.' It's a simple way to remember that even if it's good, there might be something even better for you."

"Life is a progression of events and experiences and we need to grow through them."

"Some of them are going to suck, and though it sucks to be in that suckiness, you also want to have that higher vision of, 'I'm gleaning something from this experience, because that's always the case."

Is there any scientific or biological reason as to why we should be following our true passions?

"Absolutely. This is what I did my whole dissertation on: the intelligence of the heart and that was in metaphysics, I've studied the religious aspect, the metaphysical aspect and pretty much everything in-between; I love this stuff. There's research going on all around the world about heart intelligence and looking at the heart, not just as this organ that pumps filters blood through the body, but as this intelligent, conscious entity. One of the experiments they did was they hooked-up people to an EEG and an EKG with nodes all over their body to register all the different body responses."

"They showed different images to people on the computer screen, three-quarters of the images were normal, like a glass or a car that would *not* elicit an emotional response. The other quarter of those images were designed to create an emotional response, like a snake that was ready to strike or a bloodied corpse. This was completely randomized by the computer, so that neither of the people running the experiment or the experimentees knew which image was going appear on the screen. What they found was that 4.7 seconds before one of those emotional images appeared on the screen, there was a physiological response in the body. They were like, 'Holy cow! This intuition thing might be real' because it hadn't even appeared yet, but our body was already reacting."

"They were able to trace the source of that first knowing and guess where it was? It was in the heart. Often people think that intuition comes through the head, they look at the chakra system and they think that it comes in through there and then it may be travels through the body. Perhaps that's not the case because now these scientific experiments are showing that the source of that intuition was first the heart that then communicates up to the brain that then alerts the rest of the body. If you are asking, 'Should I follow my heart?' Yes, and there is scientific proof for that. Often people say, 'What if it's not something that I can even recognize? How do I listen to my heart or how do I know what my heart is saying?' I would say use your emotions, follow what makes you feel happy, follow what makes you feel good because that's the emotional idea. I don't mean feeling good on this moment only, like instant gratification. That's not what I'm talking about. I'm talking about this greater sense of ultimate, high-level fulfillment. At your higher self, what's going to be the most fulfilling thing for you to do, because that feels better than anything and it definitely feels better than all those instant gratification things."

ZB: That's mind-exploding.

MK: "I run this wilderness retreat called Heart Path every year and we spend a lot of time looking at the science of the heart. People have come out of there saying they had a paradigm shift, a whole new way of thinking about life because it's a holistic way of thinking. Let me tell you a little bit more about why it's important to follow that as opposed to getting stuck in your head, frustrated or being paralyzed about taking that first step. The heart is also the source of courage. The word courage is from the French word, '*coeur*,' which means heart."

"Realize your heart is the essence of courage within you, not all of those fears in your head."

"I tell a story on stage sometimes about my brother and sister and I. We used to drive to North Carolina every single summer to spend a couple weeks at the ocean and we were coming from Chicago, so the ocean was this big thing far away. We'd go to the ocean and often, we'd get crashed over by the waves as we were trying to make our way out into the ocean. We quickly learned that if you dove underneath the wave, it would crash over the top of you, but not impact where you were, so you could continue to swim out farther. It's the same thing if you look at the heart. If you just dive underneath all the mind chatter, you can get underneath and it's a much smoother road than trying to go through all those crashing waves if you're up in your head."

Are there any things that we should be incorporating into our daily life such as mindfulness exercises, things that will allow us to keep us on our path?

"There are so many distractions and even cultural norms that come into our lives, even our biology. Our default is to pay attention to fear. That was a good thing way back in the day when there were saber-toothed tigers chasing us. We had to be very focused on the stuff that could kill us. Nowadays, it's not so helpful. It holds us back creates this paralysis of, I want to do this but I'm too afraid or I don't know what to do. The idea of a daily practice is brilliant and one of the things that I recommend, that they talk about in heart science, is this element of coherence. If I'm speaking to you and you can understand what I'm saying, I'm speaking coherently. If I were to start mumbling, you'd be like, 'What the heck is she talking about?' I would be speaking incoherently. The body does the same thing. It's a physiological response, so scientists can measure it to the .01 Hz of the exact dynamic that they're measuring. What they're measuring is not necessarily your heart rate but the time in-between heartbeats. It's called HRV or heart rate variability. It's the space in-between the heartbeats and you can create this nice 0.1 Hz of the flow of this beautiful smooth sine wave. What does that feel like? It feels good, it feels like stress has left the building, you're relaxed, you're calm, and you're in your empowered state. To get to that place, focus on something that you're grateful for."

"I have a client that emailed me a while back and we were working on some of this stuff and she goes, 'This gratitude shit isn't working.' I said, 'If you're looking at it like that, it's not going to work.' If you're literally saying, 'What are three things you're grateful for?' and keep it in your head, that's not going to work. What I'm talking about is the actual feeling of gratitude, letting it sink down into the heart, into the chest cavity and the way that I describe gratitude often is this feeling of expansiveness. If you think of a time in your life when you have been the most grateful, where something was so powerfully overwhelming to you in terms of gratitude, go back there get that feeling. That never doesn't work. If you get to that, that can automatically start to calm down your nervous system, spread neurotransmitters and feel-good chemicals all throughout the body and that will get you closer to being in coherence and then everything is going to be a lot easier from that point forward."

KEY TAKEAWAYS

- Understand what works for you
- Pay attention to the nudge
- Plan and create goals but don't get so attached to them that you let other opportunities pass you by
- Merge your talents and your passion
- Follow the intuition in your heart
- Find something to be truly grateful for

CONTACT INFO:

- Website: mindiekniss.com
- Book: *The Heart of Consciousness*

STEVE OLSHER
What is Your What?

Steve Olsher (www.steveolsher.com) is known as the world's foremost reinvention expert. Famous for helping individuals and corporations become exceptionally clear on their *what*, that is the one thing that they were created to do. His practical no-holds-barred approach to life in business propels his clients towards achieving massive profitability while also cultivating a life of purpose, conviction and contribution.

Why should we be looking at the *what*, as opposed to the *why*?

"If we look historically at who did what when, so I've been doing this for a while before Sinek did his *why* stuff. Some people call it semantics but from my perspective, it's really different. Your *why*, as Sinek defines it, is all about everything that is external. It's everything that is the driver for you. You do it because you want to help children in Africa, you do it because you want to put your kids into the best college, you do it because of, whatever the *why* is for you and that becomes the driver, I see the power in that, and it's beneficial to understand what your *why* is."

"My work is focused on helping people become clear on how to answer life's most important question, which is, what is your *what*? Your *what* is that which is chosen to you, as opposed to that what you have chosen, and it reflects the one amazing thing you were born to do. It is everything that is internal. Until you're clear on how you were naturally wired to excel, you could have the biggest *why* in the world but, frankly, if you don't know how to execute based upon the gifts you've been given, you're not going to be able to help those that you're compelled to serve."

Was there a time when you realized that you were chasing the *why* and you had to focus more on the *what* instead?

"It's more a function of chasing the almighty dollar as opposed to chasing the *why*. For me, it's always been that ongoing question of, what is it that I'm truly wired to excel at? After going through the Myers-Briggs and What Color is Your Parachute? and the Strengths Finder, and all of those types of things, they just left me with more questions than answers. Ultimately, that's why I ended up creating this framework. The fact that it's helped others is great, but it's something that I designed because I needed the answers for myself."

Three Steps to Discover Your *What*

"Step one is understanding what your core gift is; it's not easy. Most people go through a lifetime without understanding one piece of the puzzle, let alone all three. For a lot of folks, understanding what that core gift is, is the hardest part. There is a specific process that I take people through to help them identify what that core gift is. It varies based on the day, but somewhere between 20 and 25 core gifts is what we've identified. For instance, your core gift might be teaching, or it might be communicating or something of that nature. You're going to hone-in on your core gift after you go through a process that I created, which is lovingly called The Seven Seeds of Your Soul. That'll help bring to the surface what that core gift is. The second step is then figuring out the vehicle that you're going to use to share your gift with the world. If teaching is your gift, let's say, then how are you going to teach? Are you going to teach in a classroom? Are you going teach via writing? Are you going to teach via a video interview? Whatever it might be, what's that vehicle that you're going to use? Then, step three is all about identifying the people that you're most compelled to serve. It's a challenge to get one answer, let alone all three, but you can see how one without the other is not nearly as powerful."

What does it truly mean to reinvent yourself?

"The word has gotten overused to some extent because people talk about reinventing the hamburger like Burger King did, and it became this buzzword much to my chagrin because these are the kinds of things I've been talking about now for a long time. Long story short, what I've been talking about insofar as reinvention is concerned over the years is that it's not at all about changing anything about you. It's just getting back to the essence, to the core of who you truly are by shedding the shackles of all those personalities and character traits that we put on in an attempt to appease others. It's shedding all of that to get back to puts fire in your soul. It's not an addition, it's really a subtraction."

Do you find that those who seek purpose and meaning are not staying true to their core values?

"I'm not going to talk about values in this conversation only because values are not ultimately ingrained in your DNA; values are learned. This is more about honing-in on that blueprint. It becomes a function of recognizing that and, if you look historically, this is the thing that people hit sometimes in their mid-30s and beyond, there's way too much learning that goes on before people understand that what you were doing isn't necessarily what you were meant and made to do. It's a lot of trial and error to get to that point, but I do think that there is a fork in the road that all of us will hit eventually. The path we choose is obviously our choice, but we're all going to hit that fork in the road or we're going to wake up and say, 'Am I doing this because this is what I want to be doing and this is what I should be doing and this is what I'm compelled to do? Or am I doing this because I'm simply living by the standards that others have created for me?'"

ZB: I recently had to decide if video was my true passion and wound up realizing my true passion is storytelling. After figuring that out, a lot of things clicked into place.

SO: "Now, look at it in terms of the what is your *what* equation. So, your primary gift is communication and teaching and your primary vessel is storytelling through video. The third step asks the question: Who are the people that you most want to create stories for? That's how it all ties together. You've got your target audience and that gives you a defined path of where to go next.

Let's take it one piece at a time. Let's say the people that you most want to serve are those who have recently graduated from college and are trying to figure out what to do with their career. The question then becomes how do you help them? It's all well and good to love storytelling and video, but if you don't understand that this is something that you are naturally wired to excel at, you may go out and hire someone else to do it, even though that's what you want to do, because you may not yet realize that that communication piece, that teaching piece, is an innate part of who you are. You can then run it back through the three different steps and see how one is as equally powerful as the other."

ON THE FOUR PATHS

"The Four Paths represent where people are in their lives. It's not unusual for people to not even recognize that that's where they are. There are four typical paths and you're going to be on one of these four paths. One is what I call the birther. The birther is the path of the person who has known since the womb that that's who they are and what they're truly compelled to do, it's never been a question. You see that a lot with the musicians and athletes. They know in their heart of hearts that they were born to do X, Y or Z. These are the people that we hate because they've never had any doubt at all about what that is."

"The second path is the path of the shifter. The shifter is someone who is in a situation where things are pretty good, but their existence is not fully optimized. They need to make a subtle shift to the equation and typically, it's going to be through that what is your *what* equation. Perhaps the vehicle is right, and the gift is right, but the people are wrong, or the people are right, and the gift is right, but the vehicle is wrong – something of that nature. Just a subtle shift to that what is your what equation ultimately will make all of the difference for them. Whether they know it or not, they are on the path of the shifter."

"The third path is what I call the reinventor. This is somebody who pretty much has a come to Jesus moment or whatever you want to call it and wakes up one day and says, 'I can't do this any longer.' For instance, a client of mine was a chiropractor for a long time, had a book of paying clients, opened up his own practice and was doing quite well on paper, but internally was imploding. He woke up one day and said, 'I can't do this anymore.' Fast forward six years and today he is known as the ambassador of love and he helps single women find love. It's a full-on 180. It's somebody who does that full quantum shift and people look at him and they go, 'How did you get from here to there,' because the two paths are so incredibly disconnected, that you would never have been able to make that leap of faith if you were not that person."

"The fourth path is the path of the wanderer, which is 99% of the world. The wanderer's someone who doesn't realize there is something that they're truly compelled to do, something they're truly wired to do; they haven't figured out any element of the what is your *what* equation, and meander through life. they get there and they do their thing and, I'm not saying it's good or bad, but it's simply something that provides for an existence, I'm not sure that it necessarily provides for complete fulfillment. The reality is it's not their fault because these aren't conversations that we have around the dinner table or in classes. It's a place that most people find themselves because we don't teach people well enough how to discover who they are and what it is that they're born to do here on this planet."

For those following the path of the wanderer, could there potentially be a life-changing event that shifts them to a different path?

"Change is the result of one of two things: either something new comes into your life or you manifest something new. Those are the only two choices. It can happen where something externally hits you, like your friend has a heart attack and dies, your dad is diagnosed with cancer, or you get fired from your job. None of the paths are set in stone; all of those paths are inter-malleable, something that you can shift from one path to the other, with the exception of the birther. You're either a birther or you're not, but the other paths, you can certainly shift from one to the other throughout your life."

212

"Somebody who is unaware that it's possible for them to understand how they're naturally wired to excel and was going through life with the switch off and this wasn't even a conversation that they would have had. For that person to now recognize that it's possible to identify those pieces of the puzzle now becomes a conscious choice. Most people go through life in that unconscious incompetent state, where they're unaware of what's going on and it's not their fault. It's simply a matter of not having awareness. You don't know what you don't know. It's impossible to see it unless somebody points it out to you or something else comes into your life."

Families and financial obligations are no excuse, but don't quit your job.

"It's not an excuse but it is a reality because we end up with bills, responsibilities, and obligations and you can't in good conscience just walk away from that. If you put kids on this planet, you can't just walk away and decide you're not going to feed them. We have to figure out how to transition from that point A to whatever that point B is that you've now identified. If you've got the three pieces of the puzzle, you could go out and start doing something with it tonight and the beauty of having that day job is you're literally funding your transition with your day job. You don't want to cut off that source because it's going to take you some time, and it could take you a long time in order to start generating some real revenue from what it is that you're truly compelled to do. You continue down the path that you forged, with an eye on what your new ultimate objective is and you begin taking those baby steps towards getting there. Currently, 100% of your income is derived from what you don't want to do and 0% of your income is derived from what you do, but as soon as you understand what your *what* is and you begin down that path, now 1% of your income is derived from what you want to do and 99% is derived from what you don't, and then, 10-90, 20-80, 70-30, etc., until you figure out when you have enough income to cut that rope, but you don't cut it before then."

KEY TAKEAWAYS
- Your what is as important as your why
- Get back to what puts fire in your heart
- Identify your gift, identify your vehicle for communicating it, identify your audience
- You can't walk away from your obligations

CONTACT INFO:

- Website: steveolsher.com
- Podcast: *Reinvention Radio*
- Free Book: *What is Your What?* at whatisyourwhat.com/free

SERGEANT KEVIN BRIGGS
Guardian of the Golden Gate

Sergeant Kevin Briggs (www.pivotal-points.com) also known as the Guardian of the Golden Gate Bridge, is a California Highway Patrol officer who encouraged upwards of 200 people to either not go over the rail or come back to solid ground from the cord of the Golden Gate Bridge in San Francisco. After retiring in 2013 from 23 years of service, he has gone on to deliver a TED talk and founded Pivotal Points.

BACKSTORY

"I went into the Army right out of high school and was stationed over in Germany for three years, I developed testicular cancer while stationed there. They sent me back here to the States, to San Francisco, the Bay Area where I'm from and I had surgeries and chemotherapy, got through all that. I worked with my father in San Francisco for a year and my brother-in-law suggested law enforcement. I applied for the Department of Corrections and I got in. I worked at San Quentin when a good friend and coworker said he was going out for the California Highway Patrol. I finally said I'd give it a shot. I made it and the poor guy did not."

"I started with the California Highway Patrol in 1990 and started in Hayward which is south of Oakland with a lot of gangs and violence, and good people as well, but there's a lot of stuff going on down there. It took me about four years before I get up to Marin County, which connects to San Francisco via the Golden Gate Bridge. I started working on the bridge in 1994 and enjoyed it because I met people each and every day from around the world. But the bridge also has a dark side to it and that's the suicides. I didn't realize how many suicides took place there every year and

I had no training when I first started. It was horrible to get a call that someone was over that pedestrian rail and I didn't know what to say. I felt really responsible for whatever they might do, so it was tough those first few years."

How do you maintain your own positive mindset?

"Today, I travel all over and present to folks the experiences I had on the bridge and my own experiences with depression. Even though I have to relive these experiences every time that I speak, I get to meet so many nice people who tell me their stories, so it's a bonding experience and that's my therapy. But I still suffer from depression. As cops, we're not superheroes. Things can happen to us and they do happen to us. What we are exposed to, like horrific traffic accidents and suicides off the bridge, terrible things people are not supposed to see, it takes a toll on you. If cops don't get help for that, their average lifespan after retirement is about five years. Part of that is not only heart disease, but also because we've seen things that we didn't get help for and we become depressed and suicidal."

"I'm on two different medications for depression. Even though I'm 53 years old, I still get checked out and go to therapy. It's nothing to be embarrassed about. If I want to live life to the fullest and be functional, this is what helps me do it. I have two boys, ages 15 and 13, and I love watching them play their sports. We all have these bad mental health days, but when that starts turning into a couple of weeks, there's a problem. Don't be ashamed to go seek help."

Tell us about your first experience with someone on the bridge.

"I don't recall everything back in 1994, but it was a younger woman over the rail, and I walked up with a mindset of, 'What are you doing over there? You're trespassing, you better come back over here because you can get hurt.' I didn't fathom that she may be suicidal, and I totally didn't understand about mental illness. My approach with her wasn't anything like how I would handle it now. She did come back over the rail; I think she had a lot of empathy for me. I was scared and just didn't want to be responsible for someone losing their life."

"After that, I started seeking out veteran officers and started talking to them about how I could be better prepared for these suicidal situations. These folks were in that mindset, generally, for a brief time and if we could get them past that and over that rail, then there was a big chance they wouldn't try this again."

Did these people exhibit any signs physically? Or did they behave in a certain manner that was a warning that something bad might happen?

"Most folks show signs in one way or another, they will talk or write about it. Often, we miss these things because we think they're joking when they say things like, 'You'll be better off without me.' My main objective now is to get to folks long before they get up to that bridge or on top of a building or put a gun to their head, whatever they may be thinking of doing. When they're on the bridge, it's like stage four cancer, it's extremely difficult to deal with it at that point. If we can get to them long before they get up to those positions, we have a much better chance of a positive outcome."

"You're looking for inconsistencies in behavior. For example, they might be giving away their belongings, they feel helpless and hopeless and feel that things are terrible and they're never going to get better. There might be increased drug and/or alcohol use and they can't communicate about future plans. That's a big one because we all have things going on in the future. There may be an increased or decreased amount of sleep, you know, when people are using alcohol and/or drugs and are deeply depressed, there's a lot of sleeping because that's an escape from the pain. Financial stressors are a big, like divorce, loss of income, or being diagnosed with a big-time illness. These things don't necessarily mean an individual is suicidal, but we want to check on them and let them know you are in their corner and that is a huge plus in their life."

So, when you see these red flags, how can we convince people to open up further?

"I can't think of a tougher conversation. We call this a courageous conversation because you're possibly saving someone's life and can you imagine if you didn't approach them and they did commit suicide, how much you'd regret not having that conversation? So, if I saw someone suffering like that, try to have that conversation in a comfortable, safe place – not a public place – because you're asking folks to break down and tell you what's going on and they may cry and be very emotional. Ask them, 'Hey, this is what I've seen, and I want to let you know that I'm worried about you.' Then, let them talk. If they're talking, that's phenomenal."

"Let these folks talk 80% of the time with you talking 20% of the time. Give them your full attention with a lot of minimal encouragers like saying 'wow,' and nodding without interrupting, but to let them know that you're paying attention. Then, normalize their feelings because a lot of times, people feel that nobody understands what's going on with them and nobody has been through what they're going through. You want to say, 'You know what? If other people were going through what you are, they may think the same thing. Have you been having thoughts of killing yourself?' Let them answer and be prepared for that 'yes.' Don't freak out and say, 'How could you do this to me? How could you do this your family?' or get angry and say, 'That's stupid, don't do that, you're a coward.' Be ready for that answer and have some information with you to provide to that person. As if they've tried this before and if they have, ask them what prevented them from going through with it? If they are suicidal, then say, 'We need to get some help,' and don't let them be by themselves."

If you had a chance to put a big sign on the bridge that would make people think twice, what would it be?

"As far as the Golden Gate Bridge, they are putting up a suicide barrier in 2017, and that will greatly diminish the number of suicides on that bridge. In terms of a sign, a message of hope and information about help."

Not to be dark, but was a there a time you weren't able to save somebody?

"When I speak professionally, I don't talk about this individual. We got a call of a 30-year-old African American man over the rail. I got there about the same time as two other well-seasoned officers. We started talking with this young man and he was not under the influence of alcohol or drugs; he was a very nice man. He answered our questions, but he wouldn't tell us his name and he wouldn't tell us what had transpired to bring him to this point, but he was just a very nice guy. He shook my hand not once, but three times, and on that third time, I told him my name, and he goes, 'Kevin, I want to thank you for everything but my grandmother's down there and I have to go.' His grandmother had passed away some time prior. He shook my hand that third time and then he jumped. It hits you very hard. We had developed a bond. I'm there to save his life. To lose someone, we take it personally, it's a big hit and it's a loss of life and you think about their friends and family, but to have that connection where he shook my hand, it's even worse."

"It's a big failure on my part, but what helps us get through it is the number of folks we talk to that do come back over that rail. I don't really call it a save, so to speak. I'm not grabbing them and pulling them back over. I look at it more as a conduit for them on a very dark day in their life. I don't reach out and grab these folks for a couple of reasons. One, I don't want to be pulled over by mistake, but to come back over that rail takes a lot of courage. I am not going to be able to solve their problems. It's not going to happen. We know that and I'm not going to lie to them about that, so it takes a lot of courage to come back over that rail and face all of that stuff again."

ON POST: PEACE OFFICER STANDARDS AND TRAINING

"Around the United States, every peace officer has to go through a certain number of hours of training. For California is called POST, Peace Officer Standards and Training. For example, I was called to go to Sacramento next week with some other folks to develop training policy around recognizing and handling these types of calls for California police officers, and sheriffs. It's going to be a standardized practice for every peace officer in California and this is what we're developing."

For those who did come back over the rail, have you ever caught up with them years later?

"In general, I don't reach out to people because it could be a trigger. One individual who I have kept in contact with is a guy named Kevin Berthia and was over the rail and his picture's been around quite a bit. He was over the rail, but he came back and now he gets a chance to go out and speak about everything that brought him to the bridge that day and how he's doing now and how we can overcome this depression and these different things that are happening to us. He's a great success story."

WORDS OF WISDOM

"I have this little mantra of mine for folks who are talking to other people: Listen to understand. That's the big thing."

KEY TAKEAWAYS

- Everybody needs help sometimes, there is no shame in seeking help
- Listen more than you speak
- Watch for warning signs

CONTACT INFO:

- Website: pivotal-points.com

EPILOGUE

"Sometimes, to appreciate where you are, you have to go back to where it all began. In life, there's undoubtedly some obstacle, some struggle, some lack of faith you had to overcome before you get to where you are today. Make no mistake, there's always a tale of courage, hope or inspiration, or maybe all three, which others can learn from, or from which we can empathize. We can all grow from the experience of learning what you have to share. Everyone has a story."

-*Mark Brodinsky, The Sunday Series (Available on Amazon)*

Early on in my career, I learned the value of surrounding yourself with bright minds. JLD said earlier on in the book that you are the sum of the five people you spend the most time with. This isn't saying that you need to ditch the other people you spend time with, but rather you need to be more intentional about your actions. While these interviews might have given you insight into the minds of great thinkers and doers, I feel like this book would fall short if I didn't share my story. After all, if we are to learn from those that have "made it" it's only fair to share my story.

I feel compelled to add that if you asked me today, have I made it? My answer would likely be no. I don't feel like I've made it and can now ride off into the sunset, more on that in a little bit. I think I've figured a few things out. They say that Kentucky Fried Chicken had a secret blend of 11 herbs and spices, and that Dr. Pepper has a secret 23 flavor blend. Think of my current status as someone that figured out half of the ingredients that still make a darn tasty recipe but the other half most likely won't happen in my lifetime.

I'm ok with that.

I'm not convinced I'll discover all of the secrets to living in this short blip of an existence I have in the grand scheme of things. I'd like to think that 50% 'ain't half bad' pun intended.

There will be more interviews and stories to come in the future but it was important to me that I share mine and include it in this book so that you can see where I've landed after accomplishing and learning so much.

So, without further ado, here is "The Last Podcast" the interview I had my friend John record of me in his recording studio. I made this at the end of my time in creating the Year of Purpose Podcast as a way to say goodbye to a 2.5-year long journey but hello to a rest-of-my-life adventure.

THE LAST PODCAST

John: Welcome to the last podcast. This is your last podcast, correct?

ZB: This is the last interview for the *Year of Purpose* podcast, but this isn't like a movie where I buy my one-way ticket and disappear off into Southeast Asia or something like that. I don't think podcasting is over for me. My intention with this was really thinking, "what is my message if I were to not be here tomorrow?" I'm only twenty-seven, that's very much off into the future, but for many people, they don't get the chance to live that long, and you never really know.

Tomorrow could be the last day. So I felt that after talking to over 150 people from Los Angeles to Thailand, it made sense for my audience, and my future audience, like a time capsule, to say, "here's what I want to leave behind in the world."

We had this conversation before we started recording; people asked me when they interview me on podcasts, "What is your purpose? Did you find it?" We make a mistake by thinking your purpose is one statement. My purpose is a cause and effect relationship. I am the cause, and whatever effect it has on the world: on you, on your friends, anyone who's listened to this show, or anyone who hasn't listened to this show. That is my purpose. To inspire others. My purpose can't be summed up in a one-liner. My purpose is what will happen from here on out.

I took a leap of faith, a risk, and I put myself out there. I doubt that anyone's path would have gone the same way had I not done this. For me, it was an exploration of, "Why am I here? How can I leave behind the biggest dent in the universe?" If tomorrow were my last day, being able to sum that up in this podcast episode was important to me. It is essentially a time capsule. It will be here now, ten years from now, and long after I'm gone. That's why like this medium, this audio recording could last forever.

John: Let's start from the beginning, let's take it back right out of college, who were you, what were you doing, what was going on?

ZB: I went to college at James Madison University. A lot of what I did in college, out of college, and after that point, is a mirror image of how I was born. My mom was getting ready to go to the gym; she went to the bathroom and my feet popped out in the toilet. As most people know, babies are supposed to come out headfirst. On top of that when I was delivered by the volunteer fire department, I had the umbilical cord wrapped around my neck three times and I was not breathing.

John: You were delivered by the volunteer fire department?

ZB: The volunteer fire department. It' funny, one of the medics that saved my life became my school bus driver fifteen years later when I was in middle school.

John: It's like a Forest Gump movie.

ZB: I think that that has been a mirror for me. It was never my choice to exist in the world. In my philosophy classes in college, it was said you are thrust into existence. We're put into circumstances that can be quite complicated and suffocating in a sense. It's up to other people to give a helping hand and do as much as they can do, after that, it's really on us.

They resuscitated me, After that it was up to me to breathe on my own, to make it happen. When I look at college, it was a fantastic experience. But if I could put my life out on a wall, this is one of the bigger pictures that stands out.

My fraternity brother, a freshman in college, went home for winter break, and his mom didn't wake up one morning. He came back to school and wrote a letter to the fraternity that said, "I need your support now more than ever. I just lost my mom and it was totally uncalled for, There was no warning sign, it just happened." His way of coping with the loss was to write out his story, as it unfolded, from the experience of going home for break, to becoming infatuated with someone he went to school with. It was a distraction to get away from the stress of life. At some point, months later, he shared the script with me. He wanted to get my opinion, he asked, what do you think of this? Could I become a writer?

I read it and I thought, this is like a movie. When I told him that, he didn't believe it at first because he didn't believe in his work. I said, "hey man, I think we could turn this into something." Next thing you know we're going around to professors all through the department to try and get course credit as an independent course to make this a feature film.

Then I sat in the editing lab, picked out my editor, picked my camera guy, and I had my team. It was the four of us. We had to get a teacher to sign off to give us course credit. Everyone said, "There's no way, you don't have funding, you don't have the equipment to pull this off, it's not possible."

Every professor laughed us out of their office, until I got to the last one. We walked into his office and he said, "I'll sign off on this under one condition, you turn this into a ten-minute short." We were shocked, "Did you read the script? This is not a story that can be told in ten minutes. It deserves a full feature length." He responded, "You have to make it a short. Try for twenty, thirty minutes max, but I don't see how you guys are going to pull it off." At this point, I got up from the chair and said, "I'm supposed to graduate a year early. I busted my butt every summer to get credits so I could graduate early, to take some of the burden off of the tuition fees. I'm supposed to get out of here a year early but here's the deal…

If I don't pull this off, you can fail me and I will come back and take your class again. It will be the only class that I have next year to graduate, I only need three credits and you can make it as miserable as you want for me."

I think that this was the turning point in my life where I started taking things further to see how far I could push that limit. Sure enough, in 2010, we revised the script, we did a full casting call with the theater department, we got actors, and we raised $1000 budget by asking local businesses for money.

That summer we filmed, in the fall we edited. We had local bands donate their music for our soundtrack. Then we went through and color graded the whole thing. I was self-taught on color correction. I would edit until three, four o'clock in the morning. They gave us a little closet in the basement that had an editing suite in it. We had a private key to get in and we lived out of that room.

Finally, in December of 2010, we premiered a feature-length, ninety-six-minute long film out of this script. It was the story of this guy's life. It was unbelievable, we had pulled something off that no one else had pulled off up until that point. That became a theme for me.

I walked across the stage at graduation, I didn't care to get the diploma, I was done, I was over it. I left college and found a job, but in the back of my mind, I wanted to go to the Sundance. I wanted to go to California and live out my dream. But I didn't go to California. I was afraid. I was in a relationship at the time, I had no clue. It went from this high, to a week or so after graduation wondering where I was in the world?

John: Is it the uncertainty of every graduate the second you cross that stage, is that what was going on here?

ZB: I think part of it was the uncertainty, but part of it was also this pressure of thinking I had to live out the same story that everyone else did. Go to college, get the degree, get the job, do the same thing for forty years and hopefully you have a family and kids and retire and buy a house at some point.

John: Were you already mapping this timeline out in your head?

ZB: I didn't have specific dates of when I wanted things to happen. A piece of my brain was shouting, "Hey, dude, you know this is not what you want for yourself," so I was fighting that urge of, "Do I follow the script that everyone else is, or do I do my own thing?" I ultimately chose not to get that flight, so here I am, two weeks out of school, just job searching.

I sent out over a hundred applications; it was still a pretty bad job market. I was at the house of the person I was dating at the time, on Craigslist searching job postings. I saw a posting for a videographer nearby. I applied for it, got a phone call, got an interview the next day. At the beginning of the interview she said "We've got two or three more people coming in that we want to interview. So we're not making the decision yet." Then at the end of the interview she said, "I'm probably going to give you a call tomorrow."

I don't think I understood what getting a job at this company was going to do for me. The job looked good on paper to friends and parents and the people I met at happy hour, but when I woke up in the morning I knew something wasn't right. Every time my alarm went off in the morning I'd have that tingling sensation, that pain that goes up and down your back and in your stomach. It was difficult for me.

I got hired at Glazer Kennedy Insider Circle. It was founded by Dan Kennedy and Bill Glazer. They're copywriters and marketing masters. They had been helping business owners all over the globe.

John: Here in Baltimore?

ZB: The office was located here in Baltimore, but they worked globally. They had business owners all over the place that they were helping out. They ran big conferences that they flew me out to. I was their go-to video guy, from filming conferences to a weekly Web TV show on YouTube. I remember the day we got to a hundred thousand views on our YouTube channel. This was before YouTube stars and sensations were popular. This is 2010, 2011, it was a big deal back then to have a million views on your video.

Right around that time they were getting ready to sell the company. Things were weird, I didn't have as much of a role anymore because the new supervisor that came in didn't give me any work to do. I searched around and discovered Pat Flynn. I started to learn about passive income and what he was doing, and blogging for money. I started a website called Rookie Video Pro. The idea was to teach rookie videographers how to become more professional, or how to make your video look more professional. I ran it for three or six months until I gave up on it because I had no clue what I was doing. But there was this idea in my head of there's some freedom in what you do. You don't have to work this job nine-to-five. There was a small piece of me that was pushing me, "Hey dude, try something different. Come on, it's out there for you to grab." I wasn't quite ready yet, so I didn't end up doing that. That job lasted for about a year and a half. The owner sold a stake in the company, and the people who bought us out walked in one day with a lawyer and said, "Here's your pink slip." I thought, "I did everything right. I got the degree, I got the job, I even started 401k and all the retirement stuff, how did I fail?"

John: You were following protocol.

ZB: Yeah.

John: That insecurity, when you were hired by that company, all those initial fears that you had after graduation dissipated, correct?

ZB: Yeah. I was getting a paycheck every two weeks. I thought that equated to, "Hey, you did it right."

John: Was California on the horizon at this point?

ZB: It dissipated a little bit because I had been sucked into the job and thought things were going well. My first thoughts were: go on unemployment, get your paycheck, freelance as much as you can. I went into survival mode. I wasn't thinking into the future. I thought, "How am I going to have enough money at the end of the week?" I was living at home with my parents. It's not like I was going to be out on the street. But in my head, I thought I completely failed. I'd to end up on the street because at some point, I messed up and I failed.

John: You assumed that the pink slip was because of personal failure, not because they couldn't afford to do the same anymore with the market down. Is there a reason you took on that as a failure?

ZB: The problem was I didn't know why I was let go. We saw them in the parking lot walking in, and we knew people were being called down from their offices, so we had an inkling. Someone came in, gave me a hug and said, "Sorry, guys, they let me go, I loved working with you, but I'm out." Everybody was quiet. Word was going around, but we didn't know who and how many were getting let go because not everyone got let go that day. We had no idea what was going to happen.

John: So, you're at home, you're in survival mode, what happened?

ZB: I did what I could with what I had. I went back to basics. I've got a camera and I've got these skills. I met a lot of people through this company. I reached out to people and freelanced a little bit. It was just enough money, combined with my unemployment, that I was fine. I think I had my midlife crisis early and decided to put my unemployment check towards taking a motorcycle license class.

John: That's usually at thirty, thirty-five.

ZB: Right, and I was probably twenty-two.

John: Not even a quarter-life crisis yet.

ZB: Right. So I'm unemployed, walking out of my room to my Jewish mother and saying, "Hey mom, I'm going to get my motorcycle license," and praying that I could come home to a bed later that night. I had this point like, "I don't know where I am in life and I was always told that people who are in crisis and have no clue what they're doing go and get a motorcycle, so let's do this."

John: It's fairly inexpensive actually.

ZB: They're pretty cheap, that's why I thought maybe I could save some money, not spend as much on gas. I had done a couple projects for a local guy who ran a real estate school and he paid me here and there. At the end of each shoot he would say, "How much do I owe you?" I had no clue how to price my stuff at that time, so a three, four-hour shoot I'd say 200 bucks. No matter what I said, he'd always add fifty dollars to it and I think this was one of my first business lessons. No matter whether I said 150, $200, 250, always add fifty dollars to it. I didn't quite get it yet, I was like, "I got an extra 50 bucks, sweet." But it's important to know that there was a lesson in being unemployed, being a freelancer part-time, and how this client was treating me. I was giving him the utmost respect. I was giving him the highest quality work that I could with what I had. I was always available and on time and things like that. This lesson, I'm sure, plays out later down the road.

I'd been throwing out applications left and right, applying everywhere and I forgot I had applied to work at the Apple Store. One night I'm out driving with my friends, three or four people are in my car, music's loud, people are loud, and I get a phone call. I had no clue who it was from, but I knew that some of my job applications were out there. I quiet everyone down and answer the phone. "Hey, this is Jason, one of the managers at the Apple Store." I'm like, "Oh, hi." I'm in the car, on the way to the bar with my friends or something and like, guys, shut up.

John: Steve Jobs is on the phone.

ZB: I asked "What's going on?" He said, "I want to invite you to an interview at the Apple Store. Are you available?" I said, "Yeah, sure." I showed up for the first round where they bring you in the store after it's closed. There's forty, fifty other people in there. You have no clue how many people you're up against, no idea how many positions are open. You go through this round and they do a roundtable. I'm trying to figure out If I need to sound better than the guy next to me, what if they don't want a smart aleck? Do if I need to dumb it down? I had no clue what to do. I kind of kept it in the middle.

A week later they give me a call back. This time, I came back to the Apple Store but it was much smaller, down to ten or twelve people. I made it through that and got a callback for one final interview. We had a meeting with one of the regional managers and the store manager. I thought, awesome, I made it through three rounds, I was ecstatic. At this point in time, Apple was known for being harder to get into than Harvard University. I love Apple, I've been an Apple fanboy ever since I got my first Mac computer.

John: Apple plug.

ZB: Yeah. I remember this whole interview process thinking, this could be awesome. I could go work for a company that I've loved my entire life; I could finally find that job that I'll hold onto forever.

John: Right, and being in that environment, that creative environment, that atmosphere, like-minded people, forward thinking people.

ZB: Oh yeah, and I thought even though it's the Apple Store level, it's the very bottom of the food chain, there's so much potential for growth. Maybe I'll wind up back in California, out in Cupertino where their headquarters are. Maybe I'll finally get my dream of going out to California. This is it, this is exactly what I wanted.

John: You made it through all the rounds of the hiring process. You're working for Apple now. What was that like?
ZB: There was a preliminary period where we learned how the store works. They taught us every position in the store. There's positions that you shadow and there's things that you learn online. There's some presentations and things you watch and ultimately, you kind of graduate and you get your position.

My position was called the family room specialist. They don't have the name anymore but that's what we were known as. We were an in-between position where we worked at the Genius Bar, but for the most part we focused on iPhones, iPods, and iPads. It was rare that we touched a computer. They try to push you to work from that position into the genius role, where you learn more about computer repair. I got some of it along the way, you hang out long enough, you know exactly what people are coming in for and sometimes you can fix it for them. I started to overlap, if they needed help in sales because it was a super busy day and we were not busy in repair, I would jump in and start selling stuff. I was like the best salesman ever, I talked so many people out of buying iPhones. They would walk in and say, "Tell me why I need an iPhone" I'd say, "Well, you probably don't if you're saying that. If you know you want one, then you get it. I'm not going to persuade you to buy something only to have you come back a week later and say you hate it." I loved sales, I loved every aspect of it. I had a little bit of flexibility to move around in the store and was able to move beyond what I was required to do.

There were rumors for a long time that they were building a new store in a secret spot in the mall. We had no clue where it was, and we were excited because our store was small. We knew that we had to double or triple in size because of the amount of foot traffic through there. One day I was walking by this plywood as I was leaving and I see my manager sneaking in the door. I said, "What are you doing?" He asked, "You want to come in and see something cool?"

John: You disappeared for a year after that, I lost contact.

ZB: Right, I just went into Narnia.

John: You went into Narnia, that was it.

ZB: I walked in and he said, "We haven't made the official announcement yet, but this is our new store." He walked me through the wireframe of it. I said, "Oh my God, this is amazing." I was able to be a part of an iPhone launch, and a part of transferring stores. I closed down one store one night, then opened the new store the next day. Everything was brand new and shiny, three times the size, it was everything we had dreamed of. It renewed my excitement for working at Apple. I enjoyed being there because my coworkers were awesome. Some management and I clashed a little bit, but I think that's why I'm a good entrepreneur. I don't take kindly to people telling me what to do, but I was good in that team environment. I loved helping out everybody else. When our lineup of people coming in for repairs was busy, I was knocking it out. I sometimes did forty, forty-two appointments in a day. You can imagine meeting forty-two different people with forty-two different problems with their iPhones. It was always something different, you're constantly thinking fast-paced on your feet, throughout the day, for a regular seven, eight-hour hour shift.

John: What was the leadership like in that environment?

ZB: There was a constant push. This Apple store was for all of Baltimore City and County. People were driving in all the way from the city to get their stuff fixed because this was the only place in town. The next closest one was a solid half-hour away. We got swamped all the time.

One day, we were so busy a manager dragged me over to a table and said, you sit here. Then she started populating the chairs, eight chairs around the table round-robin style. For three or four hours, I'm just going through it, no break in sight, no clue what was going on or why we were getting slammed that day.

John: How far along is this in your career?

ZB: Probably six to nine months into working there. We had moved into the new store, still trying to squeeze into the space. We gained more people because we had a bigger space. It didn't relieve any of the pressure. That day was a turning point. I remember going home that day and thinking, "I'm going to have a heart attack by thirty if I keep doing this." I started to look for other positions in the store, seeing if I could transfer. There was a role called expert, they were in sales but they had more flexibility because they had some more knowledge. I applied for it and management said, "No, sorry, we can't move you to a different position." I said, "Why not?" They didn't have a good answer. I was their best person, I knew I was taking more appointments than anyone else in the store. They knew if they took me off of tech support they were going to get slammed. I got barred from moving into this position, then I saw a position for a video editor open up in Cupertino working for a corporate.

I thought, this is it. So, I see the details and it said minimum requirement two years' experience, I had been with Apple just over a year. I asked around and got the answer that unless you've been there for two years, they're not going to consider it. I thought, "Are you kidding me? If you knew my editing skills, if you sat me down in front of Final Cut Pro, I know Final Cut inside and out."

John: Did you submit anyway?

ZB: I did but it didn't turn into anything; they didn't even consider it. Things were starting to add up. I'm getting frustrated with the job. I'm getting tired of where I'm at. It's so busy and every month or every other month, we'd have a staff meeting where we would try this new strategy, we would change things up and transform how this all works. They wouldn't give us enough time to get it working before they would try a different way. Corporate passed this down and this is the way we're going to do it.

John: I didn't expect to hear that about them. I mean pivoting a lot.

ZB: You would think they would find one thing that works and run it. Isn't that what the iPhone is? They found something that works, they add new features here and there but it's the same darn phone as it was five years ago.

John: So, you're discouraged with the job. That change in mindset towards this job happened when? At about eight months?

ZB: Between six and nine months. As I got discouraged more and more, it became the norm. I knew I wasn't going into work to be happy, I was going into work to see the same old stuff. It wasn't going to change. The more I tried to switch to different roles within the company the more I realized they were going to bar me at every step of the way. I thought, "I won't be able to make the impact in this company that I want to make." I saw from the ground level that they could have made it much more efficient. If I could have sat down with the CEO that day I would have said, "I can show you how this store can work so much better," That could have fixed it all. It kind of got to this breaking point.

John: You were discouraged, what happened next? Did you eventually leave?

ZB: We were in the customer service role. People don't come to you to say, I love my phone. That wasn't what I got paid to do. I was essentially a therapist. I heard every sob story of people not reading instructions. Nothing was too far-fetched. I found marijuana inside headphone jacks. I had dads bring in their daughter's phones and say, "Yeah, she said it stopped working" and I thought, "well, did she tell you that it's filled with urine, because I opened it up and I can tell you, do you want to smell?" I was so tired of people lying about what happened. I had seen it all, so I knew what was going on. I'm not stupid, and there's liquid sensors inside. The craziest one was this girl who came in and said she dropped her phone in her taco salad and had enough dressing or salsa on her darn taco salad that it killed her phone. She failed to mention that she dropped it in the sink a week prior, so it was already on its way out. They try to give you some excuse because they think you'll replace it for free.

John: What percentage did you replace the phone for them, I'm curious?

ZB: If they didn't lie to me and it seemed like an honest mistake or something. Technically things were supposed to be marked as physical damage; the warranty didn't cover physical damage. They had to pay for a new phone. So, if you shattered your screen you had to pay for a new phone depending on the model. It was a complete mess.

John: Was there one thing that pushed you over the edge?

ZB: Yeah, all this builds up to one day. At the front door there's someone with a walkie talkie. Being in tech support I used to keep one on, so I could hear what's going on and kind of keep track of everybody. A lady comes in, I was the appointment guy that day. I was kind of shuffling around with an iPad making appointments for anyone who didn't have one, trying to manage the queue of people in line to get help. They call back to me, they asked if I had any available appointments within the next hour. We were swamped, it wasn't going to happen. I said, "No, I'm sorry boss, I'll have to get them to sign up for a different day." I think she heard it through his earpiece and I see her face as she comes stomping back towards me. As she's walking towards me, over the radio he says something like, "She didn't listen, she's coming to talk to you," I said, "You think?" I can watch this unfolding in front of me.

John: You see this tornado coming towards you.

ZB: As she's coming down towards me, I look up and see one of the freelance clients that I had been doing video for. I've got to give a huge shout out to Sherman

Ragland here, he started a real estate school here in Maryland. I met him through my old company because the owner, Bill Glazer, was good friends with him. That's how I freelanced while I was unemployed. I thought, "Oh crap, someone I know is watching this whole thing unfold." He was holding the iPad looking up at me, kind of watching what's going on.

John: Did you acknowledge each other at this point?

ZB: We locked eyes, he knew. She gets in front of me, starts screaming and hollering. The store's got 200 people in it and I see our plainclothes security guard perk up a little. She's screaming, "Why can't you get me an appointment? I was in here a week ago," We had no space open, if she was nice to me and said, "I had this terrible accident, I made a big mistake," I would have found a way to squeeze her in. But you do that, I have no reason to help you out. I said, "Look, you can make an appointment online for a different day, here's the laptop right here but I've got no room left for you today."

Eventually she gets taken away by the plainclothes security guy. After she's gone, I take a second to recompose myself and check in a couple more people. Then he walks up to me and asked, "What was that?" I said, "That's my job. That's what I get paid to do." I couldn't believe that someone I knew had witnessed it. He asked what I was doing later. I told him I get off work at 6:00. He said, "How about this, I'm going to come back later tonight, we're going to get dinner as soon as you get off work. I'll meet you at 6:30." Cool, awesome, no problem. The whole rest of my shift I'm thinking I can't afford to pay 50 bucks for dinner right now. I was kind of worried about that.

John: You had an irate customer come in, cause a huge scene, you're discouraged about the job in general, why didn't you quit on the spot? What held you back?

ZB: It was probably thinking "You're going off-script, man, you're not supposed to deviate from that." A part of me was concerned with where I was going and what I was doing with myself. It was saying, "Don't deviate from the script." Then another part of me thought, "Why is it working this way? It shouldn't be working this way."

So I got off work, ran down the hallway because I got off work late, ripped off my Apple shirt, threw on my other shirt, walked down to this place and thought, "I have no clue how I'm going to pay for dinner, what the heck is going to happen tonight?" We sit down for dinner, before we even order he asks the waitress to bring over a bar napkin. He pulls out a fancy silver pen from his jacket and draws out this little stepladder, these little twelve stairs and he hands me the pen and the napkin and says, "Put zero at the bottom," so I write it in. He said, "How much do you make right now, roughly?" I was at about $38,000, but for the sake of numbers, I said $30,000. So, I put $30,000 at the top. He said, "Do you know how much money you would have to make each month to replace your current income?" I had no idea. He says, "Pull out your smartphone, use the calculator, do the math here. If you do the math, take that $30,000 and divide it by twelve you figure it out. Or $15,000 over six months, break it down further over two months, that's $5,000, so once a month it's $2,500 a month." Finally, the number's getting smaller and I thought, alright, what's he getting at here. He said, "Do you know how to make $2,500 a month?" I thought, "Work at the Apple store and keep getting a paycheck. Is this a trick question? What am I supposed to say?"

John: At that point, you still had the linear career mindset.

ZB: Oh, yeah. It's funny because I freelanced for a couple months in between jobs. I got a taste of that but my mind wasn't there yet. I told him, "I have no clue how I'm going to make $2,500 a month" and he says, "Okay, well what if you broke it down more, you work five days a week, forty hours a week?" It came out to 100, 120 bucks in a day, five days a week, replacing my income. It wasn't until he broke it down that far where I thought holy crap, this is doable. I can find a way to do it. I'm not going to go open up a lemonade stand but, there are skills that I have as a tall male strong enough to lift forty, fifty-pound boxes. There was something I could do. This was the changing point to how I thought about money and how I could replace my income. It didn't click until that night. He turned to me after this realization, the lightbulb clicks on and he said, "Here's what you're going to do. You're going to quit your job tomorrow. You're going to write up a resignation letter when you get home tonight, and quit your job tomorrow." I don't like people telling me what to do, but for some reason, I listened. I went home, I typed up the letter and I told my mom, I'm going to quit and start my own business.

John: What did she say?

ZB: I don't remember exactly how she reacted but it was, "I don't know if you're making a good decision." It wasn't that she didn't support me, she was worried, she was concerned, she wanted the best.

John: She's your mom, she's worried about you, I get it.

ZB: Yeah. I told to a couple of my peers I was going to quit. One of them said, "You won't do it, there's no way, you're not going to do it" He was an older guy and I liked him. He was a photographer by trade and we got along well, had a lot in common. I remember flashing the envelope when I walked in the next day and he said, "I don't know why you're waiting, you should just go do it now." I was going to wait until I felt comfortable in my day. I didn't want to do it and then have to work my whole shift that day. It was almost like he was egging me on. I waited for a couple hours until finally, he said, "What are you doing, man? If you're going to quit, just do it." So, I took the letter and I pulled the general manager aside and I told him I would be leaving, and gave him my letter of resignation and my two weeks' notice. He was shocked, he had no idea it was coming. The manager wasn't around the store that often, so he didn't know what was going on in his store. I remember the relief of getting that done with. It was like working my shift didn't matter. You could have that same angry person come back in and have it happen again, I'd be like, drop the mic, I don't care, I'm out. It didn't matter at that point. I felt this sense of freedom already.

John: Okay, so at this point, you quit Apple, where did you go from there? Is this where you started ZMBmedia?

ZB: This was a big part of our talk when I had that dinner. If I'm going to quit, I need to have some sort of a plan. He said, "You've been doing videography for me and you do a great job with it, you've got the gear, you have the tools, why don't you do that?" It kind of made sense. I thought, "Yeah, I love doing video stuff, it's what I went to college for, it would be in alignment with where I originally wanted to go." It seemed like the logical next step. I took a day or two to research ideas and think things through. To give myself separation between the job and what I was about to do, because I knew whatever came next was going to be big. It was going to require a lot more work, it was going to be a lot tougher, so much more uncertainty. I went home to explain to my mom, "Hey, I quit my job, my plan is to start a company and I'm going to start doing this video stuff full time."

John: Were you formulating this prior to you quitting?

ZB: No, I'd never seen it as possible. It was never really an option until that dinner where he broke it down into such a small attainable goal. Using that strategy, I changed it up and said, "Okay, this top piece, this $30,000 is create a business and this bottom piece, the zero dollar sign, is where I am right now." I broke it down and thought, "Well, I know that there's a few aspects of a business. There's money, legality, getting clients, marketing, there's a couple of different pieces to this." Then it became let's figure out what we have to do.

John: So, at this point, you started to reverse engineer?

ZB: Yeah, using that same idea, big goal up here, little goal down here. There's definitely a way to get from zero to that highest point, you just have to find it. Many people are kind of lazy and sometimes don't want to put the effort forward to figure out what it takes to get there. Many of us want it to be handed to us on the silver platter. People like me, we don't operate the same way, our brains don't allow us to work in an organization, where there's this leadership above us. We want to be that creative thinker that's free to change and move as need be.

So, to figure out where I fell into place with business, I broke it down into pieces. I have to have a business checking account, but before I have a business checking account, I have to get a federal tax ID number. A lot of that came through asking questions and finding business owners that had done it already, saying, "well, what did you do?" I went to the bank and met with a banker and they told me how to start a business account.

John: You did all the research prior to jumping into the pool, right?

ZB: Yes and no. When I applied to become a business and get LLC, I didn't know about LegalZoom at the time. I didn't know I could go to this website and spend 200 bucks and have a legal entity. We found out through a family friend who was an attorney that I could use the local law office and they would do it for me. It was like $800. Being naive and not knowing of any other opportunities, I went for it. I spent the $800, they made the LLC, it was quick and painless. Then they come back and tell me I could have walked to the small business office downtown, paid fifty or a hundred bucks or whatever and done this. I'm like, are you kidding me? I'm starting from zero, I don't have $800 to spend, So, part of it was trial by fire and learning from those mistakes. I wasn't always sure what to do next, so I either A) Googled the answer or B) found someone who'd been there before and figured out what the next step was. Within about two weeks of quitting, I had the LLC, I had the bank account, I had a couple hundred bucks in the bank account, I had my business checks. I was essentially open for business, but I was still making invoices off of Google Doc templates. I had no clue how to make invoices. These were all things that I figured out later on. It was never easy, but the first thing I did was say, how am I going to get clients? When I told him that, the person I had dinner with, Sherman, he said, "Well, I'm hiring you, I am your first client. I need you in two or three weeks, what are you doing?" I said, "Well, I don't have a job anymore, so I'm not doing anything.".

John: You just told me to quit.

ZB: Right. So, he was my first client and if you go back to the invoices, you'll find it. I connected with other people I knew from the previous marketing company, before I was at Apple, and things started to pop up. I started doing more and more work and after about six months , I was replacing that roughly 30k income.

John: How important do you think it is to have that goal set up? A lot of people go into it and arbitrarily have these things on the horizon. It sounds like you always had the end game in mind, even if it was limited to a ten-yard view.

ZB: I kind of fooled myself into thinking it was a life-or-death scenario. If I don't pull this off, mom's kicking me out of the house and game over. I convinced myself if I don't do this in the next six months, I will be that person on the street that you see when you're driving to the video shoot, asking for money. I narrowed my view into a fear that that's where I could end up if I don't pull this off. I'm going to encourage myself to do everything possible to not be that person.

John: So, you jumped in, you quit Apple, you have a few clients under your belt now, you formed this new business, how's it evolving?

ZB: I knew I wanted to start the business, but I was never a fan of business plans. I did some research online, and thought maybe I had to do that, but there were all these people who were saying business plans are crap, you don't need this. I kind of thought, what do I need a business plan for, I shoot video, you pay me, we're done.

John: Right, very simple.

ZB: Yeah. So, I kept busy through the summer, but it was at this point where I thought, I don't know how I'm going to get past this notion of just $30,000. $30,000 is not going to allow me to move out of my mom's house, it was not going to allow me to get my own place, not going to allow me to support any future relationships, it's not going to take me anywhere. I'll be able to pay my bills; I'll be able to kind of get by. Wasn't I already doing that at the job? So, drastic times call for drastic measures. I was invited by my friend Mara, who was my old supervisor at the marketing company I worked at right after college. She ran the social media department and she was my direct boss. She became a good friend of mine after we both were let go from that company. We were essentially drinking buddies. We would go out, hang out with friends, grab dinner, get together for the Super Bowl, stuff like that. At this point, I never looked at her in any light other than a good friend, former boss. She became a business coach, she invited me to this conference she was putting on. It was a three or four-day conference in a hotel, probably 300 people in attendance. I thought it would be a great networking opportunity to meet local business owners and potential clients, who knows. Mara gave me some work because she used video to sell tickets to that conference, so I had already worked with her a little bit from a business standpoint. I had no clue what was going to happen next.

I went to the event with my buddy Carson, who I met when Mara and I created the Towson Young Entrepreneurs meetup group on Meetup.com. We were doing monthly happy hour meetups. The funny thing is Carson was there a week or two before I decided to quit. I was with him at a bar with him and said, "Yeah, man I don't like my job, I think I'm going to quit." That was the first time I met him, the second time we hung out was when he came to this conference with me about building and growing a business. We're sitting at the conference and she pulled me aside before she was about to make her big pitch for this coaching program she was running. She says, "Hey, we want to sell X amount of people into this program. One of the strategies we use is we plant some people in the audience so when we say, 'The first ten people to the back of the room get this discount,' we want you to take your order for them and run to the back of the room. We want you to be the first one there." It's to encourage more people in the audience to buy and that deal is going to run out. It's that urgency. She's giving her pitch, she's talking about what we would work on over a twelve-month coaching program and there were certain times where, out of a room of 300 people, I almost felt like she was looking right at me and talking to me.

John: You were digesting this yourself?

ZB: Yeah, I didn't know if she was just trying to make it seem authentic. She didn't want to fake it, , she's not talking to me and I run up and go, but there was this point where, when she was talking about the need to grow your business and what this could do for you and how this could change your life, I almost felt like she was on stage only talking to me and she was looking at me. I felt like this is something I should do, too. I was set up to think I'm planted as this fake in the audience, but as the pitch is going on I'm thinking maybe this is a good idea. I mean, she's someone that I trust, she was my boss. I knew she had this experience, she's not a stranger up on stage. I'll never forget, the time came in her pitch, first X amount of people to the back of the room get this discount, and I run to the back of the room. I've got my papers, I hand them to her assistant, who was in on it, she goes to rip it up and I said, "no, don't do that, don't rip it up, I want to do this. I didn't totally commit at first, but then, Mara invited Carson and I to a VIP lunch for anyone who had signed up on the spot. So, I go to the lunch and we're sitting here talking to other people, still faking it, convincing them we spent $11,000 on a coaching program. They're asking him what he does, at the time, he was employed at a Krav Maga gym teaching self-defense, he didn't work for himself. He's trying to pull it off like we're business partners, pretending he does videos. The whole thing was wild but through that lunch, I'm still thinking "Man, maybe this is where I need to be." It didn't quite click until a couple days later. I was on the phone with her and I asked her, "Do you really think I can pull this off?" She said, "Look, I've been your boss, I know your work, I've seen your work, I totally think you can do this. I think you can easily double what you were making at the Apple Store." The whole point of her coaching program was to get people to six figures, or as close as possible to six figures.

John: How important do you think it is to have validation from people close to you? When I started my business, I didn't share a lot of personal details even with my closest friends. How important do you think that is to have someone like her?

ZB: I think it means the difference between you failing and you succeeding because fortunately, I was thick-skinned enough to ignore my grandparents freaking out and saying, "What are you doing?" Ignore my mom, who wasn't angry but was concerned, and ignore what everyone had said. If they had all said, "Oh my gosh, you could do this, this is exactly where you should be," I would probably be ten times further than where I am right now. It probably took about two years into my business to prove that I was successful, two years to prove it wasn't just a fluke.

John: Prove to self or prove to family?

ZB: To them. Before they accepted that it was a possibility for me, they had to see that it wasn't a fluke. I was successful for the first year, then I had to get through a second year. The stats are bad if you look at them, something like 50% of businesses fail in the first year, and 70% to 80% of those that remain fail in the second year. They knew it was tough.

John: Did they support you along the way? When they saw determination, did they support you?

ZB: No one ever spoke down about it and said you're making a big mistake.

John: You're going to give up on this, come on, you got to get back on the workforce.

ZB: Yeah, I think part of it was because of how confident I was. When I really claimed what I was doing and owned it, then they got it. It clicked with them, they were like, "Okay, he's going to try this thing and it'll probably fail and then he'll figure it out and he'll go back and work at the Apple Store," or something like that. They were definitely very concerned, you know, "we're worried for your well-being and if you're making good decisions." A big part of that was because I had quit my job. I had a little bit of money in savings, but not much. I took $5,000 that I had saved up and I call it my, "If I F this up fund." I threw it into a Scottrade account and invested it in Disney stock and just let it sit there. I took her on as a coach, it was an $11,000 program, I didn't have eleven thousand dollars. I put it on a credit card. I was really hesitant to tell my mom how much it cost. It's one thing to tell mom "Hey, ma, I quit my job, I hired this coach, they're going to teach me what I need to know," It's another thing to say, "Hey, I live under your roof, I invested $11,000 that I don't have, I'm making these crazy financial decisions and I'm not even making money." We started the coaching program in September, we had quarterly retreats where we would travel somewhere and stay in a hotel for a weekend and mastermind and work on our businesses. It was either January or February of the following year, I had my first $10,000 month. $11,000 for the program made 10k within three or four months. That was the first time I was like, "Whoa, okay, I didn't make a bad choice, because I was able to pay this off, I will not be in debt because of this."

I'm going to be honest with you, I was just a kid in my bedroom, trying to make a few bucks and they're like, "Okay, what if we offered you check for $10,000?" I don't remember exactly how much but it was about that and I was like, "Yeah, that would help." I'll never forget the first FedEx envelope I ever got. I peeled it open, opened it up and there was a check made out to me, I never signed a contract or anything. It's like Eric James, ten thousand dollars. That was my first taste of a whole other world that I didn't know could exist.

John: Was that because of strategies you learned from Mara or a combination?

ZB: A combination, yeah, I think Mara's stuff worked. To a certain extent because of the way that stuff was taught. I couldn't keep up with what she was teaching because it takes you two, three times as long to implement what she can teach in an hour-long class. I was behind to a certain extent but I certainly think that I had now put myself out there, I had taken the leap, there was no looking back. I already jumped off the cliff. It was a matter of, "Okay, is the parachute going to open?" And that month it did. That 10k month where I could walk back in my system and see I did $10,000, I did five figures in one month. That's where I thought, "Alright, parachute open now. I can glide it down slowly." But I didn't sit back and coast like, "Okay, did it, I'm done, drop the mic, I'm out"

John: You didn't allow yourself to fall into the trap of thinking, "I've made it, done, locked in." Then you notice everything else starts to slip?

ZB: Yeah, I mean, for the months leading up to that there was a little $500 project here, little $300 project there, but then I get this huge $10,000 month. If the bar on the graph is not at the same height or close to it the next month you start to see that rollercoaster. I think the fear came back in at the end of the following month because I only did about 3000 that month.

John: The bar for you at that point we set at $10,000 a month?

ZB: Yeah, but then I realized it wasn't sustainable to do that, or I thought it wasn't sustainable to do that every month because the next month I did two or three grand. I' thought, "What's going to happen next month? $400? Where am I going to be?" It was not something where I sat back and let it coast, but at the same time, it hit me within the next thirty days that this was not the norm for every single month yet.

John: Right but it definitely gave you breathing room. So, then you're on that roller coaster, you start to come down the hill. Through all of this, did you ever think that you weren't cut out for being an entrepreneur.

ZB: There were definitely a couple of points where I didn't. At that time I was in a newer relationship, I was working all the time, this was not a 9:00 to 5:00 anymore. I mean, I was editing at two o'clock in the morning, sitting there on a Friday night researching when the next networking event is to put on my calendar.

John: Did you put relationships on pause, or did you not pursue relationships?

ZB: Oh, no, I very much pursued it. I don't know if it was the best decision, but I most certainly was pursuing a relationship.

John: Okay, so you were working like crazy and trying to maintain a relationship?

ZB: And stressing out that relationship because instead of going out on a Friday night and having fun, I had almost convinced myself that it would be more fun to work on the business on a Friday night. It wasn't fun, But it was more productive. I felt like I couldn't lose an hour of working on my business for anything else because the only thing that mattered was making sure that business was successful. I created this thought in my head, "If I put everything into this business and this business becomes successful, then I can take care of my girlfriend, I can build a family and everything else can fall into place because I'll be financially secure." I had a fear of money., I thought money would solve everything, money was all I needed in this world to get me to where I needed to go. This was a huge learning point as an entrepreneur. Towards the end of that year I started to not like money. I wanted to get away from it all. It was troublesome because here I am afraid to buy dinner for the girl I'm dating because it's money that I have to spend, when I could be sitting at home working on the business. Look, it's a Friday night, I'm probably sitting at home, watching Netflix but I was convincing myself that I would be more productive by not working on the relationship, that everything I had to do had to be solely based around the business. I was also getting to quite an interesting point in time because I fired my first client around then.

John: Fired your first client?

ZB: Fired a client. I won't name any names, but I had a client I was working with, who was very tough to work with. Look, some people clash, I get it, that's just how it is, but I did a few projects with them and ultimately I decided, in a very nice way, to say, "Look, we definitely have a difference of opinion and I don't think it's good for us to work together anymore."

John: Was that going to be a decent paycheck for you?

ZB: Absolutely. He never once questioned how much I was going to charge. I could double my prices overnight, he would have written the check.
John: And you were confident enough to walk away from that?

ZB: Well, it took a little bit. I had to think it through. I asked Mara's help, maybe one or two other people's opinions because I didn't know if I was making the right choice. I thought back to the Apple Store, maybe I just need to suck it up and keep going because it's going to be a nice paycheck.

John: Right. So, being an entrepreneur was clearly impacting your social life?

ZB: Yeah, but it went beyond telling friends that I couldn't go out. It went beyond not building up my relationship. My way of coping with things was going to the gym. When I got home from college, I joined a CrossFit gym. I was super into CrossFit, hardcore, eating paleo all the time, I loved going into the gym. To deal with the stress I would go to the gym at 9 o'clock at night, lift, blast some music, and have a good time. On top of my personal relationship suffering from everything going on, and me putting the business at the forefront, I was in the gym one night, and I got a call from my step mom. She said, "Where are you right now? I've got to come talk to you in person." I thought, "What is going on right now? Did somebody die?"

John: Right. You got to prepare yourself for something.

ZB: Yeah. She comes into the gym, she gives me a big hug and she says, "I want you to know that none of this was your fault, but your father and I are splitting up."

John: Oh, man.

ZB: Here I am, trying to start a successful business, looking for everyone in the world to support me, because I need anyone I can to say, "You can do this." And now, two parents are out of the equation because they've got their whole thing that they're dealing with now. Fortunately, it didn't affect me as much because I was out of college, already in the real world, but I had many younger brothers that were still very much affected by this. That gave me a clue as to why family, your personal life, and your relationships cannot fall to the backburner when you're an entrepreneur. There are certain things you can balance out, there are certain things you can push off to the side, but they always say, family first. This was the first time where I felt I needed to take a step back and look at what's happening for the people around me and not just at what's happening for me. I'd been so caught up in the business and in thinking "I'm an entrepreneur, I'm going to work every hour of the day, it's just me, this work and grind."

John: Grind, grind, grind.

ZB: Exactly. I was on the grind. This was the first time where it smacked me in the face that, "Hey, there's more to this than just you."

John: It's funny, five years ago I heard entrepreneurs say, "Grind, grind, grind." You're right, not going out on Friday night, not watching Netflix, just grinding until two in the morning, family secondary, health secondary. But now, I'm starting to hear that's not the correct way. Family first, health close second.

ZB: Right. You get moving thirty minutes, three days a week, you're fine. I'm not saying you've got to grind it out at the gym just as you've got to grind it out at work. There are certain things that you can let slip away temporarily, as long as you understand that this is giving you back that time that you absolutely must be productive within the business, in the relationship. That time that you're taking away from that investment in yourself and your own health, still has to go back and get reinvested in some other place, some other area of your life that still impacts your relationships and your health.

John: Right. So, your stepmother and your father divorced. Did you have to step in and play big brother more than you were doing before?

ZB: I actually chose to stay out of it. My dad married my stepmom when I was probably five. When I was eight or nine, he became an Orthodox Jew and since my bar mitzvah I had kind of been very far from that. At thirteen I moved in with my mom and my stepdad full-time and decided that that lifestyle wasn't for me. So, I had been out of that for seven or eight years. I wasn't really a member of that community anymore. I stopped by to see my brothers more often, partially because they got two dogs to help lessen the blow. The dogs were adorable, but I love spending time with my brothers. It's interesting looking back, I didn't spend that much time with them, but some of them I'm much closer with as they've gotten older. The age-range was nuts, the youngest one was sixteen, seventeen years younger than me, so it's not like we had much in common, we couldn't hold an intelligent conversation.

John: When you shift into your 20s and your 30s, that gap closes.

ZB: Yeah and I'm in this entrepreneurial mindset so yeah, I talk to the older ones about what I'm doing and one or two of them might be interested.

John: Do any of them have that entrepreneurial spirit that you've seen yet?

ZB: The two older ones are studying in a Shiva in Jerusalem, the middle one just started his freshman year at Drexel and he is the first of the kids that's going to a rather secular school. This was the first one going on my path. He started his own business by accident, staffing servers and waiters. All these people who had events, banquets, weddings, and bar mitzvahs always had meals afterwards with hundreds of attendees. He started this business where he built up his group of guys and he would staff these events and get paid in cash under the table, didn't have to pay taxes so he went to college.

John: Paid plenty of taxes, paid plenty of taxes.

ZB: He went to college with this experience of having started his first company in a sense. He didn't go through it building an LLC or anything the way I had, but he understood what it was like to manage and run a team, to show up on time and be professional, and to collect the money and to pay out your guys. He was the first of my siblings to get that experience of the realm that I was in.

John: Where did he learn those tools?

ZB: It's funny, it could be DNA. My dad's a chiropractor, works for himself, started his own practice. Before that, his father was jeweler and worked for himself, so I mean, it's possible but I think it was something where, by accident, he stumbled upon this opportunity and was aware enough to say, "Well, I can take this further."

John: So, you're through the first year, where'd you go from there? You're into your second year, what's going on?

ZB: This is where I started to get a little uneasy. I had finished up this coaching program, I'd paid back the $11,000, I built a business. I was on track to make 30 grand for the year. I was on track to replace everything I had made at the Apple Store, which is great. A year out, things had changed, I had proof that I can do this. But the interesting thing was, the honeymoon phase was starting to wear off. I got to this point, you know, the end of summer, starting to get cooler, that sort of winter blues started to fall into place.

Then I get this call out of the blue from two people that I went to school with. We weren't really friends in school, we just kind of knew of each other.

John: James Madison?

ZB: Yeah. So, two acquaintances that I had met in school reached out and wanted to connect with someone else in the industry and in the area and they told me, they had gone on a retreat. They found out about this group of people that were tired of where they were in life and truly wanted to move forward, not in this slow and steady wins the race kind of way. We wanted a drastic transformation.

John: Jump start.

ZB: They told me more about what it was about, where they were before they went on the trip and I thought, "This sounds like where I'm at right now." I felt purposeless, I did the business, I made it successful. Now what? What do I do next? Do I have to do this for the next forty years? Is it going to be the same thing all over again? I almost lost my meaning because I had achieved the goal that I set out to do and now I felt like there was nothing left. I mean, there was, don't get me wrong but I couldn't see it at that point in time. You set the bar to a certain point, what happens when you hit the bar? The bar continues to move up. Now you've got to hit this higher bar. For me, I'd set the bar and then it never went any higher.

So, I decided I needed to apply for this retreat. It was called the Higher Purpose Project, and it's run by some fantastic people. I scrounged up the money between asking my mom to throw an early birthday present, and my grandparents for some help financially. We spent four days up in Boston, they rented out this campground in the middle of the Berkshires, and it's just gorgeous. I mean, we're living in these junky bunk beds that they use for a summer camp, but it's in this cabin house with a den area and couches. We had fresh cooked organic meals in the cafeteria, and then there's this gorgeous lake. It's a mile-wide lake and there's a dock where you can take out stand-up paddle boards.

John: What was the group size?

ZB: It was probably twentyish people, maybe twenty-five.

John: It's not too many.

ZB: No, it wasn't that big. It was just the right amount where I could truly connect and get to meet every single person there. I felt it from the second I had watched their promo video, before I'd even signed up. They use a song by Einaudi called Divenire. Many people have probably heard this in other places, but for whatever reason an emotion was evoked within me. Before I was even done with the video, I knew I had to go. I flew into Boston and met a woman named Jeanine, who's now a great friend of mine. She was hanging out at the airport. Slowly, one by one, everybody files in and we get to meet each other, take the bus ride up to the location. I can't describe with words the vibe that was going on at the time. I met this guy Kyle on the bus who quickly turned into my long-lost brother in another life. He's a videographer, too. We were like the same person. I can't describe in words what I was feeling at that time other than I knew that if I didn't open up right away and share everything about what I was feeling and who I was and what I was about, I would not get everything out of this. I had to lay it out on the table. I was telling people about my struggle with my suicidal thoughts and depression as a teenager. Over this two-hour bus ride to where we were going, my whole life story was out on the table. It was just, "here's who I am, take it or leave it, but this is who I am in my full essence, a hundred percent of my being and I'm going to see how you guys respond."

John: How quickly did you come to find similar stories from everyone else?

ZB: Immediately. The second I started sharing certain aspects of my life, everything from divorced parents, to depression as a teenager, to suicidal thoughts, to attempting to take your life, everybody has gone through it. It was so wild to me because at the time, you feel like you're the only one, this is only happening to you. Here you are on a bus with twenty other people that are so much more similar than you thought. They created a safe environment where we were all able to open up. It was everything from doing sunrise yoga on the docks of the lake, to organic lunches, to treating your body holistically, Just really opening up your awareness to what you're fully capable of. I came back from that weekend knowing that my life had changed forever. It would never be the same. I would not be the same person who was on that plane going up to Boston.

John: Did you have a better idea of how you were going to grow your business because of the Higher Purpose Project?

ZB: I don't think I knew how I was going to grow the business, but it was more of a personal development thing. I remember , as I walked through the security line in the airport when I left this trip, it was like in Scrubs or those TV shows where you see the person is stationary and everyone's moving so quickly around them. I was almost scared to go back to the real world. The last thing we did was visit Walden Pond, where Henry David Thoreau wrote Walden. It was all about going to the wilderness to live a lifestyle that was so much simpler. He went off script and wanted this simple life that nobody else wanted. So, I'm back in this world where everyone's on their phone, in a rush, trying to get places in the airport and I thought, "I'm not the same person going home right now, I am a completely different person, everything is different from here on out." Sitting on the plane on the way home, I knew that every decision I made from there on out was going to be different. The one thing that I learned while I was on that trip was I had to go to California.

John: So you finally went to California?

ZB: I did. I made the decision. I was mid conversation with somebody, hiking up a mountain one day, and out of nowhere I said, "I need to go to California." We were talking about something else entirely and they said, "What are you talking about?"

We were having a conversation the day before asking the question, "What's the one thing that you're not doing that you need to do right now? Was there something in your gut that you felt you had to do?" It didn't hit me until the next day when we were climbing the mountain. The one thing I always said I was going to do was go to California, I never knew the goal or why I was going out there, but I knew that just the act of putting myself out there would change in my life.

I was teaching myself travel hacking by reading blogs on Reddit, watching YouTube videos and learned that if I took out some credit cards, hit some spending bonuses real quick, I'd have hundreds of thousands of sky miles and I could go for free. I bought a ticket from Baltimore to Denver with two of my friends I had made from that trip. From Denver, I went to Boulder, I visited my big brother from the fraternity when I was in college. Then flew from Denver to San Francisco. The best part about it was, one of my friends who was on the trip, who was also on this journey of self-discovery, decided that he wanted to go to San Francisco to hang out for the week. We got to explore San Francisco, visited a fraternity brother at Facebook headquarters, got to see Mark Zuckerberg in his office. The whole trip was wild, rented a car, drove highway 1, did everything. Left San Francisco, my friend went back home, I went to LA and then I went from LA to Dallas, and then Dallas back home over the course of a month. There was never really a deadline of when I was going to come home, it was just whenever I felt it was right to go home, I was going to do it.

John: You put the business on pause?

ZB: Yeah and the crazy part is when I bought that plane ticket, that voice came in the back of my head saying, "You're screwing this up." That same voice that had said, "Why did you invest $11,000 in a coach?" came back and said, "You're about to mess this up again, you're about to throw everything away that you worked so hard for. What are you doing?" It was that inner monologue that was playing devil's advocate. I ignored it and said, "You know what, I need to figure this out." I talked to my dad about it a little bit and he said, "You know what, what's the worst that can happen?" It's a little cliché because a lot of people say that.

John: But it's true.

ZB: He brought the point to mind that this is the only time in my life when I don't have a wife, I don't have kids, I don't have anything holding me back. This is the one time I could screw up massively and have forty more years to come back from it. I can't do that when I have a wife or kids or a house or anything. That's when I knew that was my confirmation. That was the first time a family member said, "This is exactly where you need to be and what you need to do," and supported it.

John: That must have been an amazing feeling.

ZB: It was a pretty big eye-opener. I got the travel bug. On my trip I had my laptop with me, I had my phone. I was answering incoming client emails. I booked six thousand dollars' worth of work from the road in advance and realized I could do it in four weeks. I got home and thought, "Wait a second, I made $6,000 and I wasn't even here," That's where my circle of awareness grew bigger. Christmas was rolling around, I was single, over that summer I had broken up the relationship. I'm single, my roommate, who's my cousin, is single. We're looking for something fun to do, what do two single guys do on Christmas Eve? Naturally, they go get Chinese food; but I convinced him to go get Chinese food and continue on to a 3,000-mile road trip. Because of the amount of days between Christmas and January 1, he could take off one or two days of work for that whole time span. We left on Christmas Eve, we got Chinese food, we drove up to Pittsburgh that night. I used some rewards points to buy a hotel room and that was the last hotel room we stayed in for the rest of that trip. Got to give a shout out to Suzanne Shafer here and the family because Suzanne and her husband had an automotive company that had been learning from the marketing company that I was originally employed by, fresh out of college. I met them at conferences, I was friends with them.

John: Coming full circle.

ZB: Yeah, so we're driving through Minneapolis and I put a feeler out on Facebook, "Do I know anyone in Indy who can give us a couch to crash on tonight?" Next thing you know, she's making us dinner, we're hanging out with her kids, we're watching a movie. It was awesome. She kicked her daughter out of her own room for the night so we could have a bed to sleep in. Suzanne, I'm sorry you had to do that but thanks. Got to give you some credit there, you guys were awesome. I can't think of a more generous family, who took us in with open arms and was said, "This is amazing what you guys are doing, what can we do to help you?"
John: Where'd you go from Indiana?

ZB: So, Indiana, we started to loop down, so we went out through Ohio and Indianapolis and then we looped down through Louisville, Nashville and then to Atlanta, all the way down to Jacksonville, Florida. We stayed in Louisville with a fraternity brother, we just passed through Nashville. We made it all the way to Atlanta and we stayed at an Airbnb, which was a unique experience. We got there late at night and we got hit on by the male Airbnb hosts who took us out for barbecue and then invited us to his hot tub later that night. Yeah, we didn't partake, but, you know, adventures in the life of Zephan. It's all another piece of the journey.

John: Airbnb was probably a new concept at that time?

ZB: It was brand new and I was all about it because I signed up and got a $25 off code or something. We wound up in an Airbnb after that in Jacksonville, Florida. This was our halfway point. We wanted to take a break from driving. We spent two days there at a small apartment on the beach, we walked ten miles on the beach, 90 degrees outside, we had been in rainy Pittsburgh a few days prior and we were loving it being on the beach, enjoying everything, the food, being in the sun, just being there.

John: Did you ever think, "I would love to move to Jacksonville at this point? It's got a great vibe," or whatever.

ZB: We didn't get to see much of the city because we stayed on the beach and the restaurants, but we were so excited that in the middle of winter in Baltimore, 20 degrees outside back home, we're laying out on the beach. This was where we started to realize that the world is very small place. We were hanging out at night with our Airbnb host and she told us she had a friend coming over to have some drinks and hang out. We're like, cool, we'd love to meet more people, we were going along with the adventure and wherever it took us. We're hanging out that night, just talking and this girl asked where we were from. We said from Maryland. She asked what part. I said Baltimore. She said, "What part of Baltimore?" I told her I'm from Pikesville and she says, "Oh, no way, my boyfriend went to Boys' Latin High School." That's a private school, ten minutes down the street. We're in Florida, a stranger's house that we met on Airbnb, her friend happened to come over and she knows the neighborhood that we live in. She knew the street name, she knew the bagel place up the street.

John: Alright, so, you went on a four-day trip with the Higher Purpose Project and this led to a journey across the US. How do other people do this? Because this sounds awesome.

ZB: I feel like this is the unanswerable question.

John: I need an answer.

ZB: This is the place that so many people get stuck in and everyone seems to have one way or the other for looking at it. So, I've got to start off by sharing a quick quote from an interview that I had with David Mead on my podcast, who's a member of Simon Sinek's team.

David Mead: "Couple other things that I can throw in there just as a couple of tips is every decision that you make will either get you closer to your *why* or farther away from it. When you're going to make a career decision or when you're going to make a decision to hire somebody or you're going to make a decision to partner with somebody, always go back to your *why* and use it as a filter and ask yourself the question is, this decision going to get me one step closer to the world I imagine or one step farther away from it. Start using your *why* as a filter for every decision that you make."

ZB: If there was a formula, I'd give it to you but everyone's journey is going to be different. I want to jump over and share a little bit of insight from John Lee Dumas. He's on the Entrepreneur on Fire podcast and here's a little tidbit from my interview with him.

John Lee Dumas: "It's a very long, it's a very hard journey. I like to equate it to a marathon, not a sprint. That's what we're on right now, we're on a marathon and that's good because there's a quote that I love that's by Earl Nightingale which is, 'Success and happiness is a gradual realization of a worthy ideal.' Having this goal that's here and then reaching it, that's good but that's not going to be sustained happiness, because now okay, what's next? Having this gradual realization of a worthy ideal over this marathon of life, that's what excites me."

John: Alright, so I can see where this is tough. Some people are implying that's a part of this journey that you take, right? You spend time trying to figure, you spend time trying out things and seeing what sticks, and staying with your happy place, so to speak. But even David said, "Start to ask yourself the question, 'is this decision going to get me one step closer to the world that I imagine or one step farther away from it.'" How do you go about defining that world and that mental space that you want to live in?

ZB: This is a great question and it's what my book, *Life Re-Scripted*, covers. I take you through some of the story of how I decided to rescript my own life, because a big part of this adventure, and this travel hacking, and working my way around the world, we could probably pull some lessons out of. Just sharing this new reality that I created for myself and designing your future through your story.

Before this trip happened, I took those twelve steps again that I used to build the business and thought, "I know I need to get to California where do these steps break down in between?" I didn't necessarily have the money to spend. I was still strapped for cash, even though the business was doing okay. I thought I could fail, I could put the business on hold and the business could be gone. If I left for a month it would be gone. I had to figure out some way of doing this. I started researching online, I heard this idea of travel hacking, and how people use credit cards to hit the bonus bends where they would spend 3,000 bucks in the first three months and they get like 100,000 SkyMiles. Having a relatively decent credit score, I took out, four or five cards, and there I was with four or five hundred thousand SkyMiles because I found ways to spend the money on the credit card to hit that spending bonus. I would put it onto a Visa gift card and then use the Visa gift card to pay off the bill of the credit card. Now, this was much easier at the time, the rules have changed, but it was super easy for me to rack up a couple hundred thousand SkyMiles in a few weeks. My new reality was writing itself because I took those twelve steps. I said, "Here I am, here at the bottom, at the zero and the 30,000 at the top is me in California or on a plane to California. How do I get there?" It meant, "Let's find a way to do it that didn't mean going online and booking the ticket right now. Let's figure out creatively how we can do this in a different way and look at it through a different lens." I read an article, started researching it, then broke it down: step one, got to take out a credit card, step two, got to do this step three, got to spend money on the card, step four, you get the bonus points when you hit that spending limit. I broke it back down to those twelve steps and that led me through that trip for roughly a month around the country. We were down in Florida and Jacksonville, then worked our way back up through Charleston, North Carolina, stayed in another Airbnb while we were there. Then stayed with my college roommate in Virginia Beach on New Year's Eve.

John: Awesome, love it. You're a videographer, right? Was there any thought your mind to make this into a movie? Did that happen?

ZB: I bought a GoPro and a little gimbal stabilizer and I have video footage outside of the Colts stadium. My cousin Dan is failing to do the limbo underneath one of those parking guard things that closes the parking garage. Then we're running up the stairs in front of the stadium. We have some footage of the trip, it's not super high quality or anything but I feel like that need to document this trip was definitely underneath of it all. I wanted to show people what can happen when you let go and just go for it. It certainly was there

We spent New Year's Eve in Virginia Beach, we bought some illegal fireworks in Louisville that were still in the trunk. So we decided at 11 o'clock at night on New Year's Eve to drive out to the middle of nowhere and blow up all these fireworks. We wound up getting the car stuck in a muddy ditch. So, it's two o'clock in the morning and AAA is towing us out of some muddy ditch in the middle of nowhere. The next morning, it was in our plan to drive home. It was New Year's Day, my cousin had to get back to work and we decided the trip had run its course.

We get home and the first thing in my mind is "Back to civilization, let's jump on Facebook, let's see where people were at, what's going on. "At the top of the newsfeed, someone who I'm connected with shared an article that said, "2015 to be a year of purpose for many people." I saw this article, and had no idea what was going to happen next.

John: Did you have any negative talk, self-limiting talk in your head at this point or was that all eradicated?

ZB: I certainly came back to that place, "You've been on the road, you're wasting your business away, you're not being productive, you're not working on it," But it wasn't as strong as before. I had the realization that I was on the road and built six thousand dollars in a month. I knew it wasn't impossible, but it definitely wasn't the same being gone that time. I didn't make the same amount of money, but I was only gone for 10 days or something.

John: Let's shift into the podcast.

ZB: I saw this article and something clicked. I had been in the self-improvement mode for the last year. I was listening to two podcasts in particular. Brendon Burchard, *Live, Love, Matter* and *The Art of Charm*, because I was single, I wanted to learn how to find a relationship. On my nights recovering from coming home from the gym I'd have an Epsom salt bath and tune into a 30-minute episode of *Art of Charm*. Jordan Harbinger was the soundtrack of my workout recovery. I thought it would be cool to start a podcast. It wasn't a hundred percent, I got back and hung on those words, "Year of Purpose." I related so much to it for the next couple days. I started to think, "How cool would it be if I did a podcast? What would I do a podcast on?" Then the words came back to me, "Year of Purpose Podcast," Why not? This has been my journey the last two or three months, I want to find my purpose. I want to know why I'm here and how I'm going to make my impact on the world. If you look at *How to Win Friends and Influence People* and all these books, Napoleon Hill, all these people, they surrounded themselves with, interviewed, and learned from other people. It made sense, "Let's go and find people that are creating life on their own terms, doing exactly what they want to do, that love every day of it, interview them to find out how they got there." The first person I ever interviewed was Adam Smiley Poswolsky. He authored a book called *The Quarter-Life Breakthrough*. He's only a couple years older than me, and congrats to him. He just launched his book because Penguin picked it up and he republished it. So, he self-published first and then he republished it and it's growing like wildfire now.

John: I read it, I loved it.

ZB: That was a huge piece of taking that leap. I met him when I was in San Francisco so I felt it was only natural to ask him to be the first podcast interview.

John: How much prep work did you put in to forming the podcast idea before you reached out to him?

ZB: About two weeks. The idea came January first.

John: You execute quick.

ZB: Oh, yeah. I jumped on it, I was reading for hours and hours every day. What mic do I need to use? How do I record this interview? What software do I need? Where do I upload this? I learned everything. It goes back to that twelve-step formula, here's your zero, here's your 30,000, figure out what's in between. If those twelve steps aren't broken down enough, break it down again. 2,500 bucks a month wasn't enough for me, so I had to break it down to a day-to-day basis. Same thing goes for all this stuff. I can't tell you that I knew what those twelve steps were, but I knew how to find out. You can learn how to tie a tie on YouTube, we're in a place where there's no excuse for not learning something.

John: Okay, so you're getting a podcast off the ground. No more excuses, it's go time.

At this point you've just started your Year of Purpose, so what were your thoughts at the time of death, legacy, and what we're going to leave behind?

ZB: It was definitely a scary thought to me. I started to think more about how we love to have control, we love to be able to control our destiny, our faith, everything that's going on. But truthfully there's nothing stopping me from being in a car accident on the way home. We don't have control over how long we're here. The lucky ones live to 90 or 100 and live out a fantastic life, but there's so many people that aren't that lucky. As I talked to others, my awareness bubble is increased even more, I was introduced to people from around the world that took life by the horns. I started to notice a pattern. Every single one of these people wanted to leave something behind, but also wanted to know that if this were their last day, they would be satisfied with where they were at. That their family would honor what they did and how hard they worked. I wanted to emulate that.

So, I started interviewing people. Sometimes twice a week. I released episodes. I hired a booking service to book people on my podcast and hook me up with people that I might not otherwise be able to get in touch with. The podcast quickly grew, that spring into summer I decided to go to the podcast movement conference in Dallas-Fort Worth. I got to stay at my friend Judy's house. It's great when you have a friend you can stay with, not have to pay for a hotel. Of course, huge shout out to Judy. I learned about podcasts and met everyone in the hallways, and next thing you know Pat Flynn is calling me out from the crowd in his keynote speech in front of 1,100 people.

John: What did that feel like?

ZB: I would never even Pat Flynn, because I want to hear every word he's saying, but for some reason, at this point in his talk, I was looking at my phone. I get a text from my buddy John and it says, "Dude, look up, you're on the screen." I look up and it's a picture of me and Pat on the screen. He's talking about me and sharing my story of how I wrote to him when I lost my job at GKIC, and told him about taking a leap of faith and starting my own business. Too many feelings to even explain what I was feeling at the time. It's so unbelievable what happens when you truthfully open up and share your story with someone that inspired you, and you thank them or tell them the impact that they had on you. That's why they're doing it. He wants to impact the lives of many people. To share that with him and not be another face in the crowd, it was a fantastic experience. I was on my way out of the hotel that day, getting ready to head back when someone drags me to the side and tells me they're doing a smart passive income meet up at this bar. The second I walk in the door, Pat walks in behind me and goes, "Hey, man, I'm sorry I didn't warn you I was going to call you out from the audience like that, I'm really sorry. I hope it's okay." and I'm like "Okay? It's more than okay! I had no clue you were going to do that. That was fantastic." Everyone was coming up to me for the rest of the conference saying, "You're that guy!" That was never my intention. I wanted to network and meet tons of people, but he knew what he was doing, he knew that that would change the plot for the story of my life.

John: How many episodes into the podcast were you at this point?

ZB: If the podcast started in January, I was probably 30 or 40 episodes. It was about a third of the way.

John: Right, it wasn't right off the bat, you weren't two, three, four episodes in.

ZB: No, this was not brand-new. He invited me to be a guest on his show many months later, but that day, he said, "Hey, here's my card send me an email, let's get you on the show." I couldn't imagine what was going to happen after that point. The year was fantastic, I interviewed a guy by the name of Chandler Bolt, who taught a self-publishing school. He teaches people how to become best-selling authors. When I interviewed him on the episode, I thought "I'd like to be a best-selling author, write a book, you never know what can happen with it." It was an idea in my mind in April or May, but over the summer I joined his program. I started writing the book throughout that year and by November-ish of that year, Life Re-Scripted was done. I had a printed copy in hand and was planning out my book launch party.

John: Executed quick again.

ZB: It was a wild year to go from New Year's Day, coming home from a wild road trip, still had no idea where my business was going, starting this passion project on the side which is the podcast, to halfway through the year writing a book. I was diagnosed with a learning disability in school, I could read the whole book and not remember any of it. I'm not the next greatest writer but the fact that I completed it, that I just did it, was a real accomplishment for me. It's not perfect, I know it's probably got a couple spelling errors but I don't care because I did it. It was the fact that I brought myself out of bed every morning and took myself to the computer to write and to do it.

John: I've talked to a lot of creatives who come from a linear career path, and jump and follow their heart. At any point with any of these endeavors, it sounds like you never had this, "I'm faking," feeling. It sounds like you got the idea, you executed, then you by surrounded yourself with people that were strong believers in what you were doing, learned how to do it and bam, done. I meet a lot of people who begin something and they think, for example, "I'm not the guy that does podcasts." But they're doing it. Did you ever feel like that along the way?

ZB: It hit me when I "made it." After the book was done and hit bestseller, the podcast had been out for a year, and my business was successful. It wasn't until I checked off all the boxes that I thought, "Who am I to get the credit for accomplishing this? Who am I to speak to the thousands of people that listen to the podcast and be that role model for them?" It's odd that it hit me at that point. Most people would hit it along the way up, for some reason I tuned it out, It wasn't in my mind. Certainly after I accomplished many of those things it hit me.

John: After you have achieved all this?

ZB: After I achieved it. It wasn't fake. I sat there and wrote that book, it's not like someone else wrote it, it's not like it was copied from anywhere. I made it.

John: It's funny that you would feel like that with the proof in your hand.

ZB: Yeah. Partially because I had an audience now. I had people that depended on me, looked to me for answers, looked to me to give them input, feedback, and to be the role model. I'm in my 20s, it's not like I've lived this long life of screw-ups, mistakes and successes. Who am I to be this young guy to set the example for people that might be even older than me?

John: Why not?

ZB: That's probably why I'm still going.

John: From everything you just told me, life got super busy for you. ZMB, podcast, beginning to write Life Re-Scripted, successful business. Your relationships were on fire at this point, professional and personal?

ZB: I was still single. I was single for the longest span of time.

John: Were you dating, retesting the waters at that point?

ZB: It wasn't even a thought in my mind. I was so focused on the business and self-improvement, so I put it off for a year or two.

John: How do you balance everything? There's got to be a breaking point, right?

ZB: You don't sleep. No, I think that that whole trip with Higher Purpose, and then that whole trip that I had built for myself had me so on fire that I felt untouchable. I was in the best shape of my life, I felt good. I woke up in the morning ready to go, I think it's because I'd ignited that passion side of things. I was so focused on the business for so long, but I never had that thing that kept me going outside of that. When the laptop shut for the day, it was like there was nothing left. But now with the podcast, I had this renewed sense that there was something there for me outside of the work. I could impact even more people than the one client who's hired me. In 2013, I had to replace $15,000 just to get by, to hit that $30,000 goal for the year. 2014, I doubled that, I made $30,000 for the year. 2015, I doubled that again, I made $60,000. Here I am in 2016, on track to make a lot more than I made last year. I was on fire from the productivity standpoint, but I think part of it was that I had made a sacrifice in not being interested in a relationship. My friendships were great, I relied on them for so long to help me get by because my friends loved to see me succeed. I was running off of that fuel, but it certainly got to a point where I discovered that entrepreneurship can be a very lonely thing.

I discovered that when I met someone by the name of Simon Smart. I interviewed him on a virtual summit, we interviewed forty-one or forty-two people over a summer and launched it to bring people in, to get to know more about me, my story and everyone that I was interviewing in the podcast. Simon talked about going into a warrior's mindset of thinking, and having a sound samurai style mindset. After that interview, he said, "I don't know how we're going to work together but I can tell you, I can feel it, at some point in the future, you and I are going to link up." At the end of 2015 he reached out again. I got on a call and he listened to everything going on in my life for forty minutes straight, just me puking everything out. As much as the success was good and the highs were high, the lows were low. He picked up on things that I was avoiding, and called them out.

He invited me to come out to a transformative experience in Arizona with him and a couple other guys. I thought, "I did something like this before when I did the Higher Purpose trip, that was a year ago." That was right around when I hired my coach. I hadn't had a coach in a year and I was starting to feel a little lost. I thought, "I'm probably overdue for a nice kick in the butt." I went out to Arizona for Warrior Protocol Training and I'll never forget it. I don't want to share the whole experience with everyone, this is definitely one of those experiences where you have a better experience by keeping it as a part of you and not telling everyone the full story. There was a part where I jumped in a boxing ring. I was put into a match with one of the guys that was in our group. I went for a round, got hit a couple times, it hurt, I did okay. In the second round, I was battling mentally some things of my past from a long time ago, and it was coming out. I was holding back from sharing it with them. The second I let my guard down, I got knocked out, hit square in the face, fell down to the floor and everything went fuzzy for a little bit. I came to and got up, and I literally felt like that negative self-talk, that negative emotion, those things that had been still eating me up inside for so long, were knocked out of me. When you ask "Did you feel like you were a fake?" Part of that comes from that negative voice, those things that eat you up, those pieces that show you that you're not perfect. I felt like that was knocked out of me that night. I'm not telling people to go jump in a boxing ring and get punched in the face.

John: We should note you were also fighting.

ZB: Right, but I think it's important to mention how transformative experiences can be when you take on a coach, when you take a risk, when you trust in others who have been there, done that and who can show you or open a door to the next place that you're going to go to. There's no way for us to know where we're going. Unless you're on a roller coaster, it stays on the track. You know exactly where it goes, it goes up, it goes down, it goes around, it comes back into the station exactly where you started. But, life is not like that. There are twists and turns, ups, and downs, but life never comes back to the same exact place you started. You will never come back the same person. Maybe if you throw up on the roller coaster you don't come back the same person, but let's hope that doesn't happen. You need to know when you need to bring on a mentor, when you need to open up to a group of like-minded individuals, when you should go on these retreats or take on these coaches. I don't think I would be where I am had it not been for taking that risk and trusting other people to help me along the way.

John: Here's some insight from your interview with Jordan Harbinger.

Jordan Harbinger: "That stuff piles up. If you don't have the help you need and you don't have your own time scheduled out, you will run into these weird blocks and you won't know what caused it or you'll go, well, it was this and then I scheduled my email and then this call ran late and then dot, dot, dot, my whole day is ruined."

ZB: That's one of the first podcasts I started listening to when I was getting in shape, working out in the gym maybe three to five days a week. My trainer and roommate Jeff was getting me into strongman lifting. We'd been following this guy John Anderson, he teaches a deep water method for working out. All I can say is it left you in so much pain each night. Each night, as I was saying before, I would soak in those Epsom salt baths, and tune into *Art to Charm*. This is before I had a relationship. So, I'm interested in learning how to be a better guy, how to attract love and ultimately live a good life.

John: It's one crazy journey I tell you. Let me bring Mitch Matthews of Dream, Think, Do. Here's one thing he said.

Mitch Matthews: "I've had some peaks and valleys, so I've had what I called bridge jobs which are those jobs that get you from one place to the next but like a bridge, you wouldn't want to live there, you can appreciate a bridge for what it is but it's not a home. I've had some bridge jobs and when you're in those bridge jobs, you want to focus on what you can learn, what you can earn and who you can meet, all of those things."

John: Was this Year of Purpose idea of a forever thing? Much like what Mitch said, you don't want to live there but you appreciate the bridge that gets you to the next place. What came next? I mean, how did 2016 play out for you?

ZB: At the end of 2015, Christmas Eve, seems to be a turning point for me. That's when we left on our trip the year prior. Christmas Eve I was able to meet someone and start a new relationship. Going into the new year, I was stronger than I had ever been. I put so much work into developing myself to the point I was now open to a relationship. I knew that the business was strong, the podcast was strong, I was passionate about everything. The book was getting ready to launch the first week of 2016. 2016 started off in a huge way. I was in a relationship, I was a best-selling author, business was moving along, I didn't have to worry so much about where money was coming from, checks were coming in. I got offered an opportunity in spring to staff a group trip. I'd been volunteering for five years with BBYO, B'nai B'rith Youth Organization. I was interested in doing more and they told me they had a summer program where, all expenses paid, they could send me to Europe with a bunch of kids to travel around and see the sights, learn about my Jewish heritage and history. It was fantastic. We went from middle of June to the end of July. it was a crazy 28-day long trip. We started in Italy, went to Vatican City, then to Slovenia. Then from Italy we flew to London for a week. Then We took an overnight ferry boat, cruise ship from London to France, and then from France we traveled we went to Bruges. We wound up and Amsterdam before we headed home. It was another crazy journey of taking a whole month off, putting the business on hold.

John: Much like the California trip, right?

ZB: But it was the first time where that voice never came in saying, "Hey, dude, you're messing up again, you're choosing to put the business on hold, why are you doing this?" It was gone now. I'd learned from so many people that I'd interviewed and met that you have to live your life, you have to do what you want to do. The crazy part was, I was in a hotel in Paris answering emails on my iPad and I closed a $12,000 project, from 3,000 miles away. I used that same strategy that I learned, just say it, "Look, I'm in France right now, I'll be home in a few weeks. So, if you're cool if we don't start tonight, then we'll be good." It was insane to realize that no longer was it five or six thousand dollars booked while I'm gone, but now double that, and minus the fear of messing up. When I let go of the fear and went for it, the world opened up and said, "Alright, what do you need? We'll give it to you." It was totally insane to see that happen, being in a successful business, building the largest income I'd ever had while being on the road and enjoying every piece of life.

John: So, you're able to travel the world on someone else's dime, build your business even further, and run the podcast from thousands of miles away. What happened with the Year of Purpose community for you this year 2016 that differs from last year?

ZB: Well, we published *Life Re-Scripted*, we launched it in January of 2016 to great success, 4,000 copies were sold to people from New York to Scotland. Through the summer while I was working with my intern Alex, we conceived, designed and developed an adult coloring book series, a gratitude journal hybrid book, and we published three volumes of it. We bootstrapped, we outsourced. Using all the methods I learned from Tim Ferriss' 4-Hour Workweek, in a couple of months' time we created three new books that launched on Amazon, all while I'm on the other side of the planet. Things changed drastically.

John: So it sounds like you didn't run into failure too often here, but I don't want to focus on just the positives here. We have to share what goes on inside your head, I mean, it wasn't perfect, right?

ZB: Oh, it certainly wasn't. Take Facebook, for example, People think that likes equate to happiness, I did this thing and took a picture of myself on this wild adventure and 100 people liked it, therefore, I'm being rewarded for show. This happens every day. Facebook was never meant for you to one-up people, it was to connect and to share. I want to jump into some of my darkest moments, but before I do, here's a quick sound bite from JLD from EO Fire again.

JLD: "Failure's part of the game. Failure's there every step of the way and that's okay as long as you're learning from those failures."

ZB: So, you see, failure's a big part of it. It's more that we don't like to talk about it, right? We only hear about it once in a blue moon. Let me take you back to a dark time in my life. It's something that still peaks out and haunts me, mostly in the winter months. It sits on my shoulder and attempts to convince me that I'm a failure.

Entrepreneurship can be a very lonely place, but the space between our ears is even lonelier. When I was in eighth grade, I was diagnosed, or labeled, with bipolar manic depression. I was thirteen, coming up on my bar mitzvah, dad's Orthodox, mom is switching houses every single day, switching religions practically every eight hours. It had a huge impact on me. It was also the first time that I experienced death. One of our classmates had taken his own life, so on Thanksgiving morning I was told that he had taken his own life. That weekend, as I went up to New Jersey to visit my grandparents with my dad and the family. I was a drummer, and I wanted to get back for this Battle of the Bands, I was supposed to play with my buddy Ari, we had a band, we were going to play, it was my dream goal. But because my family observed the Sabbath, we couldn't drive a car until the sun was down on Saturday. We wound up missing this Battle of The Bands that to a 13-year old is the most heartbreaking thing in the world. Then you come back to school on Monday, your classmate's committed suicide and within the next couple of days, someone who had just had dinner at our house, was in a car accident. He wasn't wearing a seat belt, he went straight through the windshield and was gone. He was my age.

John: It affected you, right.

ZB: I learned in eighth grade, you are not permanent. I had no clue what I was doing with myself, why I was here, and I wanted to find that meaning. So that's where the quest for meaning came out from. I rolled into a depression, and I stopped going to my classes, I would skip out and go to the nurse's office. I would have anxiety attacks and I couldn't breathe. I was eventually bed-ridden, they had me on all these antidepressants and anti-anxiety meds that I was just a zombie. I could get up and go to the bathroom and go to the fridge and that was about it. I felt so completely useless. We tried the homeschooling thing, and for some reason they let me graduate the eighth grade and move up to high school. I don't know how because I wasn't doing the work. I think they saw that through some medication and going to the therapist, things started to turn. After a few months of being in bed and being drugged up, I woke up one morning and I walked to the kitchen where my pills were sitting on the counter, as they always were, and I was like, I got to do something. I had one small tiny moment of clarity where I thought, "If I don't change right here, right now, I'm going to die. If I don't do something, I will find a way to take my own life." I took the pills and made them disappear. I stopped cold turkey which I don't recommend to anyone.

John: Yeah, it's rough.

ZB: This is a rare case where I chose to do that. For the next week, Mom would leave for work, I would sit on the kitchen floor with a butcher knife, bawling my eyes out, thinking, "Am I going to do this? Is this it? Am I really here and this is what I'm going to do? I had that battle in my head. I know there's more than this, but the knife's in my hands. I'm here at this moment, this pivotal moment, people were dying around me, life's not permanent, why should I keep going? Learning about death at such a young age, it's scary. As you're older, you don't think about it, it's a natural part of life. It happens and you come to accept it. But at thirteen my thinking was like, "That's going to suck to die and not be here and not be breathing." You almost think it's going to be painful to not exist. I wanted to die. I felt like the better thing to do would have been to get it done with already. But for some reason, I felt like I had the power in my mind to lift me out of that. I have to bring up Chanel again from How Far From Home, because she said:

Chanel: "Our rule is if it enhances your experiences, then it's worth it. Everything else you don't need."

John: How do we create this change in our own lives?

ZB: That's a really good question.

James Lawrence: "I don't think we wake up one day and go boom, I'm going to do something extraordinary. I think extraordinary happens organically and over time. I think people rush to the extraordinary and they don't enjoy all of the milestones and landmarks along the way."

Michael: "… in a lot of situations where I was able to strengthen my mental fortitude and get stronger as a person and individual and as an athlete. Then, every one of those experiences and hard things that I experienced would add to it and then at a certain point in time I was ready to do it. So, absolutely, there's no goal that's not attainable. What people need to realize is you have to have the appropriate timeframe associated with such big goals and you have to be willing to do the right things consistently over a long period of time."

- "To me, life is school, we're here to grow a soul and nothing should get in a way of maximizing our potential as much as we can."

John: That first piece was by James Lawrence, the Iron Cowboy. You interviewed him on the show right after he broke the Guinness world record and completed 50 Ironman races in 50 consecutive days, in 50 different states. For those who don't know, the Ironman race is a 2.4 mile swim, 112 mile bike ride and a 26.2 mile run. Then, the second part came from Michael, who was a correspondent for Outdoor Life TV and has visited over thirty countries, published numerous books and even shared a story on your podcast about his encounter with a bear and living dateless on an island away from civilization for quite some time. Tell me, you've met so many inspirational and motivational people, Zephan, how have you changed?

ZB: I've changed in every way imaginable. I mean, A) I want to be here. I want to live out every experience to the fullest. I'm not that person at thirteen years old, who didn't want to be here. I also think that my awareness is huge. I am so alert to the point where not only do I know where I am in physical space but I'm conscious of other people and their conversations in the room. I'm conscious of when an opportunity presents itself to me, and being able to know on the spot whether or not I should grab it and run with it.

I went from a scared person who worked a job and felt that he had to live out the script to a person who goes against the grain, who said, "Screw it, let's see how far we can go with this and how awesome it can be, build a successful business, find out what you're passionate about and just do it. Never question or look back or apologize for who you are, never apologize for who you become and take it all in." If you interviewed 150 people that had truly mastered the one thing that you wanted in life, wouldn't you learn everything you need? There's still going to be lessons for you to learn on your own. This is not something where they give you everything on a silver platter, but I've met people who have given up everything that they possessed to travel the world, to experience cultures, to go to the Galapagos. There's one family that I interviewed on my podcast, they got a boat and rode it around the world. There are other people who have broken world records that didn't seem to be humanly possible before. Now that I've seen 200 people, I feel like nothing is impossible anymore. Everyone has shown me how possible it is for you to do something that never seemed possible before. It comes down to "How far do you want to take it?" It's your life and it's your opportunity to take it as far as you want. If today were your last day, if tomorrow were your last day, why aren't you living in that manner? If you want to be that person that's breaking that world record that no one's ever done before, why are you not spending every waking second right now, working towards that? If you died tomorrow, then they would know that you were working so hard on the one thing that you wanted to accomplish more than anything else. If you accomplished it, and then died the next day, then you're forever remembered as the person that worked so hard for that one thing they wanted and they did it. If you're not spending your time working towards that thing, then what are you here for? We're not here to just Netflix and chill and give up on our dream just because our parents didn't believe in us enough. We're not here to not do the one thing that we always wanted to do just because we're a little bit afraid. It was a trip to California. I couldn't tell you at that time that I'm going to go to California and then I'm going to become this number-one podcaster and then I'm going to be a number-one best-selling author. I can't tell you that, but looking back, I can tell you had I not had the guts to take that leap, to make that decision and say, "You know what, the one thing that I always wanted to do was go to California and I never did it. I should go do that." I can tell you that I wouldn't be here where I am today. I'd be alive, I'd probably be a lot more boring. So, to me, it means the world to show how much I've changed as a human being in every aspect of my life, physically, emotionally, mentally, financially, entrepreneurially.

I think every piece of my life, my relationships are better than ever and I attribute a lot of that to learning from other people's failures, to hearing their stories and hearing what they told themselves when they thought they were going to fail or when they were scared or when someone didn't believe in them. Seeing how far they could set that bar out for themselves, how they could set that crazy big goal that they want, and knowing that you could set the bar that much higher, too. I have to throw in there something big that I learned from when I was at that conference where Pat Flynn spoke, he said, "I want everybody to put your hand up as high as you can." Everyone raises their hand up. Then he says, "All right, I want you guys to put it up even higher." He's on stage standing so he goes up on his tippy toes, but of course every person raises up a little bit off their chair. He said, "See, I told you to go as high as you could go, and then I told you to go further and all of you could go further." The point is there's always more in the tank. Being a rower and practicing for races, when you're 3/4 of the way through the race and your body wants to give out, There's always more in the tank.

John: So, you decided to call this podcast episode The Last Podcast. If I were to ask you what do you want to leave behind on this earth, what is it that you've learned from traveling the world, meeting people who have done all these things, what is the secret of life?

ZB: The secret of life came to me when I was working with one of my mentors, Simon Smart. I went through his Warrior Protocol Training. After one of the best weekends of my entire life, we were in a meditation session. I pulled out a piece of paper and wrote, "Be proud of here." That's it. Be here, not in the future, not in the past, be proud of where you are right now. If where you are right now is under a roof, sheltered from the weather, with a full belly, a few bucks in your wallet and the ability to spend time with friends and family, you have made it further than 90% of the people on this earth. That's it, be proud of right here, right now.

John: There you have it, the last podcast.

A Letter From The Author

If you read this far, thank you from the bottom of my heart! I tried my best to pour all of the knowledge I have learned over the years onto paper. This book wouldn't have been possible without the help of so many inspirational people around the globe who devoted their time and expertise to the Year of Purpose Podcast and now to This Book Won't Change Your Life.

I did my best to portray all of the events and conversations in as close to the original form as possible. In other words, to the voices shared here, I hope I made you proud.

To my reader, you are always at a crossroads in life where you can choose to make change. You always have an option, a way out or another direction to take. But it is up to you to make a decision to change your life. No one will change your life for you.

I'd love to think that there is someone that could reach down like a puppeteer and do the hard work for us but there isn't. So, enjoy the ride, put in the work and make your life, a story to be passed on.

If you enjoyed this book, please do me a favor and leave a review online. Letting the world know that you got value out of this book is one of the greatest gifts I can receive. If you ever find yourself in Baltimore, Maryland please don't hesitate to reach out.

My door is always open, should anyone ever need a chat, completely non-judgmental. You are always welcome here. Please never suffer in silence. I have juice in the fridge, tea or coffee ready at a moment's notice and I will always be here for you to talk on the phone if that's what makes you feel comfortable. You are never not welcome. You will never disturb me. Go make the choice to change your life.